W. C. Prime

Coins, Medals, and Seals, Ancient and Modern

Illustrated and Described , With a Sketch of the History of Coins...

W. C. Prime

Coins, Medals, and Seals, Ancient and Modern
Illustrated and Described , With a Sketch of the History of Coins...

ISBN/EAN: 9783337014742

Printed in Europe, USA, Canada, Australia, Japan

Cover: Foto ©Andreas Hilbeck / pixelio.de

More available books at **www.hansebooks.com**

·COINS,

MEDALS, AND SEALS,·

ANCIENT AND MODERN.

Illustrated and Described.

WITH A

SKETCH OF THE HISTORY OF COINS AND COINAGE, INSTRUCTIONS FOR
YOUNG COLLECTORS, TABLES OF COMPARATIVE RARITY,
PRICE LISTS OF ENGLISH AND AMERICAN COINS,
MEDALS AND TOKENS, &c., &c.

EDITED BY

W. C. PRIME,

AUTHOR OF

" Boat Life in Egypt and Nubia," " Tent Life in the Holy Land,"
&c., &c., &c.

NEW YORK:

HARPER & BROTHERS, PUBLISHERS,

FRANKLIN SQUARE.

1864.

PREFACE.

This volume is published without any pretence to novelty, but is intended to give, in a cheap form, information which new collectors could not otherwise obtain except at very great expense. In the mass of illustration which it contains will be found its chief value.

When this was placed in my hands to prepare the accompanying historical sketch, I shrank from the work as one which could, however well executed, result in very little credit to myself. The countless works on coins, the mere catalogue of which fills a volume of several hundred pages—the inexhaustible nature of the subject—the obscurity which overhangs even that portion of it that relates to our own country—these and many other considerations operated to induce me to decline the attempt.

I have only undertaken it with the idea that I might do something for the benefit and assistance of young collectors in this country, who are in need of such advice as I have endeavored to give them. It has been my desire to encourage in the young a taste for numismatic

5

study, and to discourage the mania for rare and curious, but uninteresting and worthless, pieces of metal which has prevailed extensively in America during the past year.

I promised myself that I would prepare a book which every parent may place in the hands of his child, with the assurance that it would not mislead him into collecting coins for the sake of their rarity instead of their historical value.

This end I hope this volume may serve. While the illustration is valuable to all collectors, the instructions are specially directed to young students, and not to old scholars. As the young collector advances in his studies, he will be able to appreciate and to use with judgment the learned and elaborate works with which our public libraries abound.

That portion of the volume which relates to America and American coins and medals has been prepared with much labor, but is sadly imperfect. I have already hinted at the obscurity which overhangs the history of American coinage. It is remarkable that such facts remain undetermined as whether the Washington coin of 1792 (commonly but erroneously called the cent of 1792) was struck from a die cut in this country, or whether there was any issue of cents from the Mint in 1815, or where or whence the Georgius Triumpho copper first appeared, and many similar questions. It is very easy to give replies to these questions, but difficult to give authorities for the replies.

It is also impossible to affirm in this day whether certain coins now very rare will remain so, since every year new specimens of rare coins are found and added to collections. For this reason the price catalogues are of only temporary value. So, too, with the silver of the years preceding 1853. For the present, most of the dates can be readily obtained; but in consequence of the change in weight which took place in 1853, the silver of earlier date than that has almost entirely disappeared from circulation, and is now sold to the melters or returned to the Mint. As this practice continues, the entire early coinage is becoming scarce; so that within a year from the present time many half dollars, quarters, dimes, and half dimes now common will become of the highest rarity and command the highest prices.

Tradesmen's cards, tokens, and medalets of all kinds, have for the same reason no fixed value or steadfast place in any scale of rarity. The mania—no other word can be correctly used—which during the past year has led to the payment of enormous prices for tradesmen's cards, received a fitting check by the reproduction in immense quantities, from the original dies, of many of the most highly prized. For this reason it is impossible to-day to say that any one card or token will be scarce or specially valuable to-morrow.

It is to these and like points that it has been my desire to direct the attention of young collectors.

When, by reason of an increase in the number of students, and a more steadfast pursuit of the science, the

prices of American coins become more fixed and certain, and the entire supply, now hoarded in cupboards or old stockings and purses, **is** brought to light, it may be possible to prepare **a book on** American coins which shall have a permanent value. At present the science of numismatics in America has very few devotees. Collectors **we** have without number, who hunt diligently for tradesmen's **cards and mistakes in dies, and who** collect **for a year, then sell their cabinets at auction and** begin **again.** But we have **very few students of** the science. Let **us** hope for better days in this respect; and meantime let us preserve all that is historically valuable, and **do all that we** can to discourage the folly of collecting worthless pieces of metal, whose sole value is in their **scarcity,** and on which so much time and money have **been** expended during the past two years.

W. C. P.

New York, *Nov.* 1, 1860.

HISTORY OF COINAGE.

I.

The Origin of Coins.

It is a trite, but by no means a worn-out idea, that a coin, could it speak, would be able to relate a stranger story than any other article to which imagination might give a voice. Such a thought can never be worn out, for it is inexhaustible in its richness. Human fancy fails utterly to trace the possible adventures of a copper that was coined even last year; and for every month that a coin has been in circulation a lifetime must needs be added to the years that would be required to sum up the incidents in which one can conjecture that coin as an actor.

Human nature has not changed very much in the ages during which men have inhabited the world. The price of joy and of pain has been about the same since men began to deal those commodities out to other men for money; and certainly imagination scarcely finds a period of time when men lived and did not sell pleasure or sorrow to each other. The silver *drachma* of Ægina, in a modern collection—which was perhaps one of the first of silver coins that men ever handled—may therefore have been, doubtless was, in its day, like silver coins of this nineteenth century: now the purchase price of bread, and now of poison; to-day the comforter of want, to-morrow flung to the street from the jeweled hand of wealth; now the winner at the board, now the last stake of the suicide; in the morning doing duty to buy flowers

9

for the forehead of purity, in the evening the price of infamy and shame.

To a thinking man, then, every coin that his collection contains opens a new subject of thought; and it is no idle employment, though it seem so, to sit quietly over Greek or Persian, Roman or Punic, French, Turkish, English, or American coins, and seek to trace, in pure fancy, the history of one and another shining piece. And if the instruction to be thus derived is not the most valuable which the collection of coins furnishes, it is at least the origin of that which is worth more; for the desire to make acquaintance with the men who used these coins leads to the study of history; and perhaps the great benefit to be derived by the ordinary collector, from his employment, is to be found in this, that his coins serve to fix historical facts with great firmness in the memory This is especially true of young collectors. The young student of history who possesses a coin of Augustus Cæsar will read up in the history of the Augustan Age, imagining the coin now in the hands of Virgil, and now thrown by Horace to the slaves of Mæcenas; and in this manner he will enter into the life of Romans, and read history as if he knew in person (and had some associations in common with) the men of Rome.

These suggestions will, without further discussion, afford an excuse and an argument for indulging the young in a taste for the science of numismatics. There is danger always that any taste of this kind may become a passion. This depends on the ability and the judgment of guardians, and of this we have nothing to say.

But aside from the considerations thus stated, the science of numismatics has a claim on all intelligent persons that no other subject of study can surpass. In coins and medals, more than in any other monuments, the past is preserved, and its heroes and great events are kept memorable. Possibly it was to the almost imperishable nature of the splendid medals of the Augustan age

10

PLATE I.

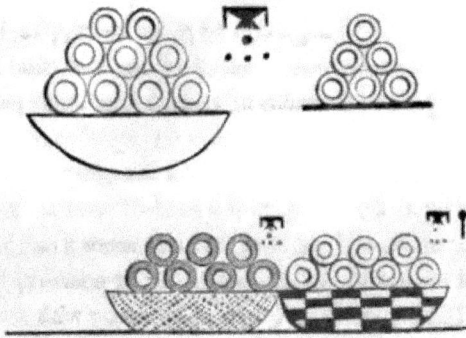

FIGURE I.—EGYPTIAN RING MONEY, GOLD AND SILVER.

(From the Wall of a Tomb.)

FIGURE 2.—ANCIENT EGYPTIAN METHOD OF WEIGHING MONEY.

(From the Wall of a Tomb.)

that Horace alluded when he spoke of a fame more enduring than brass—*monumentum ære perennius.* Then, as now, the records of coins and medals were regarded as most lasting; and it may be safely affirmed that we owe as much of our historical knowledge of the remote past to the coins of nations long since passed away, as we owe to their written chronicles on paper or parchment.

We find a coin, and we at once mark the place of its discovery. It bears the name of a king or the head of a god. We compare it with other coins, and lay it in its place among the brass, or silver, or gold memorials of the same king or country. It may be in itself of little importance; but in company with others it may form a link in a chain of evidence, a fact in a series, which will settle beyond reasonable doubt a great historical question. Forms of worship, manners and customs of nations, relationships of kings or of great families, may thus be determined. The coins which are illustrated in Plate XIII. verify this remark. They are given as specimens of a large class, from which we derive a vast amount of information on Roman subjects. Two of them—No. 10 and No. 11—exhibit the well in the forum to which Cicero and other authors refer. Two others—8 and 9—show the ancient and the new rostra. Others exhibit religious ceremonies. So the medallion No. 1, Plate IX., is a fine memorial of the tradition of the wolf and twins, the founders of Rome. The coin No. 5 on the same plate is a monument of the story of the embassy which the Senate of Rome sent to Epidaurus, about B.C. 290, with a request that Æsculapius would come to Rome and turn away the plague then raging. The embassadors brought back a sacred snake, which found its own way into the cabin of their ship, and which, when they arrived in the Tiber, swam to the island in the river on which was afterward built the temple of Æsculapius. The island itself was walled up in shape like a galley. The whole story is of exceeding historic interest, and this coin remains as an evidence that the event is not a creation of later years.

PLATE II.

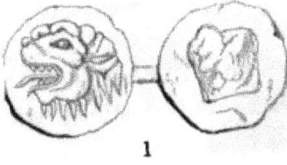

1

2

3

4

5

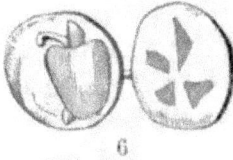

6

7

8

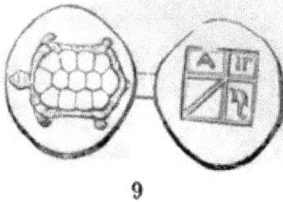

9

10

Examples might be multiplied from the illustrations in this volume; but it is no part of the design of the work to deprive the young collector of the pleasure and profit to be derived by searching out for himself the numerous historical incidents or ancient forms and customs to which these coins refer.

It is an object of much interest, in this connection, to determine the earliest date at which coins become a part of history, or aid in its preservation.

Although the article of money, in the shape of coins, is one of the most familiar objects of daily use, it is probable that very few persons have troubled themselves to consider when and where it originated. For, like all the inventions of man, it must have had a birth and a birth-place. Adam had neither purse nor pocket, and in Eden there was no one to trade with for food or clothing; and hence a means of barter was not very likely to be needed.

The origin of all human art was in necessity; or, as the proverb has it, necessity is the mother of invention. Thus the first recorded invention was an apron; or, as an old translation of the Bible has it, a pair of breeches. But when the breeches had a pocket in them, and when the pocket was first filled with small change, is a question for antiquarians.

This is worthy of remark, however, that the remains of antiquity which tombs and monuments furnish us agree remarkably with the **Scripture history of the** origin of our race. That is to say, the Scripture affirms that at a period about four thousand years ago **the world was** depopulated by a deluge, which only one family survived. Naturally we should suppose that **the** arts and sciences would progress with more rapidity, **from the** fact that this family possessed in themselves the learning and a great deal of the experience of the previous ages, in which men had lived long and learned much. But the world shows no remaining **monument** of any earlier period than this; and all its existing memorials indicate an age of **art** that dates from a time a little

14

PLATE III.

1

2

3

4

5

6

later than this flood. **Let us** record the fact, in spite of all that men have sought to establish to the contrary, that **no one** has found a relic of human existence on earth which **antedates the** period of the Noahic deluge. Bunsen has indeed founded a theory on the discovery of a piece of pottery **in a** deep boring in the Nile mud; but Bunsen failed to inquire whether the place of boring was not the site of an ancient lake, or the bottom of the ever-changing Nile itself; or, more likely still, **the** excavation for laying the foundation **of a colossal statue,** near whose **fallen** trunk as it now lies prone, the pottery was found, where a workman probably left it.

At a certain period after this deluge, when **men might be supposed** to need the convenience of money, and **not before—having** scattered, and formed nations of diverse interests—we **find it** coming into use.

It is no theory that we speak of, but a direct chain of existing specimens, leading us from the magnificent coinage of the Macedonian empire back to the earliest and rudest specimens of the **coins of men's** making. **It can not be** possible that any where in the world coined money had **been** used at a period prior to the date **of the Lydian** and the Ionian coins; so that, in this study of numismatics, **we** find at **once a** great tribute—the tribute which profane history has in **all** times paid—to the Sacred story, **a confirmation of the account of the** origin of our **race on** the earth.

The first mention that is made of money in history is eminently striking. It was used for the purchase **of a grave. There is** no **picture in all the** past **more** profoundly sad than **that of** the old **man** buying a place to bury his dead wife out **of his sight.** Who **has not** read the story with unutterable **emotions?** Who that **is** father of a family or husband of a wife, **when** the first dead **one in** the house must be buried, **has not** gone out to buy a burial-place, and called to mind that sad scene before the Cave of Machpelah? Does this first record in history, sacred or profane,

PLATE IV.

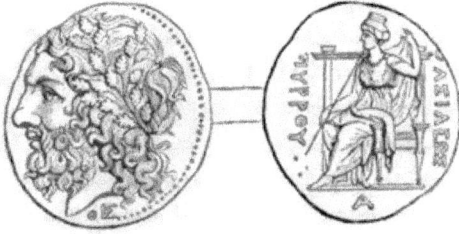

1

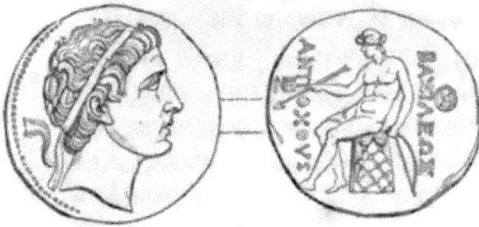

2

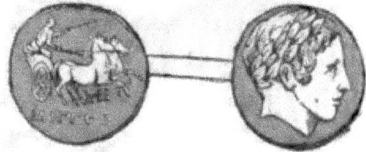

3

4

6

5

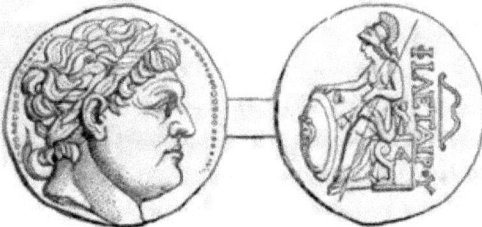

7

B

of the use of money, teach us that the shining stuff is of no higher value to a man than just the price of his grave? After he has bought and occupied that, it certainly ceases to matter to him whether his heaps are gold or copper or dust.

But let us glance a moment at this story, and see whether, in the days of Abraham, men had any knowledge of coin. For the first question before us is, When did coined money originate?

Although the Hebrew word, which, in the case of Abraham, is translated *shekels*, may have been used by Moses in writing the account with the design of fixing the value of the metal intelligibly to the Hebrew readers of the history, we are by no means to suppose that Abraham paid out the shining coins which, in the times of Simon Maccabeus, bore the emblems of the Hebrew faith. On the contrary, he *weighed* out the silver: four hundred *shekels* "current with the merchant"—not current *money*, as our translation has it; for the word money is supplied. But what was a *shekel*, or any other given quantity of silver, current with merchants in those days?

A little later the grandson of Abraham was purchasing land in the same country, and paid for it "a hundred *pieces of silver*."

The Hebrew word קְשִׂיטָה, here translated *pieces of silver*, may as properly be translated *lambs*. The question at once arises, Was it a hundred lambs which Jacob paid, or was it a hundred coins, or was it the metal value of a hundred lambs? Other speculations, too, arise on examining the uses to which the same Hebrew word, or words of the same origin, are applied. Thus, in the form of a verb קָשַׁט, we find it meaning to be true, equal, just, correct. And again, in the form of a noun, it signifies truth, equity, holiness, purity, etc. It occurs thus in Psalm lx. 6, and Proverbs xxii. 21. It has a similar signification in the Arabic, and also in the Chaldaic and the Syriac. This examination into the origin of the words first used for describing money is by no means labor wasted. For although we do not intend here to trace

PLATE V.

1

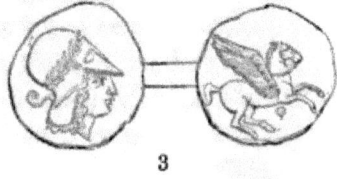

2 3

4 5

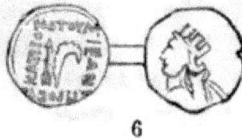

6

the history of the word, or determine whether the significations of equity, justice, etc., were primary or secondary, it is enough that we find in the word both these ideas—*a lamb* and *a just weight.*

Now what connection had a lamb with a just weight?

Egypt is the great illustrator of the Bible, and much of our speculation on Bible difficulties would be set at rest if we had the Egyptian monuments at hand to refer to whenever we needed an illustration. In this case all speculation seems to be done away with by this aid. In one of the Theban tombs, among the countless illustrations on the walls of the manners and customs of the ancient Egyptians, and especially of the Egyptians who lay in that tomb, we find a picture of a scribe weighing out the wealth of his master and counting it up (Plate I., Figure 2).

No one who sees it can doubt that the Egyptians of that day weighed out gold and silver by a weight whose shape was that of a lamb, and the half of it was like the hind-quarters of a lamb. This interesting discovery gives us reason to think that Abraham paid the sons of Heth in silver weighed out by these same weights. Mr. Layard found specimens of the weights themselves in Nineveh.

It is natural to suppose that the weights were originally determined by the value of a sheep or lamb; and this supposition derives additional force from facts that appear in the history of other nations, and even from the words which for many centuries have been used to express the idea of money. In early ages, when men led mostly the pastoral life, cattle were probably the most common medium of exchange and barter, and the value of a sheep was a fixed value, varying but little in places or years. When metals became standards of value can not be affirmed precisely, but it is evident that at this time, and for many centuries afterward, they were not coined into what we call money. The evidence, however, that the price of cattle was the earliest method of fixing the value of money, and that gold and other

PLATE VI.

1   2

3   4

5   6

7   8

metals were valued according to the number of cattle a given quantity would buy, is found elsewhere than in this solitary instance. Our own language contains a proof of it, since the word *pecuniary*, which is in common use with us, is derived from the Latin word *pecunia* (money), and this was derived from *pecus* (a flock of sheep or cattle). The evidence of the derivation is found in the oldest Roman coins extant, one of which is shown on Plate VII. This gigantic copper coin was in the Pembroke collection in England, and weighed a little less than five pounds avoirdupois. It is a specimen of the earliest known coinage of Italy, and probably dates from B.C. 500 to B.C. 600, a period not much later than that of the earliest Eastern coinage, of which we have before spoken. This piece was the *aes* or *as* (the brass or the piece of brass), which subsequently changed its size and form, but which remained a Roman coin down to modern times. We refer to it at present to illustrate the theory of the origin of money value. And when the reader has studied history with reference to the price of cattle in various periods of the world's history, and in various parts of the world, he will readily adopt the idea that the first valuations of metal became fixed with regard to the value of sheep and oxen. Homer mentions no use of coined money, but speaks of a bar of brass as being equal in value to one ox, and a woman slave as worth four oxen. The father of poetry, indeed, often speaks of oxen and sheep as the representatives of wealth, as when Achilles argues boldly that he can go elsewhere and find abundant spoil of oxen and fat sheep. It is true that in the same conversation (Iliad, Book IX., line 365, etc.) Achilles also speaks of "the gold and ruddy brass and bright iron," but not as if coined into money. Homer's is perhaps the most remarkable work in the world as a description of existing arts, dress, manners and customs, and, in short, comparative civilization. There can be no reason to suppose that he had ever seen coined money, or, if it existed in his day, that it had then existed so long as to author-

Plate VII.

Roman Quincussis.—(Exact size.)

ize him to mention it among the arts and furniture of the Grecian camp or the Trojan city at the period of his story, which is located at about the same date with our chronological location of Samson and the judges of the Israelites.

But it is also evident that gold and silver became valuable as ornaments long before they were used for coins. Thus we find Eleazar of Damascus carrying to Rebecca rings and bracelets of fixed weight; and in the 11th verse of the 42d chapter of Job we find it mentioned that each of Job's friends brought him an ear-ring as well as "a lamb" or "piece of money." That these rings and bracelets became frequently, and at length commonly, the medium of exchange, we have abundant evidence. The Egyptian monuments show that the common form of the valuable metals when in course of transfer was the ring. Numerous illustrations of these rings in gold and in silver are found on the walls of tombs (see Plate I., Figure 1). Ancient writers refer to rings and bracelets as the usual form of gold ornaments, and the modern customs in the East are doubtless accurately like the ancient.

The Oriental traveler is surprised to find the poorest woman sometimes wearing heavy gold bracelets and anklets; but his surprise ceases when he learns that, in the East, there is no investment for money which pays interest, and that, as a consequence, the poor and the rich, when they accumulate more or less gold, are accustomed to call in the traveling tinker, who, with crucible, furnace, and hammer, sits down in the court of the palace or on the ground-floor of the hut, and out of the coins handed him soon fashions a rude bracelet or anklet, which adorns the dusky leg or arm of the favorite wife, until necessity compels its transfer. When this necessity comes, there is no delay or trouble about it in an Eastern market. The owner goes into the street to make a purchase, and tenders his bracelet in payment. The convenient money-changer is at hand in every street with his scales, the weight is told—it is three, five, ten, or twenty

PLATE VIII.

1

4

3

5

2

mejiddi—and the merchant takes it as readily as coin. We have seen this transaction not a few times, and regarded it as the best evidence needed of the ancient custom of using similar bands of precious metals for currency.

But without pausing longer on this subject we may give the illustrations well known to the numismatic scholar, of the ring money of the ancient Britons, dating before the Roman invasion, and therefore at a period not many centuries later than the invention of coined money by the Greeks, and continuing in use down to a late period in the Christian era. These rings are now found in abundance in various parts of England and Ireland. At one time, in 1832, a quantity of it, valued at £1089 14s. 1d. (intrinsic value of the gold), was dug up at St. Quentin (see Plate XXIII., Figure 1). The forms varied. Some immense ornaments were manifestly worn over the shoulder; others on the arms, or around the waist. Cæsar, in his account of England, distinctly relates that rings of fixed weight were used for money in Britain. He says the same of Gaul. We find the same sort of money spoken of in the north of Europe; those found in England are all exact multiples of the same unit in weight; so that there is no reason to doubt that they had a fixed weight and passed current as coins.

But as yet no regular coin existed. The Greeks had been in the habit of using bars or spikes of metal. A bar was an *obolus* (literally translated a spike or a small obelisk), and six of these were as many as a man could grasp in his hand. Hence six *oboli* made one *drachma* (a handful), and thus originated the coins *obolus* and *drachma*, the latter being to this day the coin of Greece, and having given its name to weights and measures in all the languages of the civilized world.

It was about 900 years before Christ that the first money was actually coined. There is much doubt in the minds of antiquarians as to the precise spot where the custom had its origin. He-

PLATE IX

1

2   3

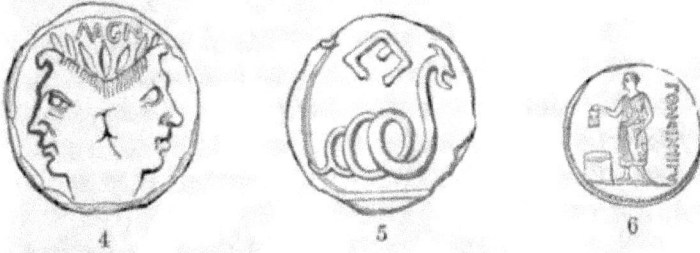

4   5   6

7   8

9

rodotus ascribes it to the Lydians, but his authority is not conclusive.

The oldest coins extant, and probably the first coins ever made, are from Ionia, in Asia Minor. Miletus, a city south of Ephesus, on the shore of the Icarian Sea, probably produced the first coined money. It was the gold *stater* (Plate II., Figure 1).

It will be noticed that the coin is stamped on one side with a deep indentation. On the other it has a rude picture of a lion's head. This form is characteristic of coinage for a long period. A die was used, the lump of metal placed in it, and a punch, struck with a hammer, drove the metal into the die and left the rude mark of the punch on the reverse of the coin. What induced the adoption of the lion's head as a design is left to conjecture. It is by some supposed to refer to the regal power represented by the lion, while others think that it had some connection with the worship of Cybele, the great goddess of the Ionians. A somewhat similar coin is also known (Plate II., Figure 2), which by some numismatists is supposed to be of earlier date than the Ionian. It is a Lydian coin, one of those referred to by Herodotus; and we give it as a specimen of one of the earliest, if not the earliest. Coins of this kind have been found in considerable quantity at Sardis, and there is reason to believe that some of these are of the period of Crœsus. The value of these two coins is the same. It was called a *stater* or *standard*, and it is worthy of remark that the value of this first gold coin known has been continued in currency among all nations, with very slight variation, down to recent times. These coins were the first specimens of stamped gold in the form that we call money.

It has been by some supposed that an Eastern coinage existed of earlier date than the Ionian or the Lydian, and that the remaining specimens, now known as gold *darics*, are possibly of remoter date than the *stater* of Miletus. This is mere conjecture, however. The gold *daric*, of which a representation is given in Plate

PLATE X.

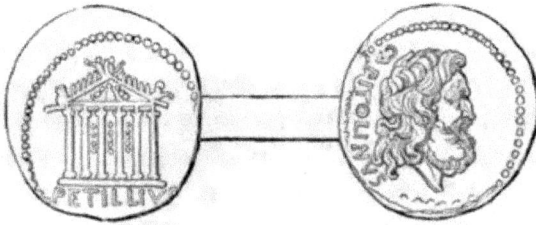

1

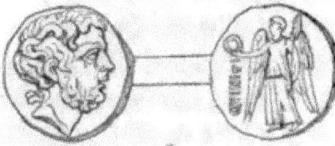

2

3

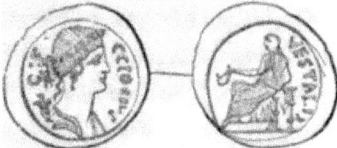

4

5

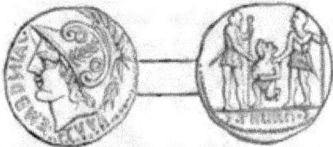

6

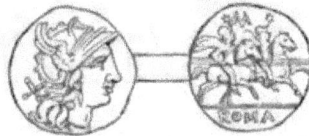

7

8

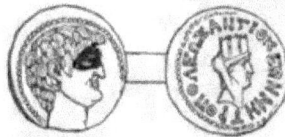

9

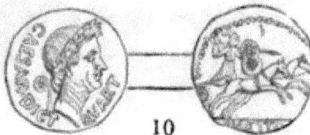

10

II., Figure 4, is a rare coin of early Assyrian or Persian times. The large *daric* of silver (Plate II., Figure 3) is not earlier than the time of Cambyses. The name of the coin has been by some supposed to be derived from Darius, by others from an old Persian word signifying royalty. It is interesting as being one of the early coins named in the Bible. In Ezra ii. 69, the word דַּרְכְּמוֹנִים, *Darkemonim*, translated in our version *drams*, is supposed to be this coin; and the same word occurs in other places, as in Daniel viii. 5; 1 Chron. xxix. 7. In the latter case the word is less like Drachma, and more like Daric: it is HADARKON. It is not impossible that the Hebrew words may have been two, one referring to the Grecian, while the other referred to the Persian coin. The *daric* was, in fact, worth twenty silver *drachmæ*. Xenophon gives us three thousand *darics* as worth ten *talents*. The value of the gold in a *daric*, as now found, is about $5 45. The pay which Cyrus gave to the soldiers of Clearchus was a gold *daric* per month (Anab. i. 3). These coins are scarce, it being probable that Alexander replaced them with his coinage when he conquered Asia.

The silver *daric* was, as remarked, unknown until the time of Cambyses, when, it is supposed, Aryandes, Governor of Egypt, first struck them.

We have thus briefly sketched what is known of the origin of gold coinage. Silver does not seem to have been coined as early as gold. The earliest known silver coinage is that of Ægina. It dates about B.C. 870, and not long after the Ionian gold. An example of it is visible in Plate II., Figure 6, and another, of a later date, showing an improved style of art, in the same plate, Figure 9. The die was at first used, as before described, with a punch, which left its mark on the reverse. The tortoise was the national emblem, and continued for a long time on the Æginetan coins.

Copper was probably first used for coins in Italy, but the exact date of its introduction does not appear.

PLATE XI.

1

2

3

4

5

6

 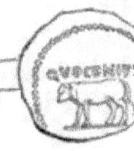

7

8

9

10

II.

Progress of the Art among Ancient Nations.

FROM these crude beginnings the art of coinage advanced to a stage of beauty in early periods which has hardly been surpassed even in our day of splendid medals. But this advance was not instantaneous. It was measured, gradual, and slow. The first step was the placing on the end of the punch some rude figure, which was indented in the coin when the blow was struck, thus producing the usual raised head or legend on the obverse, while the reverse showed the indentation of the figure on the end of the punch.

The *quarter stater* of Phocea, of which a representation is given in Plate II., Figure 5, illustrates this. The idea was further carried out in Greece by making the end of the punch to correspond with the die, but not so as to leave the impression raised on both sides. The result was a coinage of which one side presented in concave the same figures which were on the other side in relief. And this led to the production of very beautiful coins, of which we give an illustration in a silver coin of Caulonia (Plate II., Figure 7).

The first devices on coins were emblematical. The tortoise of Ægina, the owl of Athens, the seal of Phocea, and similar designs, are found on all the earliest issues. No heads of kings or heads of gods are on the first coins. The deities at length took possession of the money; and thereafter the head of a god or goddess who was the chief object of worship in a city or country became the ordinary obverse of coins. This custom continued for

PLATE XII.

1

2

3

4

5

6

7

8   9

10

11

C

centuries. It was not till very near the time of Alexander the Great that the heads of monarchs were placed on money. There is extant a coin of Archelaus I., King of Macedonia (Plate II., Figure 8), which gives us probably a portrait of that monarch; and, if it be so, it is undoubtedly the first coin which had for a device the head of a reigning prince. He reigned from 413 to 399 B.C.

Alexander I. had reigned about fifty years before, and during his reign a coin was struck bearing on its face a youth carrying two spears by the side of a horse (Plate II., Figure 10). Possibly and probably this was a representation of the fact that Alexander was admitted to the Olympic games; but it can not be considered a portrait.

The period, then, of the introduction of human heads upon coinage may be safely placed at about 400 B.C.; and from that time to the present the coins of the various nations of the world which have outlasted time and corrosion are the most valuable and faithful historians. The admirable succession of coins which some large collections contain serve as lasting monuments of the great events in national history. In some instances it is by coins alone that history has been preserved.

The Macedonian coinage has been preserved in remarkable succession, and a view of the history of that coinage would probably be the best possible illustration of the advance of the art from the rudest to the purest specimens. We illustrate, however, coins of various Eastern countries during the four centuries before the Christian era, from which the reader will be enabled to gather a very clear idea of the splendor to which the art was rapidly brought.

The period of Alexander the Great is one of great interest to the numismatist. During the reign of Amyntas II. in Macedonia, B.C. 393–369, there was a great improvement in coinage. Up to this period and during his reign the punch-mark on the reverse

PLATE XIII.

1

2

7

3

4

8

9

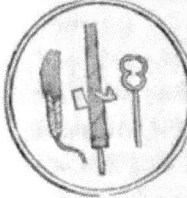
5

6

10

11

12

13

14

15

of many coins had continued in use, but hereafter it is not known.

We have now arrived at a period of high perfection in the art of coinage. In the reign of Philip II. of Macedon, commencing 359 B.C., and continuing twenty-four years, some of the finest specimens of ancient coinage were issued, and among others the gold *staters*, which became known as *Philips*, and gave this name to the gold coins of Greece for a long period, precisely as in modern times we hear of *Louis* and *Napoleons* in France.

When Alexander the Great ascended the throne and proceeded to the conquest of the world, he scattered his coinage over the continent, east and west, in an immense variety of forms. So many were they, that they are the cheapest of ancient coins even now, and in Europe, Asia, and Africa abundance of genuine coins of this monarch can be purchased for a trifle above the weight of the gold or silver. It is not uncommon, in modern times, for vases of the Alexandrian coins to be turned up by the plowshare of the farmer, and in all the towns and cities of the East men are to be found with specimens for sale in a fine state of preservation. Genuine coins of Alexander can be procured at such low prices that it has hardly been an object to counterfeit them, as has been done with many others (see Plate IV., Figures 3, 4, 5).

The Macedonian coinage, gold and silver, continued to be fine for more than two centuries. But it was not alone in Macedonia that the art was advancing, as all the illustrations given in this volume abundantly testify. In all the East, which was then the civilized world, the fine arts were progressing to a golden age. Phidias had completed the Parthenon, and a rare coin of an early time shows a rude view of the Acropolis (Plate III., Figure 3), the statue of Minerva, and the Parthenon; while another (Plate III., Figure 2) shows the theatre of Dionysius on the side of the Acropolis.

It is remarkable that we have no coins of Egypt until the pe-

PLATE XIV.

1

2

3

4

5

6

7

riod of the successors of Alexander. That old land—first in arts and sciences, far in advance of all the world in architecture, sculpture, painting, music, and every thing that adorns civilization—seems never to have felt the necessity of a circulating medium other than the ordinary use of metals by weight, and the interchange of commodities by barter. This may have been owing to the character of the country, lying as it did along the banks of the Nile, where interchange of articles by barter was convenient.

The ring money seems to have been used in Egypt down nearly or quite to Ptolemaic times (see Plate I., Figure 1). That it was in common use, and was the standard of value, the monuments abundantly testify, since we find in countless tombs the pictures of this money in the enumerations of the wealth of the proprietors, and these tombs are of all periods through many centuries.

The successors of Alexander, however, introduced a different style of money, and the coins of the Ptolemies are among the most splendid relics of ancient art. They extend to the period of Cleopatra, of whom we have portraits on very fine coins (Plate XI., Figure 1).

III.

Coinage of the Jews.

ALTHOUGH our earliest records of the use of money are found in the Hebrew sacred writings, we have no reason to suppose that the inhabitants of Palestine had any coined money until shortly before the Christian era. It is possible that the Persian coins, and those of other conquering nations, obtained currency from time to time among the Jewish people. But we may be

PLATE XV.

1

2

3

4

5

6

7

8

well assured that they had no coin of their own bearing a national device until after the captivity.

The silver *shekel* has now become quite common in collections. A few years ago it was very rare. But within the past five years a large number of them have been found at Jerusalem, near the pool of Siloam, evidently washed down by the rain from some point on the hill of Moriah, or the opposite slope of Zion.

The only extant Jewish coins are the several varieties of this silver *shekel.* In the first book of Maccabees, xv. 6, in the letter of Antiochus the king to Simon the high-priest, and to the Jewish nation, occurs this passage: "And I give thee leave to coin money of thine own stamp in thine own country." Simon Maccabæus probably coined, under this permission, the first national coinage of the Jews. We give an example of his issue. The Jewish coinage, of course, bore no head of a God on its face. The second commandment forbade it. But the pot of manna and the buds of Aaron's rod were the devices adopted, with legends varying, but most commonly "SHEKEL ISRAEL," "JERUSALEM HOLY," or "SCHISCHIMON PRINCE OF ISRAEL." The legends were in the ancient form of Hebrew. character, and not in the debased form in use since the captivity. An example is given in Plate III., Figure 6.

For what length of time this coinage continued in Jerusalem we can not say. It is not probable that it was of long duration. The Greek and Roman currency took its place in time; and although coins of Herod and of Barkochebas the rebel are extant, it seems improbable that these were issued to any great extent. We have copper coins of Agrippa, very rare, and these complete the entire series of coins of Judea.

It is impossible to give any idea of the money value of ancient coins by modern money terms. The size of the *shekels* now extant is larger than the American *quarter dollar*, and not so large

PLATE XVI.

1

2

3

4

5

6

7

as the *half dollar.* The weight is 274 Paris grains. In the 17th chapter of Matthew the temple tax, or tribute money, is spoken of as a *didrachma.* Elsewhere it is stated at a *half shekel;* and in the same chapter, 27th verse, a *stater* is made to pay the tax for two persons. The few verses at the end of that chapter give us some light on the relative value of the ancient Jewish, Roman, and Greek coins.

IV.

Roman Coinage.

WITHOUT attempting to trace the history of coinage through all the nations of the earth, we content ourselves with following it rapidly through that line in which at last we find our own coinage.

The Italians early learned the art from their Eastern neighbors, and a few hundred years later introduced it into England, or introduced there an improvement on the rude forms which the inhabitants of that barbarian island had possibly borrowed from the hordes who had overrun the north of Europe.

There are coins extant of a very early Roman period, and of the nations who inhabited Italy when Rome was in its infancy. The first coinage of copper seems to have been Roman. They commenced it in the time of Servius Tullius, B.C. 578.

ROMAN COPPER.

The earliest Roman coinage was of the metal called Aes. It has been much disputed whether there was any zinc in its composition, and if any the alloy must have been very small. The word Aes, which is ordinarily translated brass, became a synonym with money, so that Ulpian said, "We call even our golden coins *aes.*"

PLATE XVII.

1

2

3

4

5

6

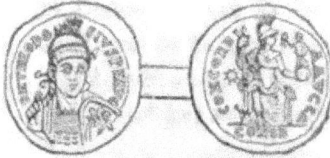

7

8

9

10

The first copper or brazen coins are supposed to have been made by Servius Tullius, Pliny being our authority. These coins were cast. Specimens have been found adhering one to another, never having been broken apart since taken from the mould. Being stamped with the images of cattle (*pecus*), they readily gave origin to the word *pecunia*, which has since given words to many languages descriptive of money and affairs relating to money. The first coin was doubtless the *as*, and weighed one pound. Other heavy coins were struck or cast, even to the weight of five pounds. The *quincussis*, of five pounds' weight, is illustrated on Plate VII., and the *as* on Plate VIII., Figures 1 and 2. According to Pliny, the weight of the *as* was reduced at the time of the first Punic War, about B.C. 261, when it appeared at one-sixth its former weight. Still later, about B.C. 217, it was reduced to one ounce, and about B.C. 191 to half an ounce. Indeed so numerous were the changes, that the *as* has been found of almost every weight, from the full pound down to one-fifth of an ounce. The value decreased with the weight, and it seems probable that this was met by a slight increase in the value of copper. The subdivisions of the *as* were numerous, of which the most common were the *semis*, or half-*as;* the *triens*, or third part of an *as;* the *quadrans*, being the fourth part of an *as;* the *sextans*, or sixth part of an *as;* the *uncia*, or twelfth part of an *as*. Illustrations of the *sextans* and the *triens* will be found on Plate VIII., reduced in size one half. The two balls on one and four on the other indicate the number of ounces in each coin.

The *as* was used by the boys of Rome as coppers are now, and instead of " Head or Tail," they cried " Heads or Ship"— "Capita aut Navem"—alluding to the heads of Janus and the prow of the ship on the opposite sides of the coin; and this cry, "Capita aut Navem," continued in use among the Roman boys centuries after the heads of Janus and the ship's prow had disappeared from the coinage of the country. The origin of such

PLATE XVIII.

1

2

3

phrases in various languages is one of the most interesting studies connected with the science of numismatics.

ROMAN GOLD.

The Roman gold coin, which was the standard, was called the *aureus*, or the *aureus nummus*. Its value in modern American gold would be within a small fraction of $5 10. This coinage was first made about B.C. 207. No gold had been previously coined in Rome. The smallest gold coin was the *scrupulum*, which weighed 18·06 grains, and was of the value of twenty *sestertii*. Other coins were struck of forty, sixty, and eighty *sestertii*. The coin of sixty *sestertii* will be seen illustrated in Plate XII., Figure 4. The *aureus* is the same coin known in later times as the *solidus*.

The value of gold, as compared with silver, of course changed in different ages, and the changes seem to have been more frequent in ancient than in modern times. Herodotus, in the 95th section of The Thalia, in estimating the tribute paid to Darius, calculated gold as worth thirteen times the same weight in silver, showing that in his day the relative value was estimated as 1 to 13. This was about B.C. 450. Livy (xxxviii. 11) makes the proportion 1 to 10. This was B.C. 190. From Suetonius we learn that Julius Cæsar once exchanged them in the proportion of 1 to 9; and it appears that under the Roman emperors the value increased until it became, under Justinian, 1 to 14, or 1 to 15.

ROMAN SILVER.

Silver was first coined in Rome B.C. 269. The style of the most common early silver coins may be seen in the illustrations, Plate X., Figure 7, and Plate XII., Figures 3, 8, and 9. These bear the Dioscuri and the bigatus and quadrigatus, from which last devices the coins were called *bigati* or *quadrigati*. The principal silver coin was the *denarius*, so called because its value was

PLATE XIX.

1

2

3

4

5

6

7

8

ten *ases.* Originally there were eighty-four *denarii* to a pound weight; but a reduction was made to ninety-six, although the period of the change is somewhat uncertain.

The value of the *denarius,* under the former weight, was about seventeen cents American, and under the latter weight about fifteen cents. The Romans coined silver of as low a value as the fortieth part of a *denarius,* the smallest coin being the *teruncius.* Other silver coins were known as the *sembella,* which was two *teruncii,* or a *half libella;* the *libella,* one-tenth of the *denarius,* and of course the equivalent of the *as;* the *sestertius,* or *quarter denarius;* and the *quinarius,* or *half denarius,* which was also known as the *Victoriatus.*

Although the *drachma* of Athens was originally somewhat heavier than the *denarius* of Rome, it is probable that, in later periods, its weight decreased, and the two coins would probably pass equally well in either country. This *denarius* continued to be a Roman coin, was introduced into Britain, and, finally, reduced to be the silver *penny* of England; and to this day appears in English coinage as the letter D, which represents pence in the notation of £ *s. d.*

The collector who proposes to devote his attention to Roman coins will find the field inexhaustible. It would be vain, in a volume like the present, to attempt any instructions on the subject, and we must leave him to examine the numerous and learned works on the subject with which our public libraries abound.

Through the long course of Roman history the art of coinage had its periods of elevation and depression. In the Augustan Age it flourished. The splendid medals, the noble coins of that period may well have been the origin, as before intimated, of the celebrated line of Horace: "*Exegi monumentum Ære perennius;*" for the next line is by no means necessarily connected with it, as some have supposed, confining the idea of the monument to a brazen pillar. In the Eastern empire the art of coining never re-

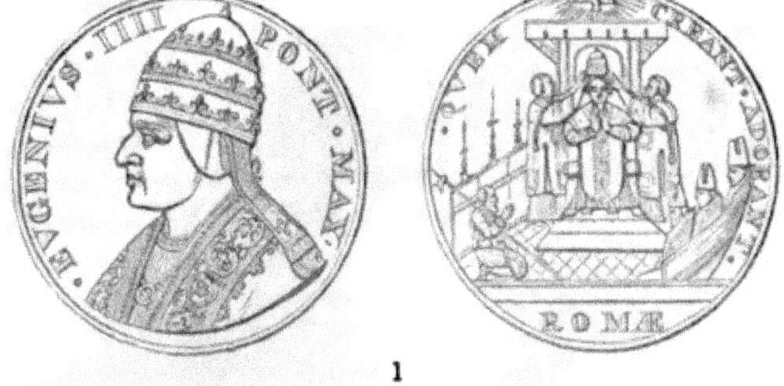
EVGENIVS · IIII · PONT · MAX ·
QVEM CREANT ADORANT ·
ROMÆ

1

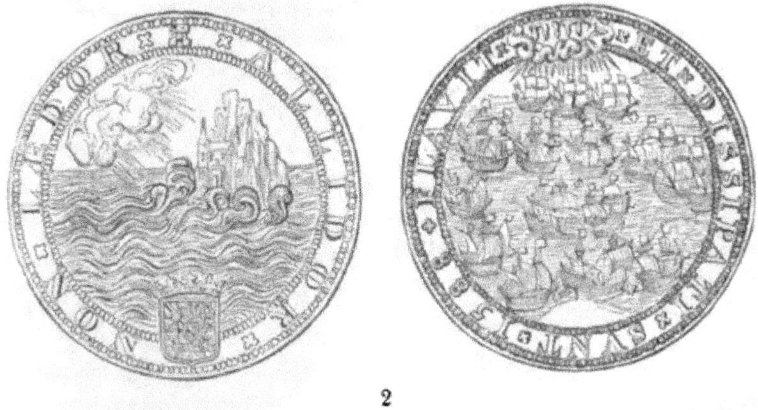

2

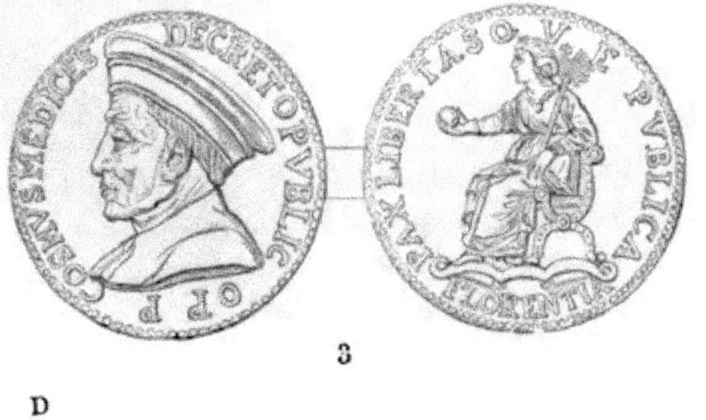
COSMVS MEDICES DECRETO PVBLIC
PAX LIBERTASQ VE PVBLICA
FLORENTIA

3

D

ceived much attention, and few coins or medals, among the immense number which are extant, indicate even a mediocre skill in workmanship. A medal of Justinian (Plate XVIII., Figure 1), and some few coins of different periods, on Plates XVII. and XIX., illustrate our subject better than pages of description. Long before these coins were struck, the history of British coinage had commenced.

V.

Coinage of Britain.

THE history of the British coinage is one of the most remarkable illustrations of the progress of art in the world. A glance at the illustrations which this volume contains will show the reader a series of coins in unbroken succession, through all the changing events which have marked the history of the British Islands. These are, of course, but few of the coins of England. But if every other relic of art were lost, if all the volumes of written history were destroyed, we should be able out of these materials to reconstruct a large portion of the history of England. We could, at least, give the succession of monarchs from the period of the Norman invasion, without loss of a name.

The Romans, according to Cæsar, found no coinage in England. The inhabitants, for the most part, used the torques, or ring money, before spoken of and illustrated (Plate XXIII., Figure 1).

Some coins of apparently a very early period, and bearing names of individuals contemporary with Cæsar, have been found. These coins, illustrated on Plate XXIII., have given rise to much interesting discussion. More than forty have been discovered in various places which have the name of Cunobelin (the Cymbeline of Shakspeare). A very interesting coin is extant with the name

PLATE XXI.

1.—A COINER AT WORK.

(From the Capital of a Column in Normandy.)

2.—A COINING ESTABLISHMENT.

(From an old German Wood-cut.)

of Boadicea or Boduodicea, and others with the name of Segonax, one of the Kings of Kent who attacked Cæsar. The letters TASCIA occurring on many of these coins, have given rise to the idea that they were coins of Tasciavanos, the father of Segonax. But another opinion holds that all these coins are of a much later period, and that they bear only such names or legends as the makers thought fit to put on them. That they were, in fact, tokens; or that they were struck to pay taxes with, and that the word TASCIA is an English corruption of the Latin *taxatio*. The idea has also been advanced that they were tickets of membership of certain orders or societies, of much more recent date than Cæsar.

It is quite certain, whatever may be true of these coins, that England had no coinage prior to the Roman invasion. Immediately after that event, it is probable that the Romans introduced the art; and the coins we have referred to, if struck at all as coins, doubtless appeared between that time and the reign of Claudius; and although there are coins of Claudius relating to Britain, which were struck about A.D. 46 (see Plate XXV., Figures 2, 3), yet it is impossible to affirm that any mint was established in England, or that any coins were actually struck on the island until the time of Carausius. He being, in fact, an English emperor, struck coins which are extant, and there is no reason to doubt that they were struck in England (see Plate XXV., Figure 6, and Plate XXVII., Figure 1).

The Saxon *sceattæ* were the first purely English coins in circulation of which we have any knowledge. Their value is doubtful, but they would seem to have been worth not far from a *penny*. In the laws of Athelstan it is said that 30,000 of them are spoken of as equivalent to £120, which would make them worth a little less than a *penny*. They gave place to the silver *pennies* of the Saxon kings, of which some illustrations are given on Plate XXVII.

PLATE XXII.

1

2

3

The word *penny* was derived either from the Latin *pecunia*, money, or from *pendo*, to weigh. We have already said that it was of the value of the Roman *denarius*, and its successor in England. The word cattle was also adopted by the English from the Norman, and used to signify, in general, a man's property; whence came the word chattel, applied to any species of moveable property. How far this use of the word has connection with the Latin use of *pecus* and *pecunia*, we leave to the conjecture or examination of the reader.

The first silver *penny* now extant is of a period after the middle of the eighth century. This is of Ethelbert II., King of Kent and Bretwalda (Plate XXVII., Fig. 8); but the genuineness of this coin has been doubted. There are, however, coins of Cuthred, A.D. 798 to 805, and of Baldred, A.D. 823, both Kings of Kent.

Of Offa there are interesting coins (see Plate XXVII., Fig. 2). He was King of Mercia, A.D. 757 to 796. A curious Arabic coin has been found with his name on the reverse, whence it was supposed that the Arabic coins of Spain obtained circulation in England at that time. It is recorded, however, that Offa promised the Pope's legate 396 gold *marcuses*, and these Arabic *marcuses* may have been coined in England expressly for the present. They are curious coins for a present to the legate of the Pope, bearing as they do the usual Arabic legend: "Mohammed is God's apostle." We shall not pause to speak of the other Saxon coins, of which numerous specimens exist. Egbert and Ethelwulf left many coins. Of Ethelbald (855 to 860) none are with certainty known. Of Ethelbearht (856 to 866) we have many, as well as of Ethelred (866 to 871). Then came Alfred the Great, and from his time the succession is very perfect down to the Anglo-Norman dynasty.

William I. introduced the Norman *shilling* of twelve *pennies* as a name of money, but not as a coin. The Saxon *shilling* (*scil* or *scilling*) was at first five, and afterward four *pennies;* but the Nor-

PLATE XXIII.

1.—ENGLISH TORQUES AND RING MONEY.

2.—EARLY ENGLISH COINS.

man value prevailed at a later day, though the coin was never struck till the reign of Henry VII.

The word *shilling* has been by some derived from the Latin *sicilicus* (a quarter ounce), and by others from a Saxon word signifying a scale. The *pound* was, of course, a weight originally, but it is remarkable that the standard gold coin of all nations and times continued to be of about the value of the ancient Grecian *stater*.

The word *sterling*, in connection with the English *pound*, is said to have been at first *easterling*, which was a name given to the mint examiners, who perhaps made an annual visitation at Easter. The term literally signifies "according to the mint rules." Others derive the word easterling from German traders who frequented English markets in those times, and who dealt only for pure gold or silver coin.

In the reign of Henry III. a few gold *pennies* were issued as a sort of trial piece; but the beginning of English gold coinage was not till Edward III., when *florins*, *half florins*, and *quarter florins* were issued. They were at once recalled, however, and a new coin, the gold *noble*, deriving its name from the nobility of its metal, made its appearance. This coin, with its reverse showing the king at the helm of the ship of state, is the first specimen of great advance in the art of coinage in England (Plate XXIX., Figure 8). This monarch also adopted some curious legends on his coins. This one, for example, has the passage, "JESUS AUTEM TRANSIENS PER MEDIUM ILLORUM IBAT;" the *half nobles* have, "DOMINE NE IN FURORE TUO ARGUAS ME." A variety of this last coin has been found, and is in the British Museum, on which the word *ne* is omitted, making the prayer decidedly contrary to what the monarch intended.

The series of illustrations which are given herewith afford to the reader a very perfect history of the British coinage down to a recent period.

PLATE XXIV.

GREAT SEAL OF EDWARD THE CONFESSOR.

The chief departures from the regular series have been in the issue of siege-pieces, of which some illustrations are **given**. There have been times in the history of most modern nations when the monarch had either lost possession of the mint, or when the exigencies of the times compelled the immediate conversion of bullion or plate into money without the minting process. Thus at sieges of cities it has frequently been found convenient to cut plate into squares, diamonds, or irregular shapes, and stamp on the pieces their respective values. These pieces are known as siege-pieces, and are prized by collectors as curious. Such are the Newark and Scarborough, Colchester and Beeston Castle pieces of Charles I., shown in Plate LXV.

PLATE XXV.

1

2

3

7

4

8

5

6

VI.

Coin in America.

THE necessity of coin as a medium of trade was felt in America at an early period after the settlement of the country. The wampum of the Indians was used by the white settlers of Massachusetts to a considerable extent, at first. Wampum seems to be a primitive form of money, unlike that of any other part of the world. The value of gold depends on its scarcity, and of silver as well. Sheep and cattle were worth more or less as they served the purposes of men for food or labor; but wampum is the result of labor only, and its value seems to be only the value of so many hours' work of a man's hands. It consisted of strings of white shell, a valueless article itself, except as it had cost time and labor to make it on the sea-shores of New England.

Is there not a lesson in this North American Indian medium of circulation to which, in a more civilized nation, and a later period, we may turn with some degree of respect? Are we not arriving at an age in the world when gold is becoming more plenty, when its proportionate value to other metals is vastly decreasing, and when some new standard of value will be necessary? Have we not already arrived at an age when the true standard of value is labor? It is worth thinking of, to say the least of it.

The earliest coin supposed to have been struck for American circulation was a piece of brass called the *Somers Islands piece*. The Bermudas were discovered in the sixteenth century, but after-

PLATE XXVI.

GREAT SEAL OF WILLIAM THE CONQUEROR.
(A.D. 1066–1087.)

ward named the Somers Islands from Sir George Somers, who was wrecked there in the early part of the seventeenth century. There is extant in England a specimen of a coin, with a hog on one side and a rude ship or vessel on the other. The legend is SOMERS ISLANDS XII. This coin has no date. Not more than three specimens are extant. The coin is of little interest to us as a nation, not being continental. It is not even certain that it ever reached the islands, and it is quite certain that it never was used there as a currency. A very handsome copy of this piece has been recently struck by a coin-dealer in Philadelphia.

The first coins strictly North American were the New England coinage of the Massachusetts Mint, in 1652. First came the New England coins of *one shilling and sixpence* (Plate XCIX., Figures 1 and 2), bearing on their faces the simple legends N. E. XII., and N. E. VI. This was as rude an attempt at coinage as that of the Ionians or the Miletians of old time. But it answered all the purposes of a young nation for a little while. It appears, however, that so long ago as 1652 there were among our Puritan forefathers some who would clip the edges of a coin before they passed it out of their hands, and this coin was eminently convenient for the dishonest uses of such individuals. Hence the New England coins were soon suppressed, and the coins known by the general term PINE-TREE COINAGE took their place. The New England coins are now very scarce, and most highly prized by collectors. They have been very successfully counterfeited.

The Pine-tree coinage was issued in large quantities—in *shillings, sixpences, threepences,* and *twopences.* Of these there were several dies. The trees were according to the fancy of the artist. We have one known as the *Shrub* or *Scrub Oak shilling,* and others as before named. They differ also in size and in weight. This coinage was continued for thirty-three or four years, the date (1652) being never changed on the coins. The *two-penny*

PLATE XXVII.

1   2

3   4   5

6   7   8

9   10

11   12

piece was not issued till 1662, and always afterward bore that date.

The Massachusetts Mint was a source of quarrel between the colonists and the crown. It grew out of the necessities of the colony, for the only money in circulation in America was the Spanish coinage, rude, clipped, and uncertain, while the supply was small (a specimen, of a later date, is given in Plate CV., Figure 2). The history of the quarrel is full of amusing incidents, which will be found related in the histories of the times. The mint was once saved by a witty Massachusetts man, who told Charles II. that the oak on the coin was the tree that saved his majesty's life, placed there in honor of him!

There is a story told of John Hull, the mint-master of Boston, who coined the *Pine-tree* money, which sounds more romantic than it appears in fact. Hull received one shilling out of every twenty he coined for his labor and expenses. It was a great grist that was brought to his mill, and this was a toll in silver which made him in time one of the richest men in the colony. When his daughter was married to Samuel Sewall, he gave her, for dowry, the *Pine-tree shillings* which equaled her own weight, she being placed in one side of the scales and the shillings poured in the other, the wedding-day being selected for the trial. If the girl was of modern mould we might think a hundred pounds a fair light weight, and the dowry would then not seem large, for a hundred pounds of silver were not then worth much more than $1600, and the girl was not worth much if that were all her value. A very different weight from the $150,000 which, in several articles and works on numismatics, has been placed as the weight of the dowry. "Lumping" the young lady in such style would make her weigh nearly ten thousand pounds!

There was as yet no copper coinage for America. In 1694 a token made its appearance in England bearing on one side an elephant, and on the other a legend, GOD PRESERVE LONDON.

PLATE XXVIII.

GREAT SEAL OF WILLIAM RUFUS.
(A.D. 1087–1100.)

Where or by whom issued does not now appear, and it remains probable that it was a tradesman's issue to attract attention, or to serve for copper change. The device, however, attracted some one's eye who thought it the basis of a good colonial speculation, and two coins or tokens shortly after made their appearance with legends varying on the reverse, GOD PRESERVE NEW ENGLAND, 1694, on one, and GOD PRESERVE CAROLINA and THE LORDS PROPRIETORS, 1694, on the other. These do not seem to have gone into circulation at all. The wants of the colonies now began to be pressing for copper money. But their appeals to the home government were vain till 1749, when ten tons of copper money were exported to Massachusetts. At the present day we find among the old copper in circulation many very fine specimens of English *half-pennies* of 1749, always in better condition than any other year. It may be owing to this importation that these coins remain in America in such fine preservation.

The Colony of Maryland had at an early date taken means to supply some of their wants, and had ordered the coinage of silver as early as 1661. Lord Baltimore issued coins, bearing on the obverse the legend CÆCILIUS, DNS: TERRÆ: MARLÆ: & CT, around a bust of Lord Baltimore, and on the reverse his arms with the motto CRESCITE: ET MULTIPLICAMINI (Plate XCIX., Figure 6). Copper *half-pennies* were also issued at or about the same time, but they never went into circulation. There is but one specimen of this copper coin now known. It was sold in England within the past year at auction, and brought $362.

The silver coins were a *shilling, sixpence,* and *groat.* The *groat* was *fourpence;* the name derived (by error of pronunciation among the illiterate) from *quart* (*four*). The coin was long known and common in English coinage, but is wholly unknown in America at present.

We should mention, in passing, a variety of the Massachusetts silver, which has caused not a little dispute. There was in En-

PLATE XXIX.

1

2

3

4

5

6

7

8

gland, some **time** since, a coin known as the *Good Samaritan shilling*, closely resembling the *Pine-tree shilling*, except that in place of the tree was a group representing the story of the Good Samaritan. This coin was pronounced a forgery by common consent, until quite recently **an** American collector has obtained one, the second specimen **known**, and is very confident **that** it is a genuine coin. His judgment is to be relied on, and **it** may therefore with confidence be ranked among the American coins.

France probably struck the first copper money which obtained circulation as a coin on this continent. In 1721 the Mint issued a small copper coin, apparently though not certainly, for use in Louisiana, having for its obverse a double L, the initial of the monarch's name (Louis XV.), crowned, with the legend Sit Nomen Domini Benedictum (Plate XCIX., Figure 5). The same legend is found on a large portion of the coins of this monarch. **The** reverse was simply the legend Colonies Françoises, 1721, **H. The second issue of the** same coin was made in 1722, after which **it did** not appear again **until** 1767, when it was enlarged and the metal changed in quality, so that we have a larger coin at that period, of nearly perfect brass, with similar legends, but in much better style.

At almost the same period the "Wood money," as it has been called, was introduced into America (Plate XCII., Figure 4).

The English Government issued, in 1722, to one William **Wood** a patent for coining various copper pieces for the use of **Ireland.** The grant was made for a period of fourteen years, **and the** quantity limited to 360 tons of copper. The money issued by Wood was certainly more beautiful than had before appeared in English dominions. The **three** reverses were all fine specimens of art for the period, but its small size attracted attention, and a storm of rage **in all** of Ireland broke out against it. Dean **Swift, then in** Dublin, led on the attack with his cele-

PLATE XXX.

GREAT SEAL OF HENRY I.
(A.D. 1100–1135.)

brated anonymous letters known as "Drapier's Letters." The Government offered £300 reward for the discovery of the author of one of them—a reward that was laughed at in Dublin. The money failed in Ireland, and large quantities of it were sent on speculation to America, where it probably failed as well. Even at the present day these pieces are frequently to be found in circulation in our country.

But other pieces were coined by Wood, under a special patent for America, which were somewhat more successful. This was known as the *Rosa Americana* coinage (of 1722, etc.), so called from the device on the face of the pieces (see Plate CI., Figure 1). The issue consisted of a *penny*, a *half-penny*, and a *farthing*. They were all issued in different varieties. Thus we have each coin with a rose crowned, as in the illustration, and also each coin with a rose not crowned. The penny appeared also in 1733, with a different rose, and a head looking to the left. This coinage circulated chiefly at the South. It found no favor at the North.

A tin piece issued by James II. has been usually classed among the coins struck for America; but there does not seem to be any evidence that this coin had any special relation to the Western Continent, or that it was ever seen here in the last century. We may, therefore, safely reject it from the series.

The earliest copper coin which it can, with any degree of certainty, be affirmed was struck in America, was a private coinage in the little village of Granby, in Connecticut. This was the production of one Higley, or Highley. We prefer to call him Higley, since that is the sound commonly given to the name, and that is the true Connecticut orthography. He was an inhabitant of Granby, but his condition in life has been subject of dispute. By some he is called a blacksmith, by others a physician. On reference to the Colonial Records of Connecticut, edited by J. Hammond Trumbull, Esq., we find that in October, 1682, one John Higley suffered an execution against him for twenty-six

PLATE XXXI.

1

2

3

4

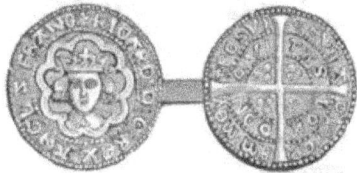

5

6

7

8

gallons of rum; and after that we trace John Higley's trouble with his creditor, one Trueman, through the usual course of supplementary proceedings and appeals. Possibly he is the same Higley who, at a later period and a very advanced age, introduced into America the art of coining copper money. Or, if it should seem that he was too old a man fifty-six years after 1682, when he **was** old enough to have a bill for rum, it may have been his son. In either case, and whatever may have been the name or the business of the man, Connecticut has the honor of introducing to the Western Continent, or at least to that portion of it now called the United States, the art of striking copper money, as Massachusetts had introduced silver.

In 1737 Mr. Higley, of Granby, **made** or procured a rude **set** of dies, and out of copper dug in Granby (where they dig it now) he coined various coppers, one of which we illustrate (Plate XCIX., Figure 7). These coppers circulated in Connecticut and New England; but being of excellent metal, soft and easily rubbed, they wore off and became smooth. They have almost entirely disappeared, **and** the **few specimens** now **in cabinets** are highly prized.

There are several varieties. One is like the illustration in the devices, but the legend around the deer is THE VALUE OF THREE PENCE, and around the hammers, CONNECTICUT, 1737. Another has, instead of the hammers, a broad axe, with the legend, I CUT MY WAY THROUGH.

The value of this rare **coin** has recently given **rise to** a suit at law in Connecticut, in which a purchaser, who brought his action **for the** value of a Granby which the seller refused to deliver, actually recovered $50 as the value of the coin. This valuation is exorbitant. The Granby copper brings from $13 to $25 at auction in New York city.

In 1773 a copper coin was struck in England for use in Virginia, which was a very beautiful coin. It has been said that the

PLATE XXXII.

GREAT SEAL OF STEPHEN.
(A.D. 1135–1154.)

issue of this coin had some reference to an interesting historical fact; namely, the invitation which had long before been extended to Charles II. by Virginia to come over and establish his throne in the Dominion—an invitation which the King did not forget, but subsequently honored by allowing Virginia to adopt his own arms. We know no authority for this statement, but the coin remains as one of the most beautiful of the early coins of America (Plate XCIX., Figure 4). It was struck in two sizes, but the sizes probably did not differ in value. Copies are known in silver, but it never circulated as a silver coin.

On the approach of the Revolution a token or coin, now known as the *Pitt* or *No Stamps* token (Plate CI., Figure 4), made its appearance in Massachusetts. It referred to the odious Stamp Act, and may have been popular as a medalet, though its history is lost. Some have supposed that it was struck in Boston, and have given the credit of it to Colonel Revere, whose memory has to bear the weight of a large number of poorly-executed copper coins, which do more credit to his patriotism than his taste. We know of no authority for attributing this coin to him, and it appears to us of English origin; but it is a rare and highly interesting relic of the times.

Other coins are known which are supposed to be the issue of Massachusetts experimenters in patriotic times. Thus there is a Janus head, rudely imitating the Roman *as* on a very small scale, with a reverse, the Goddess of Liberty. Another is a pine-tree copper, with the legend AMERICAN LIBERTY; and another has the words INDEPENDENS STATUS around a bust. These and others are illustrated in Dr. Dickeson's work on American coins, all of them very rare, some unique, but one and all of very doubtful origin.

During the war no coins were issued, unless the pewter medalet of 1776, with its CONTINENTAL CURRENCY legend, can be called a coin (Plate CIX., Figure 3); but when the war was ended the

PLATE XXXIII.

1

2

3

4

5

6

7

demand of the country for coin was loud and imperative, and was answered in all directions.

The *Georgius Triumpho* copper was among the first in the field (see Plate CIII., Figure 1). It was modeled on the *half-penny* of the English King, and struck in England, but the legend manifestly referred to George Washington. There is not the slightest reason for the common appellation of *Tory cent* which has been given to this coin. Liberty standing behind her barrier of thirteen bars (the engraver has mistaken the number in our illustration) sufficiently attests the character of the coin. A large supply of copper coin, probably struck in England, appeared in immense quantities in 1783. These were the *Nova Constellatio* coppers (see Plate CI., Figures 5 and 6). Of these there are five very distinct varieties and many inferior varieties. A similar coin, of larger size, with the same legends, is said to exist in silver, having under the letters U. S. the figures 1000. Another, of the size of the copper, having the figures 500, is also described; and the piece known as the *Immune Columbia* silver piece has the *Nova Constellatio* obverse, and Liberty seated on the reverse, with the legend IMMUNE COLUMBIA. All these pieces will be found fully described, with their varieties, in such works as Dr. Dickeson's. The plan of our sketch forbids more than a reference to them. (The Washington tokens of 1783, which now appeared, we shall describe in another connection.)

The *Pine-tree shillings* never circulated out of New England, and in time silver money became very scarce. One J. Chalmers, in 1783, struck at Annapolis, Maryland, silver coins, which appear to have obtained considerable circulation, and are known as the *Chalmers shilling, sixpence,* and *threepence* (see Plate CV., Figure 4). Specimens are now rare and highly prized.

STATE COINAGE.

Various States established Mints. Connecticut in 1785; other

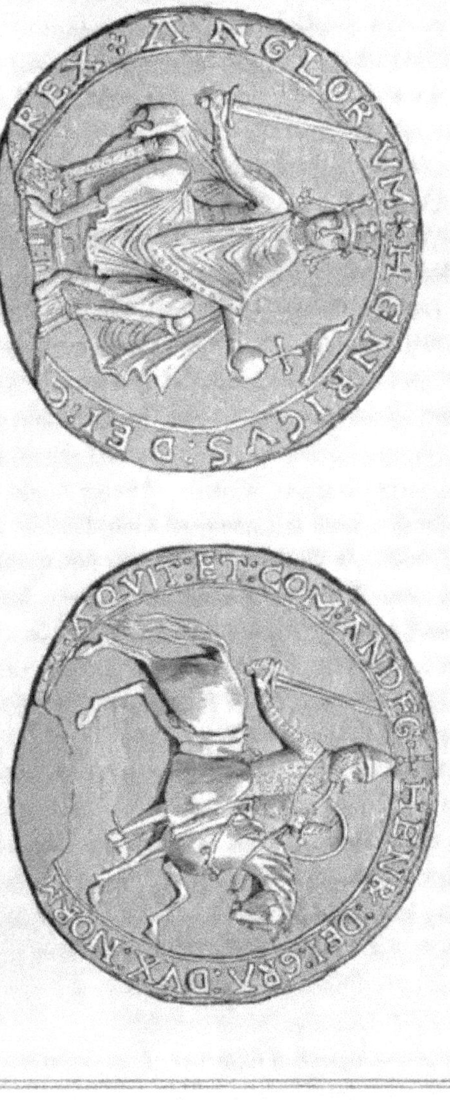

PLATE XXXIV.

GREAT SEAL OF HENRY II.
(A.D. 1154–1189.)

States as soon or immediately after. We can only glance rapidly at their issues.

Vermont soon issued many coins. The most common were those with the simple legend VERMON. AUCTORI. (By Authority of Vermont) on the obverse, around a laureated head (Plate CI., Figure 3), and on the reverse a seated figure with the words INDE. ET LIB. (Independence and Liberty). This form of legend was adopted by Connecticut, as will appear hereafter (Plate CIII., Figure 3).

Other Vermont coins had for a device the sun rising over the mountains, and the legend VERMONTENSIUM RES PUBLICA, with a reverse bearing the words QUARTA DECIMA STELLA (the fourteenth star) (Plate CI., Figure 2). This coin is somewhat varied in other specimens, the legend being VERMONTS instead of VERMONTENSIUM, and the reverse being differently executed. The Mint of Vermont seems to have been very active, and great quantities of coin were issued from it. Among others we have found coins with the head and name of King George, and the reverse INDE. ET LIB. A curious combination for a coin, but possibly resulting from the counterfeiting of English *half-pennies* which then passed current in the northern part of the country, or perhaps from the attempt to recoin *half-pennies* with the Vermont legends and devices. In one coin in our collection, however, the latter supposition is clearly impossible.

Connecticut was industrious in coining as in all other departments of art. The number and variety of Connecticut cents or coppers, from 1785 to 1788, is absolutely beyond computation. Every day a new one is discovered. The variation is not always important, but quite sufficient to indicate the use of a separate and distinct die for each coin. Thus the dots, stars, or lines of the legends are different, the head faces to the right or to the left, or some equally distinct mark is found.

The uniform legend is like that of the Vermont coppers, AUC-

PLATE XXXV.

1   2

3

4   5

6

7   8

TORI. CONNEC., with the reverse, INDE. ET LIB. (Plate CIII., Figure 3). Occasionally an error was made in the lettering. Thus we find an AUCTOBI, or an AUCTOPI, or an AUCIORI, or a CONNFC.; and these errors make coins of special rarity for those collectors who prize coins for their oddity rather than their historic value. It is probable that vast numbers of counterfeits were issued by private parties, and to these many of the varieties are to be attributed.

New York did not coin so largely as the other States. In fact the State never authorized a coinage, and most, if not all of those commonly called New York coins, because bearing the name or arms of the State, were struck in England. All the coins of New York are of a higher degree of rarity than those of the other States. The most common at present found, and that one of which it is probable the largest number was issued, was of English origin. It is that bearing the legend NOVA EBORAC around a head on the obverse, and VIRT. ET LIB. around a seated figure on the reverse; the date being 1787 (Plate CV., Figure 5). Of this there are two varieties, the seated figure in one facing to the right, and in the other to the left. There is also a difference in the head-dress of this figure.

The arms of the State form the reverse of several New York coins. The original type was probably the Eagle copper: obverse, an eagle, E PLURIBUS UNUM, 1787; reverse, the State arms, EXCELSIOR. Very few specimens of this coin are known.

The rarest of the New York coins, and one of the rarest coins of the American copper series, is the George Clinton piece of 1787, which we illustrate (Plate CV., Figure 1). This is the first time, we believe, that this coin has been illustrated (except in *Harper's Magazine* for March, 1860, where the same illustration was used). The coin in our own collection, and one owned in Boston, were, until quite recently, the only specimens known; but a third

PLATE XXXVI.

GREAT SEAL OF RICHARD I.
(A.D. 1189-1199.)

F

specimen has come into our possession within a short time. We have heard of no others. It is an interesting numismatic memorial of the first governor of the State, as well as of the early coinage of the country. It is remarkable that each of our specimens is struck, as the engraving indicates, over an IMMUNIS COLUMBIA. The remains of portions of the former coin are visible on each. There is another New York coin, sometimes called the New York Washington piece, from the supposed resemblance of the head on the obverse to that of the great patriot. This head is surrounded by the legend NON VI VIRTUTE VICI (Not by force, by bravery I have conquered). The reverse of this coin has a seated figure of Liberty, and the legend "NEO EBORACENSIS, 1786" (Plate CV., Figure 6).

A gold coin is known as the New York *doubloon*, having the legend NOVA EBORACA, COLUMBIA, EXCELSIOR around a landscape, the sun rising over the hills; on the reverse an eagle, and the legend "UNUM E PLURIBUS, 1787." This coin was never circulated, and we have heard of but two specimens in existence.

The IMMUNIS COLUMBIA token is ranked as a New York coin. On the obverse is a seated figure holding a flag and the scales of Justice, surrounded by the legend IMMUNIS COLUMBIA, and the date 1787. The reverse is an eagle, with the legend E PLURIBUS UNUM (Plate CIII., Figure 6).

Another New York coin had on the face an Indian chief, the legend LIBER NATUS LIBERTATEM DEFENDO; the reverse the arms of the State, on one variety; and on another the crest of those arms only, an eagle, with the legend NEO EBORACUS EX-CELSIOR, 1787.

A coin, known as the *Confederatio* copper, made its appearance in 1785 and 1786. Its history is entirely lost. We illustrate a unique specimen from the collection of Benjamin Haines, Esq., of Elizabeth, New Jersey (Plate CV., Figure 2). Another specimen, differing from this in the reverse, is known, but this copy in

PLATE XXXVII.

1

2

3 4

5

the possession of Mr. Haines is the only one extant of its kind, and is justly regarded as one of the rarest numismatic treasures of America. The reverse, as will be noticed, is dated a year later than the obverse.

New Jersey coined in great profusion. The coins of this State bear the uniform appearance indicated in the illustration (Plate CIII., Figure 4). The varieties differ only in the shape of the shield, the punctuation, the occasional omission of a letter by mistake, as in one die (which is E PLURIBS UNUM); and in one instance the horse's head is turned to the left. The latter coin is very rare.

Massachusetts struck two State coins in 1787, and reissued them in 1788—a *cent* and a *half cent*—of which large quantities were sent out. The *half cent* is now rare, but the *cents* of both dates are common, that of 1788 being a little more rare than 1787 (Plate CIII., Figure 2).

There is a coin known as the Kentucky *cent*, or copper (but so called without reason), which is a favorite with collectors, and which we illustrate (Plate CIII., Figure 5). The ground for the name appears to be that, in the pyramid of States on the obverse, Kentucky happens to be uppermost. It was struck in England, is a fine specimen of coinage, and may be prized by any one who possesses it. There is extant a token of P. P. P. Myddelton, with the legend BRITISH SETTLEMENT, KENTUCKY, 1776. But whether it was ever used in America, or is only an English token, is very doubtful. A splendid specimen, in silver, is in the collection of John F. McCoy, Esq., of New York.

In 1794 a French company proposed a settlement, and did attempt it, in the northern part of New York, which they named Castorville. It was located where Carthage, in Jefferson County, now stands, and is said to have contained families of rank and respectability. A coin or medal is extant known as the Castor-land piece. This was probably struck in France for the use of this

PLATE XXXVIII.

GREAT SEAL OF JOHN.

(A.D. 1199–1216.)

colony, and **though** it never passed into circulation, it is interesting **as the only permanent memorial of an** attempted colonization **of this State which** failed and has **been** forgotten. The dies of **this coin are still** extant in France, **and fine** specimens **are easily** procured. It may never have **been** intended as a coin, but only as a monument of the colony, and **as** such it remains, a very beautiful specimen of art.

WASHINGTON COINS AND TOKENS.

The head of the great patriot had, of course, formed the subject of more or less numismatic art in England and America; for it must be borne in mind that the American market **was** the constant spur to English labor, and that the necessities **of this** country, in the matter of coin, were thoroughly **appreciated by** ingenious artists on the other side.

In 1783 the *Washington and Independence* tokens made **their** appearance. These must not be confounded with the *Washington* **cents** of later issue (1791 and 1792), of which we shall presently **speak.** It does not appear that any of these tokens obtained extensive circulation, **nor that they were used** at all as money. They are interesting, **however, as relics of the** times in which **they** appeared, **and as indicating** the respect and veneration paid **to the** illustrious Washington **by** his contemporaries.

Of **the tokens of** 1783 there are four varieties, **of** which we illustrate the obverses of **two (Plate** CVII., **Figures** 8, 9). The four may be distinguished **easily thus: the first is the** *Washington and Independence* token, **with a** large head **laureated, and** the reverse a seated figure, the **legend** being the **words** UNITED STATES. The **second has a** similar **obverse,** but the **reverse** resembles the cent of **later years,** the legend being ONE **CENT** in a wreath, and around the wreath UNITY STATES OF AMERICA. The third has **a small head** on the obverse, and in other respects resembles the **first.** The fourth has the small head on both sides, the legend on

Plate XXXIX.

1

2

3

4

5

6

7

one side WASHINGTON, on the other side ONE CENT. The cuts show the two heads.

A very beautiful little token in brass also appeared at or near this period, of which we give an illustration (Plate CVII., Figure 3). There are two other sizes of this token extant, one smaller than the other, and both smaller than this. The legends and devices are the same on all.

When a national coinage was devised, the European custom of placing the head of a king on the coin of the realm of course suggested the idea of placing the bust of Washington on the American coins. This idea led to the production of the *Washington cents* of 1791, which are now so highly prized as numismatic treasures. These (and not the tokens of 1783) are the *Washington cents* which command such high prices, and which are the ornaments of collections of American coins (Plate CVII., Figures 4, 5, 6). Young collectors will do well to bear in mind that the tokens of 1783 are not to be confounded with these. It is not uncommon for an inexperienced collector to be induced to pay a large price for one of the tokens under the impression that he is purchasing a *Washington cent*. The most common error is made with the double-head token, which has the legend ONE CENT over the head, or with the UNITY STATES token, which also has the legend ONE CENT within the wreath on the reverse.

The cent of 1791 was made in England. This is evident from the character of the dies and the specimens of the coins extant. We have four in our own possession. The first is that commonly known as the large eagle. The second is closely like it on the obverse, though the head is not precisely the same, and the date is under a smaller and different eagle on the reverse. These are the large and small eagle cents of 1791. There are other varieties of the small eagle.

On one specimen of the large eagle cent in our cabinet the following legend appears around the edge of the coin: "BRADLEY,

PLATE XL.

GREAT SEAL OF WILLIAM OF SCOTLAND.
(A.D. 1165-1214.)

WILLEY, SNEDSHILL, BERSHAM" (the last letter is doubtful). The other specimens have on the edge " United States of America." We have heard of another specimen of the coin with this same legend.

A copper piece, bearing the date 1792, and commonly known as a *Washington cent*, is found in some collections and highly prized. It differs materially from the cent of 1791, bears another legend and a different head, and has no mark indicating that it was intended for a cent. This coin of 1792 has been claimed for Philadelphia as the work of Peter Getz; the evidence which we have received from his descendants, although purely traditional, seems to justify the claim.

This coin of 1792 was originally designed as a pattern for silver money, and the copies existing in copper are to be regarded only as medals. This is evident from various considerations. The coin is much too large for a cent. The word cent is nowhere visible on it, as it is on the true Washington cents. The work is more carefully done, and a copper coin of this size could not have taken a position in circulation in America or Europe in the year 1792. It was struck in silver, and the few specimens in that metal now existing are the highly-prized *Washington half dollars*, which are so rare (Plate CVII., Figures 1, 2). The specimen of this splendid coin which we illustrate was struck over an English piece of silver: the engraving shows the remains of some letters of the old coin. This was a common course pursued with new dies for coins, especially in new countries, where the machinery for rolling silver and cutting the planchets was imperfect, or perhaps as yet unknown. This coin brought a handsome price in 1859, no less than $57, and is well worth a much larger sum of money. Indeed the collector, once possessed of it, will hardly be induced by money offers to separate it from his collection. There is another coin claiming the name of *Washington half dollar*. We have not seen a specimen; but from an engraving

PLATE XLI.

1

2

3   4

5

we find that it resembles the genuine *half dollar* on the obverse, while the reverse bears the mark of the engraver's chisel struck across the eagle. This would indicate that the die was disapproved and destroyed by the engraver himself, and that the coins struck with it must have been produced for the amusement of some person in his work-shop, who tried his hand with a rejected die. The only copper coin of 1792 which can with propriety be called a *Washington cent* is a rare coin, of which we give the obverse (Plate CVII., Figure 7). The reverse is not very unlike the small eagle cent reverse of 1791, with the word CENT over the eagle.

Altogether there are some eight or ten distinct varieties of what are commonly called *Washington cents* of 1791 and 1792. In neither 1791 nor 1792 did these coins go into circulation. They were offered as patterns for the national coinage, then under discussion, and met the decided disapprobation of Washington. They were of course prized as specimens, and their value has since become very great.

Other coins appeared at about this time, or a few years later, bearing the name of Washington; and although in order of date they were mostly preceded by the regular American copper coinage, it is as well that we mention them in this connection. They were of English origin, and struck, apparently, for circulation there. One resembled closely the *Washington cent* of 1791, on the obverse, so closely that we have no doubt the same artist produced it. The legend around the bust is the same; and on the reverse is a ship, with the legend "Half-penny," and the date 1793. The edge has the words, "Payable in Anglesey, London, or Liverpool." This coin would seem to be conclusive in establishing the foreign origin of the *Washington cent* of 1791. The obverse of the specimen in our cabinet is identical with the obverse of the *small eagle cent* of 1791, and is without doubt the same die.

PLATE XLII.

GREAT SEAL OF HENRY III.
(A.D. 1216-1272.)

Another variety of the same coin has no date on the reverse, but two branches of leaves under the ship.

Another English token was issued with a head of Washington, and on the reverse a grate. This is called the *Washington Grate cent* or token, and was issued by Clark and Harris, a firm whose name it bears. The die is doubtless still preserved in England, as fine proof specimens are furnished to order in any quantity. It is a coin of little interest or value, and only to be noted as a compliment paid to the American patriot by an English house of tradesmen. The legend around the bust is " *G. Washington, the firm friend to peace and humanity.*"

In later years the head of Washington has formed a favorite subject with engravers and medalists, and the number of coins, tokens, tradesmen's cards, etc., which bear the head of the patriot on them is, probably, over two hundred and fifty. For a fuller description of them we must refer the reader to works which are devoted to details.

NATIONAL COINAGE.

In 1786 the Congress of the United States established a Mint. Its first and only issue for many years was the *Fugio* or *Franklin cent* (Plate CIX., Figure 2), so called, which was extensively circulated. The pewter or lead coin which had made its appearance in 1776, of which we have spoken (see Plate CIX., Figure 3), seems to have been the model of the *Fugio* copper. This coin was specially ordered by resolution of Congress, July 6, 1787. The name "Franklin copper" is derived from the pithy sentence on it, which sounds very much like the philosopher. He did recommend the adoption of such sentences on our coinage, but there is no evidence that he had any thing to do with the *Fugio* coin. Although a United States coin, this was struck by private contract, and a large portion of the issue was minted in Connecticut. It formed the chief article of copper currency down to the

Plate XLIII.

1

2

3

issue of the cent of 1793, and even later. Within the past year a keg of these coppers was found in the vault of a New York city bank, in fresh proof condition. This statement has been doubted; but we are indebted to the cashier for fine specimens of the contents of the keg, which abundantly prove the truth of the story. A recent discovery of the old dies, and possibly a manufacture of new dies, or repairing and retouching the old, has made these coins very common in various metals.

In 1791 Congress again resolved that a Mint be established, and authorized the President (then George Washington) to carry out the design of the resolution. It is supposed that the *Washington cents* of 1791 and 1792 were patterns issued to meet the plans of the President under this resolution. He rejected them. In 1792 a small quantity of silver was struck in *dismes* and *half dismes*, as they were called. These coins had on one side a head, and the legend LIBERTY PARENT OF SCIENCE AND INDUSTRY, 1792; the reverse, a flying eagle, and the legend UNITED STATES OF AMERICA; on one the word DISME, on the other HALF DISME. Tradition says none were coined but a few for Washington himself, out of silver sent by him to the Mint. They are now very rare. A few copper patterns for a cent, with a similar legend, were issued the same year. One of these was sold, in January, 1860, at a Philadelphia auction, for $66 50, and another for $50. These prices will give an idea of the present rarity of the coins. Some other patterns were struck about this time; but the Mint did not get fairly into operation until 1793, when the first United States copper cent appeared. This first cent was of the pattern shown in Plate CIX., Figures 5 and 7. It did not give universal satisfaction. Alexander Hamilton was at this time Secretary of the Treasury, and the new coin met with such criticisms as this from the *Argus*, a Boston paper, of March 26, 1793: "The chain on the reverse is but a bad omen for liberty, and Liberty herself appears to be in a fright. May she not justly cry out, in the words

Plate XLIV.

GREAT SEAL OF EDWARD I.
(A.D. 1272-1307.)

of the Apostle, 'Alexander the coppersmith has done me much harm; the Lord reward him according to his works?'"

No other coin was issued by the Mint this year. In 1794 a *dollar*, a *half dollar*, and a *half dime* were struck (Plate CIX., Figure 4). These were the first silver coins of the American series. The first *quarter dollar* and the first *dime* were issued in 1796. The devices on these coins were original, and certainly more beautiful than have since been adopted.

The form of the coins, or, rather, their devices, changed from time to time. The *dollar* reappeared in 1795 in similar style with that of 1794; but before the close of the year a new head was adopted, which continued in use until 1804. The reverse was changed, and a different eagle adopted, in 1798. From 1804 to 1839 no *dollars* were coined except the flying-eagle patterns of 1836, 1838, and 1839. In 1839 the obverse pattern of the *dollar* was struck. In 1840 it appeared with new devices, which have remained in use, with little variation, until the present time. The *half dollar* underwent several changes at different periods. In 1796 the fillet head was adopted. In 1801 the eagle wore a shield. In 1807 the bust, with a turbaned head facing to the left, appeared on the *half dollar*, and the eagle was again without the shield. The coin then continued with little change until 1836, when a smaller planchet, with a milled edge, was introduced. In 1839 the old bust of Liberty disappeared forever, and in its place came the nondescript design commonly called a seated figure of Liberty, which has since been the unvarying obverse, with the slight exception of mint marks, such as the arrow-heads of 1853.

The first *quarter dollar* was struck in 1796. The changes in the *quarter* occurred in 1815, 1831, 1838, and 1853.

The first *dime* was struck in 1796, and the changes occurred in 1798, 1809, 1837, 1838, and 1853. Two varieties appeared in 1837 and 1838. One of the varieties of 1838 came only from the New Orleans Mint—namely, the die without stars.

PLATE XLV.

1

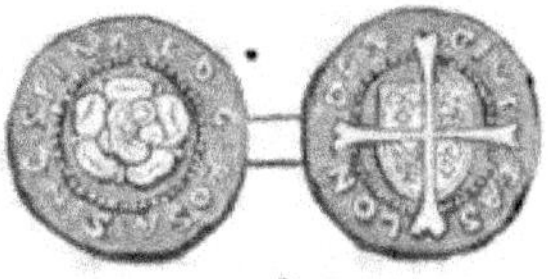

2

3

4

5

6

The *half dimes* were first struck in 1794, changed in 1796, 1797, 1829, 1837, 1838 (in these last two years resembling the *dime*), and 1853.

The *three-cent* pieces were first coined in 1851, and changed in 1853.

We are alluding now only to marked and important changes in the devices on the coins. Slight variations occurred in other years, and there are many slightly different dies of the same years; so that a complete collection of all the varieties of the different years will require at least ten or fifteen specimens of each coin of each year. The illustrations on Plates CIX., CX., CXI., CXII., and CXIII. show the variations in the gold and silver coins.

The attention of collectors has been more devoted to the *cents* and *half cents* than to any other coins.

The *cent* of 1793 appeared in many varieties.

1. The *link cent* (Plate CIX., Figures 5 and 7) before mentioned. On one variety of this *link cent* the legend is UNITED STATES OF AMERI. Some have plain edges, others have stars and stripes on the edge.

2. The *wreath cent*. The obverse of this *cent* is shown in Plate CIX., Figure 6. The reverse has a wreath instead of the links around the words ONE CENT. There are nearly or quite twenty varieties of this die, the chief marks of difference being in the shape and arrangement of the leaves under the head.

3. The *Liberty-cap cent*. This variety has a head of Liberty with a pole across the shoulder bearing a Liberty-cap, which hangs back of the head. The reverse is like the *wreath cent*, and on the edge ONE HUNDRED FOR A DOLLAR.

In 1794 the *cent* was issued with the Liberty-cap head.

In 1795 there was a thick die, with the words ONE HUNDRED FOR A DOLLAR around the edge, and a thin die without them. There was a reduction in the weight of the coin, which originated the latter variety.

PLATE XLVI.

GREAT SEAL OF EDWARD II.
(A.D. 1307–1327.)

In 1796 the Liberty-cap **head** was used during **the early** part of **the year,** and changed **for the fillet** head (so called) **in the** latter part of **the year.** This fillet head **is** illustrated on the silver coins.

In 1808 the fillet head was used on a few coins, and then the turbaned head, facing to the left, was introduced (as on the silver coins **of** that and later times).

In 1815 no *cent* was struck, but in 1816 the coin appeared with **the head facing to the** right, which has been the familiar die on **the copper cent ever since.**

The *nickel cent* **was introduced in 1856.** The varieties of this *nickel cent* during the few **years of its** issue we pass **over.**

Many inexperienced collectors waste a vast amount of time in examining smooth and worn coppers. The rule in **regard to** American cents should be to throw away a specimen of which the date **is not** perfect. Indeed a collector should never value **worn coins, and a good collection should contain** only good specimens. **Of some coins** poor specimens alone can **be had.** Of others, poor **specimens** may be kept until better can be substituted.

In examining worn specimens to find rare dates, the collector **will** save himself much **trouble** by remembering the general **divisions.** All *Liberty-cap cents* are prior **to** 1797. All *Fillet-head cents* are from **1796 to** 1808. All *cents* with heads facing **the** left are from 1808 to 1814. All copper *cents* from 1814 to **1857 have** the large head facing the right.

Plate XLVII.

1

2

3

4

VII.

Medalets and Tokens.

BESIDES the regular series of coins which have formed the subject of the preceding pages, there is a large class of pieces, belonging strictly to a numismatic collection, which are not ranked as either medals or coins, but which might be correctly gathered under the general name of medalets. These are political cards or tokens, tradesmen's cards, and innumerable small pieces of metal bearing impressions received from dies, all which are more or less prized by collectors. All countries have them. The English tokens of the latter part of the last century are very numerous. It need hardly be remarked that the collection of tradesmen's cards is the lowest department of numismatics, and although it becomes an interesting, and is in many respects a worthy part of the collector's employment, yet the extent to which it has been carried on in America of late is at once absurd and ridiculous. Prices have been paid for the cards of tradesmen equaling the prices of rare colonial coins; and bits of brass, copper, and white metal, possessing no interest or value whatever, historical or otherwise (unless as recording that some individual kept a billiard saloon or a bath-house at a particular place), have been the subjects of rival bidding at auctions to a fabulous rate of prices.

While copper coin was very scarce in this country, in 1787, Mott & Co., jewelers in the city of New York, imported a lot of copper tokens, having their names and place of business with a clock on the opposite faces. This, as being the first American tradesman's card, has a certain historical value. In 1794, Talbot

Plate XLVIII.

Great Seal of Edward III.
(A.D. 1327-1377.)

Allum & Lea issued their token, which is illustrated in Plate CV., Figure 7, and in 1795 they issued another variety. The latter is now very rare, while the 1794 is comparatively common. Our venerable friend, Dr. John W. Francis, one of the historians of New York in person and in his published works, has told us that he well remembers going to the store of Talbot Allum & Lea with silver to buy these coppers, for convenience in making change. The United States cent of 1793 and 1794 had not yet supplied the wants of the country.

After this time no tokens appear to have been issued by tradesmen until nearly or quite the time of the opening of the Erie Canal, when two or three New York houses had them struck, with reverses alluding to the completion of that great work. From this period the issue of such cards became more frequent, until now the catalogues show more than five hundred extant, and large numbers have appeared which are not catalogued and are unknown to collectors. The die-cutters of New York and Waterbury, in Connecticut, are now constantly occupied in cutting these cards for tradesmen in all parts of the country. Hundreds of thousands of specimens are struck in every successive year by the Scovill Manufacturing Company and the Waterbury Button Company. They appear in copper, brass, and white metal, and are largely circulated by their respective proprietors. But they disappear almost as rapidly as they appear, especially since the issue of the nickel cent, which keeps them out of general circulation.

But there are other tokens which possess a historical value, and form, therefore, an interesting part of a cabinet. We allude to political cards and medalets. In the various National and State elections it has been customary to issue such medalets, bearing either the head of a candidate with appropriate legends, or some device indicating the party who issue it. These issues belong strictly to the class of medals. They are metallic and lasting

PLATE XLIX.

1

2

3

4

5

6

7

records of national events. The number of these is much greater than even the ordinary collector imagines, nor has there appeared as yet any catalogue of them which can be considered as approximating toward completeness. They were not common until in the days of Jackson, when many appeared. Still larger numbers are extant of Van Buren, and every President and candidate for the Presidency since that time has secured a fame that is at least "as lasting as brass" in these medalets. In New York Gulian C. Verplanck and William H. Seward, when candidates for the office of Governor, were thus immortalized.

In 1837 and about that time a large number of copper coins were issued from private sources, some praising and others abusing and satirizing the administration. The most of these are familiar to all persons. Some of them are, however, of great rarity. Thus the common die, "Millions for Defence, not one Cent for Tribute," of which there are numerous varieties, is, in three or four kinds, of great rarity, while all the other varieties are very common.

As the nickel coinage is rapidly displacing the old copper cent, these tokens are fast disappearing, and they will in time be among the rare specimens of coins. They are now known in New England as "Bungtown Coppers;" in New York generally as "Shinplasters;" in New Jersey as "Horse-heads." The New Jersey name is probably derived from the colonial coin of that State.

VIII.

Counterfeit Coins.

THE history of coinage involves some history of counterfeits as well. From the earliest dates of coins men have been found to imitate them in inferior metals for purposes of gain. Nor is it at

PLATE L.

GREAT SEAL OF RICHARD II.
(A.D. 1377–1399.)

all uncommon now to find ancient coins which were manifestly the work of forgers. Even the earliest coins, those of Ægina in particular, are found of this description. Herodotus states in the *Thalia* LVI., that he considers the report a very absurd one, but he nevertheless gives it, that Polycrates purchased the departure of the Lacedemonians from Samos by striking off "a large number of pieces of lead cased with gold like the coin of the country," and paying these to the unwary soldiers. The reader of Herodotus will couple this remark with the amusing and characteristic statement of the preceding section, that he (Herodotus) had talked in person with a son of Samius, who was the son of Archias, who was present at the siege of Samos. It is very manifest that in the day of the old historian bogus coin was a matter of common talk, and that it was well understood that it could be made so as to deceive even an army of hungry Lacedemonians. There are extant specimens of forged gold coins of Lydia, which Humphrey suggests may be specimens of the very coins made by Polycrates, Herodotus to the contrary notwithstanding. We have certainly no occasion to doubt the perfect readiness of Polycrates to adopt such a course. His general style of life and conduct, and his associates in Greece, were of a similar class to those we now expect from counterfeiters and forgers. From that day to this the manufacture of bogus coins has been the employment of the dishonest in all ages.

It may seem incredible that a bogus coin should be manufactured which is of higher intrinsic value than the genuine, and yet this singular instance did occur in Hayti within the last half century. The Government coined base money; and while it regulated the importation of silver, so that the value of the coin should not be affected, it gave by decree a high value to the base issue. The result was that purer silver coin of the same weight or size with the genuine, and, of course, of greater value, were made in New York, smuggled into Hayti, and there passed at

Plate LI.

the rate of the genuine coin. Of course the bogus coin was worth more than the genuine coin of the realm.

A species of forgery which more concerns the coin collector is the manufacture of ancient or rare coins in modern times. Many collectors, and even writers on numismatics, have been misled by forged coins, which were not even imitations of genuine. In Padua, about 1540, two engravers, Jean Cavino and Alexander Bassiano, were manufacturers of copies of coins and medals. They pursued this honest line of business until they became so skillful that their copies could not be detected from originals, and then they began to sell them as genuine coins and medals. Hence came the name Paduan, applied by collectors to any ancient coin of modern make. Dervien, a Frenchman at Florence, Carteron in Holland, and Congornier in France, were afterward celebrated in the same line. The latter is stated to have confined his work exclusively to coins of the Thirty Tyrants. The list of coiners might be largely multiplied. Sestini published, in 1826, a catalogue of the forged coins of Becker, who died at Hamburg so late as 1830. The number was immense of coins which he made from imagination purely, without any historical authority. The result of this is that there are now thousands of these coins in collections, and offered for sale by collectors throughout the world. The cheat has been carried so far that, in some of the cities of the East, it is not uncommon for men to have supplies of these manufactured coins buried, and "excavate" them before the eyes of travelers, to whom they at once sell them at enormous prices.

It is impossible to give any directions by which forgeries of ancient coins can be detected. Experience is the only guide.

But a much more dangerous system of forgery is practiced in America. This consists in the manufacture of rare American pieces, for which very high prices are obtained. The art of electrotyping has done much to aid counterfeiters, but in general electrotypes can be detected by the ring, or the absence of a clear

PLATE LII.

GREAT SEAL OF HENRY IV.
(A.D. 1399-1413.)

ring, in the coin. A manufactory exists now, however, in which exact copies of rare coins are produced, with quite a clear ring. Nevertheless, if the purchaser will examine the edges of the coin carefully, he will be apt to detect a line or mark extending around it. If he balances one of the coins on the end of his finger, and a good copper on the next finger, he will find that the ring of the coins is very different. These coins are filled with silver solder, or with silver. The Elephant pieces, the Granby, the rarer New York pieces (except the Clinton), the U. S. A. Bar cent, and indeed nearly all the rarer American copper pieces, are thus reproduced, and the specimens are for sale freely in the market. We speak with confidence on this subject, as we are not only familiar with these coins from examination, but could without great difficulty point out the manufactory in the city of New York.

All the specimens that we have seen present a slightly rough appearance on the surface, as if they had been dipped in acid, or as if they were castings. Many collectors have, on examining their coins, found these counterfeits among them, and all should be on their guard against them.

PLATE LIII.

1

2

3   4   5

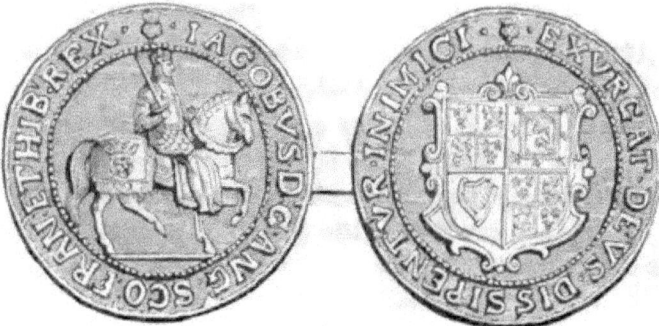

6

IX.

Coinage of Continental Europe.

AMERICAN collectors have very little opportunity of making large additions to their cabinets from the coins of continental Europe. But it is not uncommon to find a stray coin, of great interest and value, brought to this country by an immigrant or in some other way thrown into the market of old silver. No collections on this side of the Atlantic offer any opportunity for the study of these coins, and we have preferred, for the purposes of this volume, to condense a sketch of some of them from the excellent manual of Mr. H. Noel Humphreys, published by Bohn. We do this without hesitation, for the reason that the present volume can not be regarded by any one as a substitute for Mr. Humphreys's admirable works, to which we shall elsewhere refer the reader. The following remarks on the coins of European states are abbreviated from the Coin Collector's Manual.

COINS OF MODERN ITALY.

After the Roman Empire had fallen the art of coinage seems lost in Italy. After the extinction of the race of Gothic kings, the coins of the exarchs of Ravenna appear as viceroys of the emperors of the East. These coins are only small copper, and generally bear the inscription FELIX RAVENNA.

The gold and silver of the Eastern Empire were found to form a sufficient circulation in those metals for Italy.

The Lombards, who subdued the north of Italy A.D. 572, and occupied it for two centuries, have left no coinage to record their

PLATE LIV.

GREAT SEAL OF HENRY V.
(A.D. 1413–1422.)

rule; and we find no Italian coin belonging properly to the modern series till the issues of Charlemagne, at Milan, about 780. He also struck coins at Rome. His Milanese coins have a cross, and on the reverse the monogram of Carolus, with MEDIOL. These types of Milanese coins are found of successive German emperors till the thirteenth century.

About the period of Charlemagne the modern Italian coinage of silver pennies commences, founded, like that of France, Spain, and England, on the old Roman denarius.

Soon after the time of Charlemagne, the counts or local governors of towns and provinces became more or less independent, and their offices very generally hereditary. These petty governors all issued coin, and a detailed account, therefore, or even an outline of the progress of all the various coinages of modern Europe, would occupy many ponderous volumes; a few examples only can, therefore, be glanced at.

The modern independent coinage of the city of Rome, under the Popes, began, like most others, with a series of silver pennies, the first being those of Pope Hadrian, from A.D. 771 to 795, who received the privilege from Charlemagne. This modern Roman series has generally the name of the Pope on one side, and SCVS · PETRVS on the other. Some few have rude portraits, such as those of Benedict II., Sergius III., John X., Agapetus II., etc.

For above a century, from 975 to 1099, there are no coins except those of Leo IX. From Paschal II. to Benedict XI., 1303, the Popes having no power in Rome, the pennies are of the Roman people, bearing on one side a rude figure of St. Peter, with ROMAN · PRINCIPE, and on the other SENAT · POPVL · Q · R ·, accompanied by the name in succession of the chief senator, who was then governor of the city of Rome (Plate XIX., Figure 6). Some have also the arms of this personage, as on the coins of Brancaleo, 1253, which have a lion on one side, with BRACALEO S · P · Q · R ·;

PLATE LV.

1

2

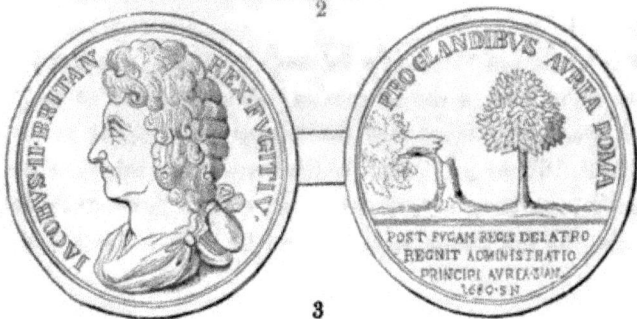

3

and on the other side a female figure, with a crown, a globe, and a palm-branch, and the legend ROMA · CAPVT · MVNDI ·, etc. (Plate XIX., Figure 8). Charles of Anjou, when elected senator of Rome, issued coins with the inscription CAROLVS REX . SENATOR VRBIS.

A few of the Popes issued patrimonial coins, with PATRIMO-NIVM; but in general the coinage of the Popes, up to a very recent period, may be considered as that of a series of bishops, like that of the Bishops of Metz, Liège, etc.; or even those of the Archbishops of York and Canterbury, in Saxon times.

Of Clement V. there are groats, with his portrait, three quarters length, as of nearly all his successors, till Sextus IV., in 1470—with whose coinage the profile portraits begin, as they do in England with his contemporary, Henry VII. The first gold coinage of modern Rome is of the reign of John XXII., 1316. After this period the coinage of the Eternal City begins to improve rapidly in excellence of execution, the money of the infamous Alexander VI., the luxurious Julius II., and the politic Leo X., being as remarkable for fine execution as any of the period. The larger silver, the scudi, etc.—equivalent to our crowns—and the German thalers, first appear in those reigns.

In Milan, the first remarkable coins, after the series of the German emperors, are those of the Visconti, the independent dukes of Milan. The first are those of Azo, 1330. Ludovico il Mauro has on his coinage the legend LVDOVICVS · M · SF · ANGLVS · DVX · MLI ·; the meaning of ANGLVS has not as yet been satisfactorily explained.

The coinage of Florence is celebrated as being the first to introduce the general use of gold, which commenced as early as 1252, a century earlier than the famous issue of gold nobles in England. These gold pieces, which bore on one side the Florentine lily for principal type, and on the other a figure of St .John the Baptist, the patron saint of the city, were imitated first by

PLATE LVI.

GREAT SEAL OF HENRY VI.
(A.D. 1422–1461.)

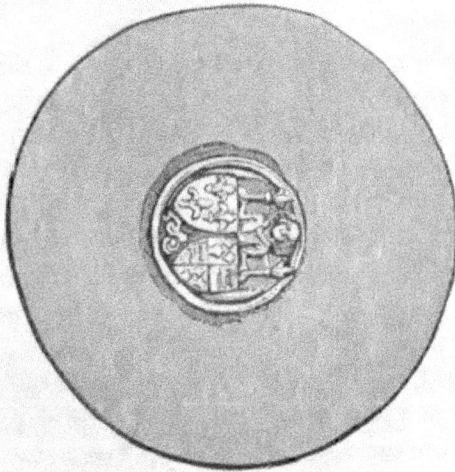

the French and the Popes, then by the Germans and English, and were the first gold coins issued in Europe after the eighth century.

The first copies of the Florentine gold not only bore the name of Florins, from that of the city where they were first issued, but also their types; nothing but the legend or inscription being changed. At a later period, however, though the name florin was still preserved, the national types of the countries in which they were issued gradually superseded those of Florence. These Florentine gold coins bore around the standing figure of St. John the legend s·IOHANNES·B·, and round the large and elegantly designed *fleur-de-lis* the legend FLORENTIA.

It is thought the national arms of France originated in the copying of these Italian coins, as those flowers do not appear as a national badge till the reign of Philip le Hardi, about 1270. These celebrated coins weigh one drachm, and are no less than twenty-four carats fine, being intrinsically worth about twelve shillings English.

The modern coinage of Venice begins with silver of the tenth century, marked Venici; and one of the earliest with a name is that of Enrico Dandolo, doge in 1280. Silver groats of Venice appear as early as 1192, and copper about 1471; while the gold followed close upon that of Florence, and appeared in 1280. Humphreys, in speaking of the ancient coinage of Cyzicus, mentions that the gold of that ancient Greek state was the forerunner of that of Venice, from which the modern name Zecchino, *Anglicè* Sequin, was derived; and it is probable that the coined gold of Cyzicus was in circulation till late in the Eastern Empire; and especially at Venice, at the time of the issue by Florence of her new gold coinage, upon which Venice, in emulation, also issued a national gold coinage, but founded upon the value and preserving the name of the ancient Cyzicenes.

Among the earliest modern coins of Genoa are those of the

PLATE LVII

2

1

2

3

3

4

5

4

6

6

Emperor Conrad, **1129,** DVX IANVAE.; and those of the dukes of **Savoy** begin **in the same** century.

The Patriarchs of Aquileia issued **coins** from 1204 to 1440, and **Ferrara** has coins **of its** Marchesi **from** 1380; while several free towns issued their own money with peculiar types, those of Mantua being honored by the effigy of Virgil, the modern Mantuans not forgetting that their city was the birth-place **of** the great bard **of the** Augustan Age.

The **Neapolitan** series begins as early as Duke **Sergius,** A.D. **880, with which are** classed **the coins** of the powerful Dukes **of** Benevento, forming **a fine early series;** and those of Roger I., of Sicily, Roger II., William **I. and II., and** Tancred, belong **to the** Neapolitan series in collections; **as also those** of Sicily **under the** Normans. In 1194, Naples and Sicily were subdued **by the** German emperors, whose Neapolitan coins are **extant.** Those of Manfred **next** appear, in 1225; and those of **Charles of Provence, in 1266; then those of the** celebrated Queen **Jeanne, followed** by **those of the house of Aragon, and** the **later series,** which begin **to improve like other modern series toward the** close of the fifteenth century; and **after that** period **assume** a strong family likeness to those of **the rest of modern** Europe.

Spain formed, **till the irruption** of the Moors, in 714, **one compact and powerful** kingdom, **to the princes of which the privilege of coining gold had been very** early **conceded by the emperors of the East.** The **consequence of** this independence **of Spain** was the **issue** of a gold **coinage of** great interest, consisting of *trientes,* or **thirds of** the Byzantine solidus, which, under **the** name of Bezants, **long** circulated in the **west** and north **of Europe.** These *trientes* of the Gotho-Iberian princes occur, of Leirva, 567; Liuvigild, 573; Weteric, 603; **Gundemar,** 610; Seseburt, 612; Svinthila, 621; Sisemond, 631; Chintila, 636; Tulga, 640; Chindas-

PLATE LVIII.

GREAT SEAL OF EDWARD IV.
(A.D. 1461-1483.)

vint, 642; Recesvint, 653; Womba, 672; Ervigo, 680; Egica or Egiza, 687; Witiza, 700; and **Rudric or** Roderic, the last of the Goths, the hero of Southey's celebrated poem, in 711.

After Amalric, **who** was the first acknowledged **King** of Spain by the emperors of the East, the kingdom became elective; the power of election residing chiefly in the bishops. The coins above alluded to, however, **bear** the portraits of the kings **as** of **hereditary** sovereigns, accompanied by their names, **the reverse having a cross with the name of the** place of mintage, **generally in the province of Bætica, where Roman** colonies had **been most abundant.**

On the subjection **of the country by** the Arabs, an Oriental coinage was issued, which, as the Mohammedan creed forbade the imitation of the human figure, present only Arabic inscriptions, generally sentences from the Koran.

The generic term of the Arabs for a coin is *markush*, from which **the term** *marcus*, common **in monetary** statements of the period, **is derived; payment of so many gold marcuses** being often stip**ulated, which no doubt referred to these coins** of the Spanish Arabs, which not only **circulated** among, but **were** imitated in *fac-simile* by, other nations who did not understand the Arabic characters. One **of** these imitations of the Arabian *markush* is **known,** which is supposed **to** have been issued by **the Saxon Offa,** King of Kent. **(See page 54.)**

The Gothic inhabitants of Spain, driven into the fastnesses of the **Asturian** mountains, step by step recovered their territories from their Oriental **invaders;** and in the tenth century, **when** the kingdoms of Aragon **and** Navarre were thus founded, **coins were** issued **by** the sovereigns of those states, closely resembling **the** silver pennies **of** the rest of Europe at that period. The kingdom of Castille **was next** founded, and the Moors were finally expelled from their **last strong-hold,** Granada, **and the** whole Iberian peninsula (1492) in the **reign** of Ferdinand and Isabella, who, as

PLATE LIX.

1

2

3

4

heirs of the kingdoms of Castille and Aragon, which had previously absorbed all the lesser states, became sovereigns of the whole of Spain.

Since the re-establishment of the Christian states, the Spanish coinage had taken the course of that of the rest of Europe, gradually increasing in excellence from the middle to the end of the fifteenth century.

After this period the discovery of America, and the vast influx of gold and silver from the mines of Mexico and Peru, caused the coinage of Spain to become, for a time, the most abundant of Europe, dollars and half dollars of silver being coined in amazing numbers, which were for a time the only European coin accepted in India, China, and other Oriental nations where European commerce was now fast spreading.

The coinage of Portugal, founded as a separate kingdom in 1126, followed a very similar course to that of Spain.

COINAGES OF MODERN GERMANY.

Germany, after the time of Charlemagne, exhibits an immense number of small independent states, each coining money on its own account, a description of all of which would be an endless task, even if the space for so doing was unlimited. About the year 920 the Emperor, Henry the Falconer, conferred independent privileges on many German cities; and from about that period the independent issues of coin commenced at Augsburg, Hamburg, Frankfort, Strasburg, etc., which may be regarded as true republics in the heart of the empire. The coins of Nuremberg generally surpass those of the emperors of corresponding dates in both execution and purity, while they are equaled by many of those of the bishops, the electoral princes, and many petty sovereigns. As examples of the coinage of the small states of Germany, as well as those of France, those of the city of Metz, the County of Bar, and of the Dukes of Lorraine, will form as good

PLATE LX.

GREAT SEAL OF EDWARD V.
(A.D. 1483.)

I

examples as could be selected, and the following notice will be found to explain their character pretty clearly.

MONEY OF THE COUNTS AND COUNT DUKES OF BAR.

Frederic of the Ardennes, the first Count of Bar, was a son of Wiegeric, Count of the Palace, under Charles the Simple. He married Beatrice, a daughter of Hugh Capet, in the year 951; and the Emperor Otho, in consequence of the marriage, conceded to him the County of Bar. His dynasty remained in hereditary possession till the death of Frederic II., in 1034; when his daughter Sophie married the Count of Monteon and Montbelliard, and lived till 1093; and her son, Theodoric II., succeeded her. The authors of "L'Art de vérifier les Dates" state that he was the first who bore upon his state-seal two *bars*, a kind of native fish, in allusion to the name of the district.

There is no money of Bar known, either of the first dynasty, or of the one of Montbelliard, which succeeded it, nor until after the reign of Thibault II., who died in 1297.

The coins of his son, Henry III., who married Aliénor, a daughter of Edward III. of England, are the earliest known of Bar.

In 1342, John, the blind king of Bohemia, and Duke of Luxemburg, afterward killed at the battle of Cressy, and Henry IV., Count of Bar, concluded a treaty, by which they agreed to strike money for the common currency of both their dominions, more especially in Luxemburg. Their coinage struck under this engagement (the original written document concerning which is still in existence) bears the inscription ✠ IOHANNES : REX : ET : HENRICVS · COMI · on a shield; on the obverse the arms of Bar and Luxemburg are quartered; and on the reverse, MONETA SOCIORVM, etc.

There are silver pieces described by De Saulci, of 68, 24, 15, and 19 grains; and of billon of 90 grains.

PLATE LXI.

1

2   3

4

5

Some of the money of **Bar, soon** after this period, closely re-sembles in type that of the **kings** of France, especially the *gros Tournois*. Coins bearing the arms of Bar and Luxemburg quar-tered were also issued, under Robert of Bar, and John Duke of Luxemburg, between 1378 and 1380.

The same Duke Robert appears to have struck gold *florins*, the first gold in this series, which are copies, except the name of the prince, of those of Charles V. of France; and have for device of the obverse original Florentine type the figure of St. John the Baptist, with s · IOHANNES · B ·, and on the reverse the well-known Florentine lily, with ROBERTVS DVX ; while those of the kings of France have KAROLVS REX; both being, in other respects, *fac-similes* of the original coins of Florence.

Réné of Anjou succeeded to the Duchy of Bar in 1419, and reigned till 1431; and during his reign some very excellent money **was struck.** He married the daughter of the Duke **of Lorraine;** and thus the **arms of** Lorraine, of Bar, and of the kingdom of Jerusalem appear **on** the very handsome coins issued in Bar at this time.

The Duke Charles II. of Lorraine, who was regent of the Compté, appears to have issued the money in his name.

MONEY OF LORRAINE.

The first two Dukes of Lorraine were only holders of the titles **and** privileges for life; but on the death of Gozelon, the second duke, **the** emperor, Henry III., having given the duchy to Gerard, **Duke of** Alsace, instead of Godfrey, son of Gozelon, Godfrey **caused** the Duke Gerard to be assassinated; but the emperor, nevertheless, persisted in carrying out his views, and appointed **Albert,** the nephew of Gerard, to the duchy, at the same time making the office hereditary in his family, in order effectually to shut out the claims of Godfrey: and thus commenced the heredi-tary power of the house of Lorraine, which endured for seven

PLATE LXII.

GREAT SEAL OF RICHARD III.
(A.D. 1483-1485.)

centuries; issuing a series of money little inferior to that of the great European monarchies.

Fine coins are extant of Thibault II.

The money of Farri IV., who succeeded, is still better executed.

Of Jean or John I., taken prisoner by the Black Prince at the battle of Poitiers, and carried to England with John of France, a few coins are known, similar in art, though not in type, to the Anglo-Gallic coins, struck by the Black Prince and Henry V. in France.

Réné II., from 1471 to 1508, carried on a war against Charles the Bald, Duke of Burgundy, and issued silver money on which his arm appeared issuing from a cloud, and holding a sword, with the inscription ADJUVA NOS DEUS SALVTARIS NOSTER, or, FECIT POTENTIAM IN BRACHIS SVO.; in allusion to the greatness of his cause.

Gold money first appears in this reign; and the florins have for type a full figure of St. Nicholas in episcopal robes, at whose feet is a vessel containing three children; on the other side are the arms of Hungary, Naples, Jerusalem, Aragon, Nancy, and Bar, all alluding to territories or alliances of the reigning family

The ducat of gold was also issued, the principal types being a ducal effigy, in front of which is a shield with the arms of Bar and Lorraine, with "S. Georgius," and "1492"—one of the earliest examples of a date on a coin of a sovereign prince. Some of the silver coins of this reign are of large dimensions.

The transition from the mediæval style of art to the modern took place in Lorraine in the long reign of Charles III., who began to reign in 1545, and reigned till 1608. The later coins are of finer execution than any English coins of the end of the reign of Elizabeth or beginning of James I. The portrait is found on the early coins of Charles III., in extreme youth, and resembles some of those of Edward VI.; and the larger pieces correspond

PLATE LXIII.

1

2

3   4

in size to the crowns and half-crowns of that English reign. They are dated 1557, and have for reverse seven small shields arranged in a circle, with different arms; and in the centre, with an inner circle of beading, a somewhat larger shield bears the arms of Lorraine. There is no legend on this side of the coin.

A magnificent écu, or crown, was struck toward the close of this reign (1603), the style of which is similar (but finer) to those of Henry IV. of France.

Francis III., the heir of Lorraine, becoming Emperor of Germany, the series of Lorraine coins ends with Charles III. In this last reign the coinage of Lorraine was equal to any in Europe.

COINAGES OF HOLLAND, BOHEMIA, ETC.

The coinage of the Counts of Holland and Flanders followed much the same course as that of Bar or Lorraine. In the east of Europe the coinage of the Slavonic races was even somewhat more imbued with the style of the Byzantine coinage of the still existing Eastern Empire of Rome.

Bohemia, the most westerly of the purely Slavonic states, has the earliest coinage; it commences with that of Duke Boleslaus, in the year 909, the coins bearing both his portrait and name. These are followed by coins of Bocelaus II. and his wife Emence, about 970. Bocelaus III. in 1002; Jaromin, 1020; Udalrich, 1030; Bracislaus I. and Spitihenetis. Wralislaus, the first king, in 1060 issued coins with the regal title, and then follow those of Wadislaus, etc., which space does not allow me to particularize.

The Bracteate money, however, of Ottocar, issued about 1197, must not be passed over, as it is the type of a peculiar class issued about that time in several parts of Europe. This species of coin is of very thin silver, and only impressed with a type on one side, the back having the hollow indent of the same form. These coins form a modern variety, somewhat analogous to the ancient

PLATE LXIV.

GREAT SEAL OF HENRY VII.

(A.D. 1485-1509.)

incused money of **Magna Græcia,** but they are much thinner, and
of course greatly inferior in execution and totally different in the
style of types. This kind of money was **struck in** the greatest
quantity about the twelfth century, and bears various types, the
cross being the most common; **but the** heraldic badges, of different
states, such as the lion, etc., are found upon the *bracteates* of
different countries.

The coinage of Hungary belongs to a similar class **to** that **of**
Bohemia.

The coinage of Poland is that of an allied race, and consequently follows a similar **course in its** development and progress to
that of Bohemia.

COINAGE OF RUSSIA.

In Russia, when Vladimir, or Volodemir **I., Duke** of Russia, in
981, married the daughter of the Byzantine **emperor,** art first began to dawn on Russia. The Tartar conquest of 1238 interrupted the course of civilization for a long period; and not till 1462,
when the foreign **yoke was** thrown off, **can the** modern race of
sovereigns be said to **commence.** The capital was anciently Kiof,
but the custom of dividing **the** territory among all the sons of the
duke caused many independent states to arise, so that there **are
also** coins of the Princes of Twer, Rostovia, Tchernigor, Suenigorod, Mojaiski, Pleskow, Riazin, and Caschin. The most ancient
money bears the names **of** princes, without **dates, and,** as many
of the same name were **reigning in** different districts, renders it
exceedingly difficult to classify **the** Russian money of the early
epochs; but it **may** be fairly stated that no Russian money exists
much **earlier than** the thirteenth century. The earliest coins
of that **country** have generally a man standing with a bow, or
spear, for principal type, somewhat similar to the coins of the
Scythian **dynasties,** who **subdued the** north of India; and on
the reverse **rude figures** of different animals. Some have St.

PLATE LXV.

1

2

3

4

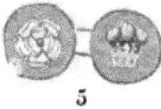

5

7

6

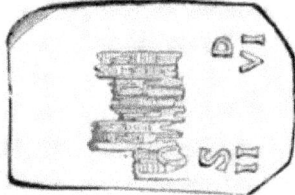

George and the Dragon. These are nearly all *kopecs*, or silver pennies.

Under Ivan, or John, in 1547, the Russian dollar, or rouble, commences, and also its half. Those of the Pretender Demetrius are very scarce.

The recent coins of Russia are too well known to require notice.

COINAGE OF PRUSSIA.

The first Prussia silver pennies were coined by the Teutonic Order at Culm. In the next century the rulers of Prussia coined *schellings, groats*, and *schots*, the latter being the largest, and consequently the most scarce. The types were generally an eagle surmounting a cross, with a scalloped border, forming a quatrefoil or cinque foil, with the legend MONETA DOMINORUM . PRVSSIE. The reverse is a cross fleurie with a similar border, with HONOR . MAGISTRI . IVSTITIAM . DILIGIT. In the same century the first gold was struck.

In 1466 Poland acquired the eastern portion of Prussia, and the Teutonic knights became vassals to that crown for the rest.

Albert, Marquis of Brandenburg, was the last master of the Teutonic Order, and in 1525 was made Duke of Eastern Prussia, to be held as a fief of Poland. At this period the money was so debased that thirteen current marks were only worth one mark of pure silver. In 1657 Eastern Prussia was declared free from vassalage to Poland, and the princes of the house of Brandenburg assumed the title of Kings of Prussia, since which period the coins of Prussia are well known.

COINAGE OF DENMARK AND THE NORTHERN STATES.

Of the northern states of Europe, Denmark, Sweden, and Norway, the progress of the coinages resembles that of the English monarchy. Of the Danes, the earliest coins known are those

PLATE LXVI.

GREAT SEAL OF HENRY VIII.
(A.D. 1509–1547.)

which were struck in England and Scotland. After Canute the Great the national Danish series may be said to commence.

Those of Magnus Bonus, 1041, have a half-length figure of the king, with Runic reverses, and are of neat execution. On those of Sweno II. the portrait has an arched crown; and the reverses have curious ornaments of a tesselated form running across the field, with a series of IIIIII's on either side, apparently an imitation of Roman letters, not understood. The coins of Harald II., 1074, have generally two heads, the throne being contested by his brother, and the moneyers being apparently anxious to keep in with both claimants for supreme power.

The coins of Canute or Cnut, the Saint, have CNVT R. for CNVT. REX., and on the reverse SIVORD. I. ROCI. (*Roschild*), then the name of the Danish capital.

The coins of King Nicholas, called in Danish Niel, are very rude, as are those of Waldemar and his successors, including those of the celebrated Margaret, whose coins have no legend. The coins of Olaf (1376) have a full-faced portrait, with a crowned O for the reverse.

Eric (1426), after his return from the Holy Land, issued billon coins, that is, of base silver, which is the "black money" spoken of by the chroniclers of various states about this time.

The later coinage of Denmark is similar to that of the rest of Europe.

The earliest coins of Sweden appear to be those of Biorno, about 818, which resemble those of Charlemagne, having a cross for principal type, though it would appear that Biorno was not a Christian.

The next well-authenticated Swedish coins do not occur till those which are probably of Olaf Skolkonung, in 1019, with the legend OLVF. REX. SVEVORVM., and those of Anund, 1026, with ANVND. REX.; and on the reverse, THORMOD. ON. SIHTV. Sihtu being Signuta, the ancient capital of Sweden. On the coins of

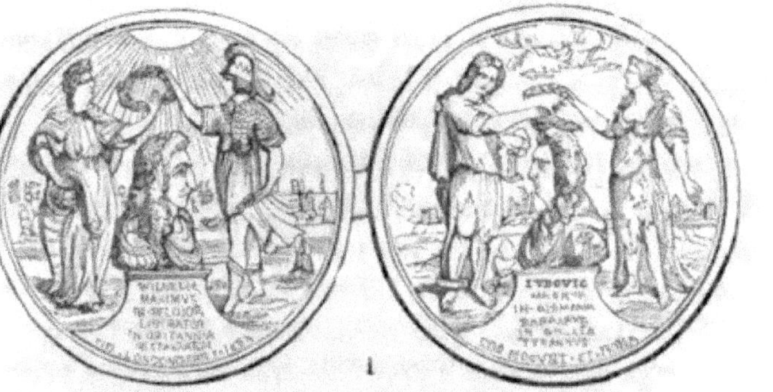

1

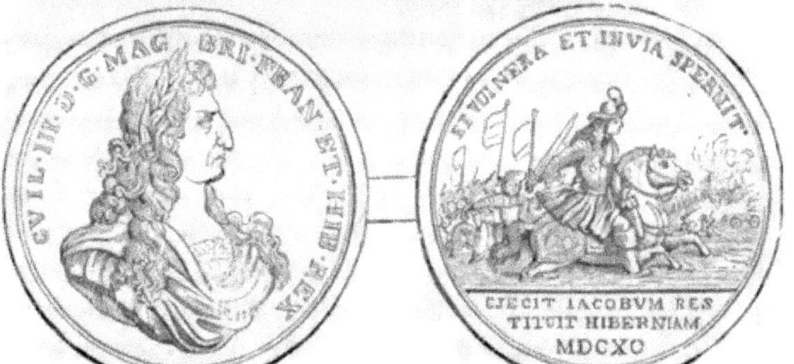
GVIL·III·D·G·MAG·BRI·FRAN·ET·HIB·REX
ET INVIA SPERNIT
EJECIT IACOBUM RES
TITUIT HIBERNIAM
MDCXC

2

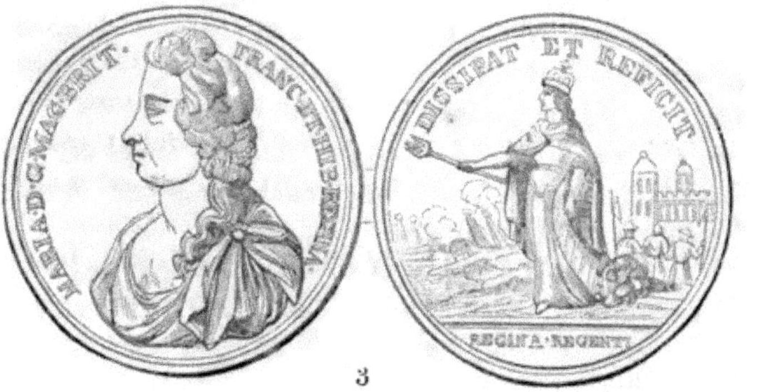
MARIA·D·G·MAG·BRIT·FRANC·ET·HIB·REGINA
DISSIPAT ET REFICIT
REGINA·REGENTE

3

Hacon, 1067, the name reads AACVNE. A similar series brings the Swedish coinage to 1387, when we have those of Margaret, Queen of Denmark and Sweden, but all very rude, Brenner's plates conveying the notion of very much better coins.

From this period to that of Gustavus Vasa, Sweden was subject to Denmark, and the coinage of that country superseded the national one; the Danish types being only distinguished from those struck in Denmark by legends Moneta *Stockol*, or Arosiensis, or Lundensis, etc. Dano-Swedish coins of this class continue to the reign of Christian, 1550, during which time coins struck by Danish governors appear, as those of Cnutson, Steno Sture, Swanto Sture, Steno Sture II., etc.

Till 1470 there are only silver pennies in the Swedish series; after that year there are half-pennies also; and Gustavus Vasa, on re-establishing the national independence, greatly improved the coinage, issuing, in addition to the pennies and half-pennies of former periods, a larger class of silver coins, similar to those then beginning to appear in other European states. In 1634 gold ducats were coined, with the head of Gustavus Adolphus, though he was killed in 1632; for his only child, Christina, being an infant at the time of his death, the portrait of the deceased king, the glory of the Swedish annals, was continued upon the coinage.

In the reign of Charles XII. such was the waste of the national wealth, caused by the insane mania for military glory of this prince, that the Baron Goertz endeavored to supply the deficiency by issuing copper coins, bearing the heads of Saturn, Jupiter, etc., which were ordered to pass for dollars, a political experiment for which the unfortunate but loyal projector was eventually brought to the block.

The coins of Norway begin with those of Olaf, in 1066, and bear the legend ONLAF REX NOR. Some Norwegian coins have on the reverse the letters NI. for Nidaros, Nidrosen, or Nidsen, now Drontheim, the capital. On the coinage the heirs-apparent

PLATE LXVIII.

1

3

2

4

5

6

K

to the crown were termed Dukes of Norway, and among the coins bearing the title of **Duke** are those of the Duke Philip, with PHILIPPVS. **DUX. NORWEGLÆ,** which have on the reverse MONE-TA. EASLOENS. Those of King **Eric, 1280,** and those of Hacon, 1309, which are good of the period, have also this title, and the legend on the last-named reads HAQVINVS. **DVX. NORV.** Copper coins of Magnus **Smek occur as early as 1343.** The last Norwegian coins are those of another Hacon, 1379. After which period **Norway was united with** Denmark. Of Sweden, Denmark, and **Norway, there are also coins of** Bishops, as in France, Germany, **and England, those of Sweden and** Denmark being **more** numerous than those of Norway.

As an example, the following may be **cited:** Olaws Archbishop Drontheim. **On the** obverse are the titles of the **king,** SANCTVS OLAWS · **REX.** NORVEG, and on the reverse **the name and** title of the Archbishop, OLAWS · DEI · GRA · ARCEP · NID'SEN, for *Nidrosiensis,* referring to Nidsen or Nidrosen, now Drontheim.

COINS OF THE FRENCH MONARCHY.

The earliest coins of the Frankish monarchy are those coined after permission **to strike** gold money was conceded by the Eastern Emperors to Clovis, **or his** immediate successors, about **the** time that a similar right was granted to Amalric, the Gothic King of Spain. The series of gold *trientes,* coined by these two states for upward of two centuries, form one of **the** most remarkable **features** of the early history **of the** coinage **of modern** Europe, **especially when it** is considered that this **issue** of modern gold **took place at a** period when **all** the other emancipated portions of **the Western** Empire were in a most barbarous condition as regards the **coinage.**

After the remarkable gold coinage of the first race of Frankish kings—the Merovingian dynasty—the gold coinage disappears. The trientes were of the value of one third of the Byzantine soli-

PLATE LXIX.

GREAT SEAL OF EDWARD VI.
(A.D. 1546-1553.)

dus; and there were also coined a few *semisses*, or halves of the same coin. They have generally a small and not ill-executed head of the king, with his name, though sometimes the name is that of the moneyer. On the reverse is a cross, with the name of the city where the coin was minted.

With Pepin commence the coins of the Carlovingian race, which are as remarkable for barbarous workmanship as those of the preceding dynasty for good execution. Those of Charlemagne have generally merely the name of CAROLVS, without a portrait, only a few struck in Rome having a rude bust of the emperor. The reverse has generally R. F., for Rex Francorum, or some such brief inscription.

The coins of Louis Le Debonnaire are, however, much better executed, and seem to show, by their Roman style of treatment, that there yet existed Roman Mints in Gaul, or rather France, where the ancient skill in coining money was still lingering.

The coins of the third race, commencing with Hugh Capet, remain—inferior in the art of coinage, with few exceptions; and in the reign of Philip I., contemporary with William the Conqueror, a species of money was issued formed of a piece of leather, with a silver nail fixed in the centre. It is not till the reign of St. Louis, 1226, that the French coinage greatly improves, and that the groat appears. This coin, of the value of four pennies, appeared first in Italy, where it was known as the *grosso*, or *large* coin; and in France it became the *gros;* in Germany the *groote;* in England the *groat;* where, however, it did not appear permanently till the reign of Edward III., nearly a century later than its first appearance in France.

Gold did not reappear in France till a considerable period had elapsed after the issue of the Italian florin, as the gold florins, given by Le Blanc to Philip Augustus and Louis VIII. belong evidently to Philip the Bold, or Philip the Fair, and Louis X. Under Philip of Valois—from 1328 to 1350—no less than ten

PLATE LXX.

1

2

3

kinds of gold coins are enumerated by French numismatists, among which are *la chaise*, being such as exhibit the sovereign seated in a chair of state, or throne; *the lion*, having a figure of a lion for principal type; *the lamb* (l'agneau), etc.

The difficulties which ensued about this period, consequent upon the English invasions, caused great deterioration in the French mintage, and base coin of all kinds got into circulation in the epoch of confusion and distress which ensued.

In the time of St. Louis, *black* coin had been issued, that is billon, or bad silver. Of these there was the *liard*, or *hardi*, which was equal to three *deniers*, or silver pennies; and the *maille*, or obole, half the *denier;* with the bourgeoise, or *pite*, of one quarter of the *denier*.

The *blancs*, or *billon* groats, were also issued about this time, but received the name of *blancs*, from being silvered over to hide the baseness of their metal.

The celebrated French gold of the period of Charles VII., called the *ecus à la couronne*, or *crowns* of gold, were so called from the crown, which formed the type of the reverse, and gave us the term *crown*, which in France was first applied to gold, though it afterward became the denomination of a silver coin. The ecus à la couronne continued to be issued by succeeding French sovereigns; those struck by Anne of Brittany, after the death of her first husband, are remarkable for their elegant workmanship.

In the reign of Louis XII., the new silver, of about the value of a modern franc, issued with the large portrait of the king, were termed *testons*, or *great heads*, a term afterward applied to the shillings of Henri VIII., in the anglicized form of *testoon*.

In the reign of Henri II., the elegant piece, called the *Henri*, was issued, which has for type a personification of Gaul sitting on a group of arms, with a Victory in her hand, with *optimo principi*, and *Gallia;* evidently suggested by ancient Roman coins, which now began to be studied—the celebrated Budée hav-

PLATE LXXI.

GREAT SEAL OF MARY.

(A.D. 1553–1558.)

ing written his treatise on the Roman coinage in the reign of Francis I. There are other coins of the Cardinal Bourbon, who, at the time of the League, was put forward under the title of Charles X.

The silver crown and its half had now commenced in France, as in other countries; and on subsequent crowns of Louis XIII. the title of *Cataloniæ princeps* is assumed.

The first Louis d'or appeared about 1640.

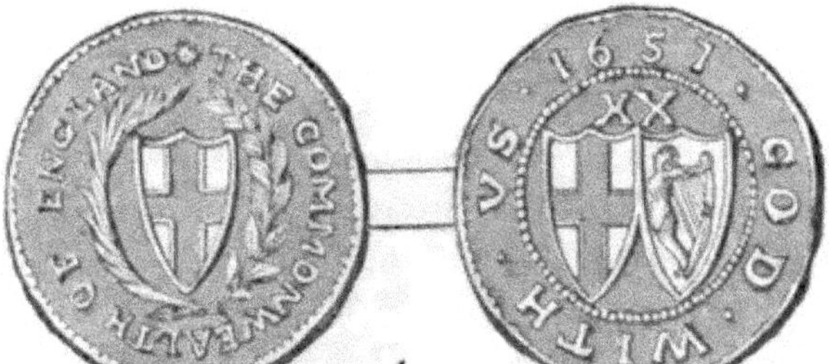
THE COMMONWEALTH OF ENGLAND
1651
XX
GOD WITH VS

1

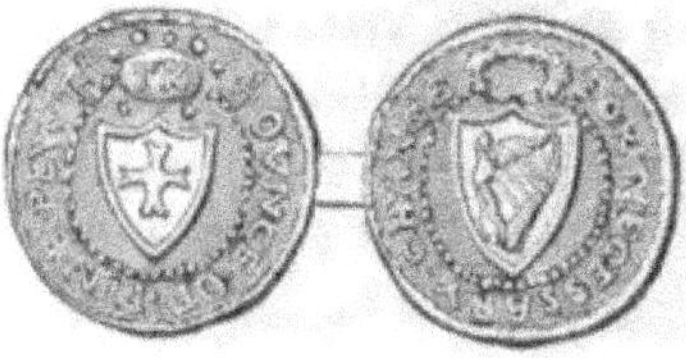

2

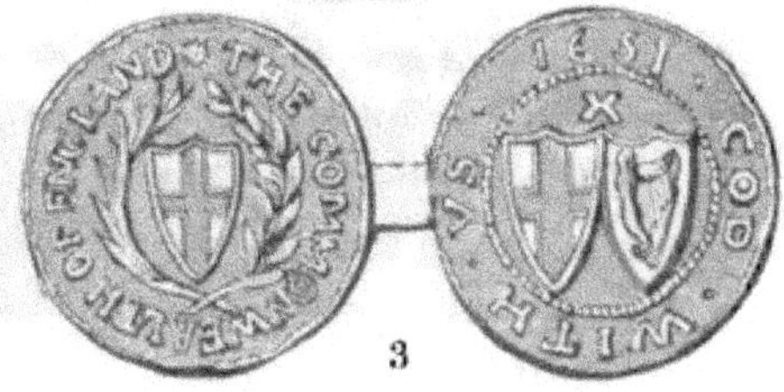
1651
GOD WITH VS

3

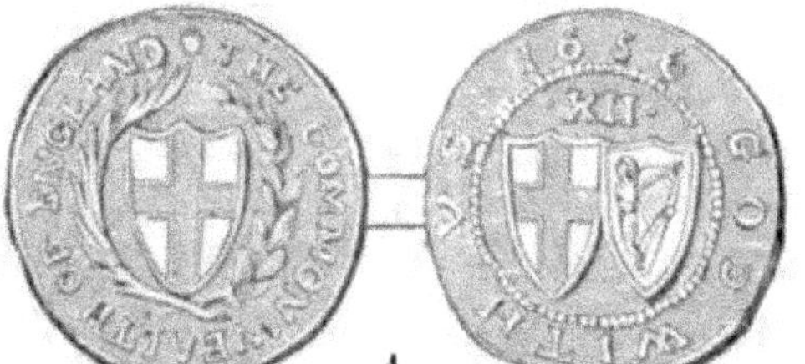
THE COMMONWEALTH OF ENGLAND
GOD WITH VS

4

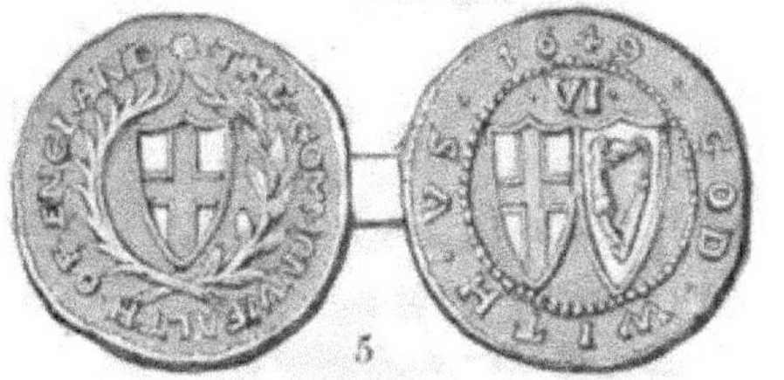
1649
VI
GOD WITH VS

5

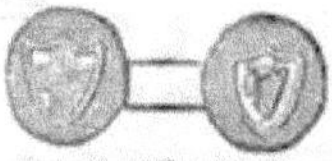

6

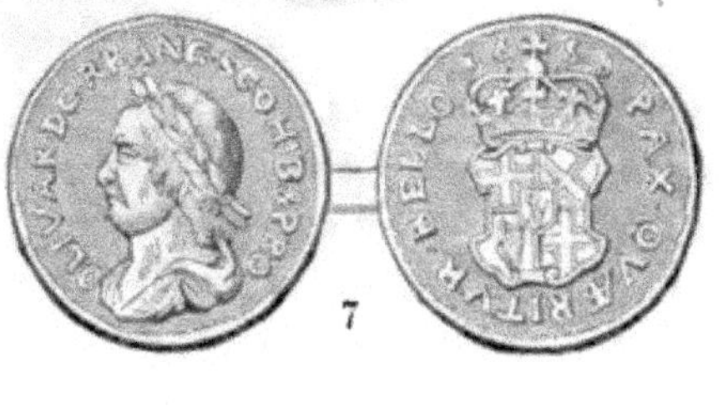

7

X.

The Striking of Medals and Coins.

It was no part of the design of this work to go into a history of medals, or attempt any description of those which are illustrated in this volume. The art of making coins and that of making medals is one art, and the splendor of national coinage has always been accompanied by a corresponding splendor of national medals.

It may not be amiss, for the benefit of young readers, to describe briefly the process of making a medal or a coin, and there may be in this description some points not known to all adult readers.

The first work in the art is the preparation of the dies. These are in all cases two: one for the upper and the other for the under side of the medal. The die is cut by a die-sinker. The hub or die is first made by a blacksmith out of steel. It is usually a cylinder or a cone of steel, of a size varying according to the size of the medal to be produced. This lump of steel is turned in a lathe, so that the upper end of it shall be round, of the size of the medal to be struck, and so exact as to fit a steel collar or ring that is made for it. The two dies are of exactly the same size, fitting this collar, and so arranged that the two will easily go into the collar face to face. On the smooth surfaces of the dies the die-sinker or die-cutter with his tools cuts the designs intended to be in raised letters and figures on the medal. Not infrequently a design is ordered which the die-cutter has executed before. In this case he may possibly have a small lump of hard steel on

PLATE LXXIII.

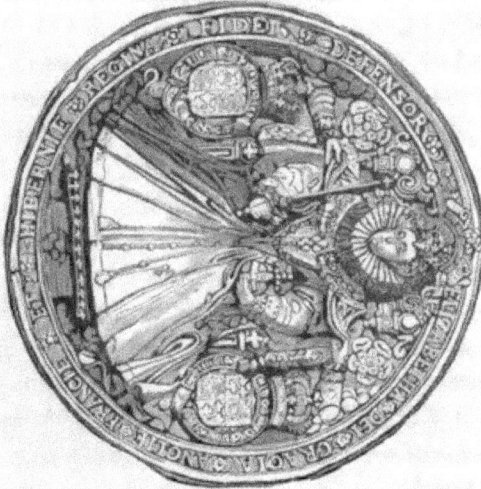

GREAT SEAL OF ELIZABETH.
(A.D. 1558-1603.)

which is a raised copy of this design. This he calls a punch, and he drives this into the surface of the soft steel die with a hammer or with a press, thus saving the time and labor of cutting it out. This process he generally uses with letters, wreaths, and all common ornaments.

When numerous copies of a die are needed, as in Mints for coinage, the first die cut from the die-cutter's hands is called the master-die. This is cut in soft steel, hardened by heating and cooling in water, and then soft steel is forced into it by a tremendous pressure, thus taking an impression of it in soft steel, which is again itself hardened. Thus we have a coin in steel. This is a punch which can be forced into a dozen or a hundred dies of soft steel, which being in turn hardened, will thus produce as many dies for use in striking coins.

The dies being cut and hardened, the collar is hardened also. If it is desired to place an inscription on the edge of the coin, or to mark the edge with any design, this is done by engraving the design in the collar; for, as will be seen, this collar is to receive the metal which is to be pressed between the two dies and prevent its expansion, and, of course, if there be any engraving on the inside of the collar it will appear on the edge of the coin or medal.

The metals used for medals are various. The softest, cheapest, and most easily struck is commonly called white metal. It is either pure tin or Britannia ware, which is a composition metal. The composition is varied by different workmen. The medals commonly called bronze are usually struck in pure copper, and bronzed afterward. Brass is a harder metal to strike than copper or silver, requiring more force, and more likely to break the dies. German silver is esteemed the hardest to strike of all composition metals.

In striking medals the dies are placed in a press made for the purpose. Tokens and small coins are usually struck by the

PLATE LXXIV.

1

use of a drop weight. (We are not now speaking of the Mints where steam power and coin presses are in use, but of the die-cutting and striking establishments of New York, Waterbury, etc.) The drop is a heavy iron weight, in the bottom of which one of the dies is fixed. The lower die is made stationary, with the collar resting on it. The planchet or planket (a piece of copper or other metal cut of the required thickness and size) is laid in the collar on the face of the lower die, the drop falls and ascends instantly, leaving the planchet impressed with the designs—in fact, a complete coin or medal.

For larger medals, however, a screw press is generally used. This is simply a large screw passing through a heavy solid iron frame. The dies rest on the lower part of the frame. Across the head of the screw is a lever, with heavy weights attached, which is used to turn the screw down. The dies are placed in position, with a planchet between them, in the collar. A blow is struck by sending the lever around with more or less force.

It is not often that a copper medal is completed at one blow of the press. The metal is compressed by the blow to its full extent, but fails to fill the lines cut in the dies. This is always the case where the die contains deep work, and the medal is to be in high relief. The process then is, after striking the first blow, to anneal the planchets, that is, heat them to a red heat. The metal is thus expanded and softened. It is then washed off with a weak acid, and subjected to a second blow. It may require a third, fourth, fifth, or a tenth blow to bring up a copper medal to a sharp and perfect impression, and the same annealing and washing process is repeated before each blow.

In the Mint the machinery is carried to a stage of perfection that none but experienced machinists can understand. The issue of coins is so large as to require labor-saving mechanism; hence the entire work that we have described as done by hand, is there accomplished by steel and iron sinews, nerves, and fingers.

PLATE LXXV.

GREAT SEAL OF JAMES I.
(A.D. 1603-1625.)

It is hardly necessary to remark on the vast changes in this respect which the art of coinage has undergone. The wood-cuts on Plate XXI. illustrate the manner in which the art was exercised only a few hundred years ago. It is worthy of notice that the entire process of coinage in that age can be illustrated in one small wood-cut of this kind, while to show the present perfection of the art and the detail of machinery employed would occupy nearly all the Plates in this volume.

The art of coinage has never received great attention in America. The national Mint has employed excellent talent, and some of its issues compare favorably with those of other nations, but many pieces have been struck which are no credit to the country. Let us rejoice at the disappearance of the copper cent with the idiotic head of Liberty which so long defaced it.

We have produced but few medalists; yet we are not without some fine artists. The late C. C. Wright has left a very high reputation, and his medals are justly prized by collectors. His partner, Bale, was also an admirable artist.

, Robert Lovett, and his sons George H. and John D., in New York, and his son Robert in Philadelphia, have all executed fine works. So also have George W. May, once a partner of Bale, and George Glaubrecht, now the partner of May, both in New York. Smith and Harttman in New York, rank among the first of American medalists; and Key in Philadelphia, has also a well-merited reputation. The great number and variety of agricultural and other prize-medals which these gentlemen have cut from year to year show at once their industry and their success.

PLATE LXXVI.

1

2   3

4

5

L

XI.

Hints to Young Collectors.

CONFINE your attention as closely as possible to one class or series of coins at a time. Do not reject other coins or medals not belonging to this series, but do not give time, labor, or money to their accumulation. Thus, in commencing a collection of American coins, start with the design of making a complete set of cents. You will easily accomplish this, with the exception of 1793, 1799, and 1804. But do not content yourself with poor specimens. Always take the first specimen you find of any cent, good or poor, but exchange it for a better specimen when you can find one. Never waste a moment of time over a coin whose date is doubtful. It must be too poor, in that case, for any collection.

Having completed one series of coins, or having all but the very rare dates, turn your attention to another series and complete that. By diligence and patience you will in this manner collect a valuable and interesting cabinet.

When your collection justifies it, have a case or cabinet made to hold it. An immense number of coins can be laid in a small space. A case two feet high, two wide, and one deep, with folding-doors, filled with drawers each five-eighths of an inch deep, a few being deeper for medals, will hold several thousand coins. Cover your drawers with cloth or cotton velvet. Let slats be tacked across the drawer from side to side, but do not separate the coins in one row from each oth-

PLATE LXXVII.

GREAT SEAL OF CHARLES I.
(A.D. 1625-1649.)

er. **The only danger of rubbing** is in opening and shutting the **drawers, and this will be** prevented by the slats from side to side.

Arrange **your** ancient, foreign, and colonial coins by States, your regular series of United States coins by dates; your tradesmen's cards alphabetically, and your political tokens **as** best suits **your** taste.

Clean your coins very carefully. For brass coins (by brass I **mean** what **we** now commonly call brass as distinct from copper) **use** ammonia (common spirits of hartshorn) two parts, **prepared chalk** one part, **by weight.** Place **them in** a phial **together;** shake well when **used. Wash the coin,** rubbing **it hard with** flannel, and clean off quickly with clear water; then **polish with** dry flannel.

Clean silver coins with soap and water and a soft brush. **Never touch** acid to silver or copper coins, unless very cautiously.

Clean copper coins with soap and **water, and** then polish **them with** powdered soap-stone on flannel. **Never** wash a cop**per coin to** give it a bright copper color. The result will **be to** show all the scratches and bruises on the **coin. It** is **better to** leave the **dark** color untouched, and the soap-stone **will** almost bronze it. Do not touch ammonia or acid **to a copper** coin.

White metal can be cleaned with alcohol, or soap **and water, or the** ammonia and chalk.

Never be induced to pay extravagant prices for worthless **coins.** There are some coins which command and are worth a large price. But these are, in fact, very few. Even the rarity of a coin **is no** test of its real value to a collector. It may increase the **price of** the article; but the **young** collector should **bear** ever **in mind that the high price** asked for a coin because it is rare ought not to make him desirous of possess-

Plate LXXVIII.

1

2

3

ing it. The moment that the collector begins to value coins because of their rarity, he descends in the scale of science; and when he seeks to possess rare coins merely because of their being rare, he becomes a speculator, envious, and uncomfortable in the presence of others, and ceases to be a genuine numismatist.

Read as you collect. Never let a coin lie in your cabinet that you can not give the history of, or connect with some historical event, if it be possible. Be careful that your collecting does not become a mere matter of curiosity. Let it rather be a constant aid to your study of history.

In directing your attention to works on coins and medals, it is impossible to do more than name a few of the most accessible and reasonable in price. Mionnet's great work will prove too expensive for the ordinary collector, if indeed a copy can be procured at any price. If purchased at $125, it might be esteemed cheap. Eckel is important to the collector who devotes himself to ancient coins, and may be had for $20 to $30. But books of this class are not for the beginner. Humphrey's Coin Collector's Manual, and Humphrey's Coinage of the British Empire, the first of which may be procured in Bohn's Library edition at a very cheap price ($2 50), and the second at about $7 in America, will be the first works on foreign coinage to which you will direct your attention. Even before procuring these, you can not do better than to buy and study the admirable 25-cent compilation of J. Thompson of New York, Thompson's COIN CHART MANUAL, which will give you at a glance a general idea of the styles of coinage of various nations of the world, and will aid you in determining coins to which you might otherwise devote a vast deal of useless speculation. We have received numerous letters of inquiry as to the name, quality, and value of coins, which the owner could have determined in a moment for himself with the aid of this excellent manual. It also contains illustrations of nearly all the American

PLATE LXXIX.

GREAT SEAL OF THE COMMONWEALTH.

(A.D. 1649.)

gold and silver series, including the various California, Mormon, and other issues.

For information on the American series, you can not find any work so complete as Dr. Dickeson's AMERICAN NUMISMATICAL MANUAL, published by J. B. Lippincott & Co., Philadelphia, which, although far from complete, is a valuable work, the result of much care and study, and will prove a great aid to the collector.

For store cards and tokens you will be obliged to depend on the ordinary sale catalogues, which it is well to keep yourself supplied with, and if you can not attend a sale and mark the prices yourself, borrow from a friend a priced catalogue and make a copy. These priced catalogues will form a valuable reference when you have occasion to purchase coins or medals.

It would be vain to attempt any farther directions on the subject of books. There have been almost as many books published on coins as there are extant varieties of coins. One sale of a numismatic library in England occupied nine consecutive days. A catalogue of all the works on coins would form a volume of over five hundred pages, printing only the briefest titles.

In closing these hints we can not do better than direct the attention of the young collector again to the folly of paying enormous prices for worthless coins. Do not be misled by the idea that a curious piece of metal with an old date is highly valuable. Do not buy coins because they are rare, but buy to complete your series. Make your collections slowly, cautiously, and enjoy your work as you go along with it.

The tables which follow will prove of use to the young as well as the experienced collector. On very many ancient coins a few letters are found, which taken together form no word, and are exceedingly puzzling to the inexperienced. The Tables of Ab-

PLATE LXXX.

1

2

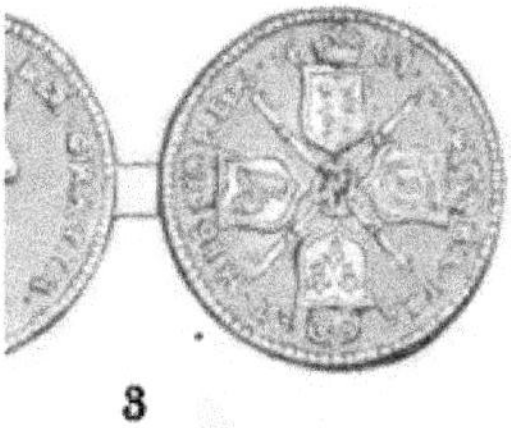

3    4

5

breviations on **Greek** and Roman Coins are the result of many years' study by **all the** most learned numismatists. **Wc have taken** them from Humphreys, as the latest and one of the most careful compilers. With the aid of these many coins can be at **once** located, over which, without them, much unavailing time might be spent.

PLATE LXXXI.

GREAT SEAL OF SCOTLAND UNDER CROMWELL.
(A.D. 1656.)

ABBREVIATIONS ON GREEK COINS,

TRANSLATED AND EXPLAINED.

A . . . . Athens, Argos, **Aulus**, Asylum. (The **letter** A sometimes **stands** for *First*, as, Εφεσιων A. Ασιας—" Of the Ephesians, the first people of Asia.") Abbassus, Abdera, Abydus on the Hellespont. Ambracia, Arcadia, or Aeginum. Atna.

A . . . . **Abydus in Egypt.**

ABAK . . . . Abacaenum.

ABY . . . . Abydus on the Hellespont.

AΔ . . . . Addada.

AΘ, AΘE . . . . . Athens.

AΘΡΙΒ . . . . . . Athribites.

AI, AIΓ . . . . . . Aegina.

AΙΓΟΣΠΟ . . . . . Aegospotamus.

AIΛ . . . . Aelius, Aelia Capitolina.

AIN . . . . Aenos.

AITΩ . . . . Aetolia.

AK, AKΡAΓAN . . Agrigentum.

AKAN . . . . Acanthus.

AKI . . . . Acilium.

AKT . . . . Actium.

AΛE, AΛEΞAN . . Alexandria.

AΛEΞ· ΤΟΥ· N·. . Alexander, son of Neoptolemus.

AΛΥ . . . . Alysia, Alvona.

AM . . . . Amyntas, Amphipolis, Amorgus.

AMBP . . . . Ambracia.

AMΦI . . . . Amphilochia.

AN . . . . Ancyra.

ANA . . . . Anactoria.

ANΔEΓ . . . . . . Andegaei.

ANΘ. (**Ανθυπατορ**) Proconsul.

ANΘH . . . . Anthedon.

ANT, ANTI . . . . Antium.

ANT . . . . Antoninus, **or Antioch.**

ANTAIO . . . . . Antiopolis.

ANTIΠ . . . . . . Antipolis.

ANTIΣ . . . . . . Antissa.

ANΩ . . . . Anolis.

AΞ . . . . Axia and Axus.

AON . . . . Aonitae.

AΠ . . . . Appius.

AΠA . . . . Apamea.

AΠO . . . . Apollonia.

AΠOΛ . . . . Apollonopolis.

AΠT., AΠTA . . . Aptara.

AP . . . . Aradus, Harma.

APΓ . . . . Argos.

APΓE . . . . Argennos.

API . . . . Aricanda.

APIM . . . . Ariminum.

APIΣ . . . . Arisbas (King of Epirus).

APK . . . . Arconensus.

APKA . . . . Arcadia.

APΣI . . . . Arsinoë.

APΥ . . . . Aryea.

APX . . . . Arxata.

APX. (**Αρχιερευς** High-priest or magis- or Αρχον) . . . . trate.

A. Σ. (**Πρωτοι Συριας**) . . . . . First of Syria.

AΣ . . . . Ascalon, Assylum, Axus in Crete.

AΣI . . . . Asinium.

AΣIAPX . . . . . . Asiarchae. Presidents of the games of Asia.

AΣK . . . . Ascalon.

AT . . . . Atabyrium.

PLATE LXXXII.

1

2

3

ABBREVIATIONS ON GREEK COINS.

ΑΤΑΡ . . . . Atarnae.
ΑΥ., ΑΥΤ. (Αυτο-
  κρατορ) . . . . . Emperor.
ΑΥΓ . . . . Augustus.
ΑΥΔ . . . . Audoleon.
ΑΥΕ . . . . Avenio.
ΑΥΡΗΑ . . . . . . Aurelius.
ΑΥΤΟΝ. (Αυτονο- Enjoying their own
  μοι.) . . . . . . laws.
ΑΥΤΩ . . . . Automale.
ΑΦ . . . . Aphrodisias.
ΑΦΙ . . . . Aphyta.
ΑΦΡ . . . . Africanus.
ΑΧ . . . . Achaia,   Acheens,
                    Achaii.
ΑΧΙ . . . . Acilium.

B. (Βουλης) . . . Council, Berytus, By-
                    thinia.
ΒΑ . . . . Battus.
ΒΑΡ . . . . Bare, Bargoda.
ΒΑΓΗΔΑΟ . . . . Bagadaonia.
ΒΗ . . . . Berytus.
ΒΙΑΤ . . . . Biatei (an unknown
                    king).
ΒΙΖΥ . . . . Bysia.
ΒΙΤΟΝ . . . . . . Bitontum.
ΒΟ, ΒΟΙ . . . . . . Boeotia.
ΒΡΥΝ . . . . . . ·. Brundusium.
ΒΥ, ΒΥΣΑΣ . . . . Byzantium.
ΒΥΤ . . . . Buthrotum.

Γ . . . . Gaius (for Caius).
Γ., ΓΡ., ΓΡΑΜ . . Grammaticus   (or
                    Keeper of the Rec-
                    ords).
Γ. (Γνωρμου.) . . Illustrious.
ΓΑ . . . . Gallus, Galerius, or
                    Gallienus.
ΓΑΜ . . . . Gambrum.
ΓΑΡ . . . . Gargara.
ΓΕΛ . . . . Gelas.
ΓΕΡ . . . . Germanicus.
ΓΝ . . . . Gneius.
ΓΟΡΤΥ . . . . . . Gortyna.
ΓΡΑ . . . . Gravisca.
ΓΡΥ . . . . Grumentum.

Δ . . . . Decimus, Dymae.
ΔΑ . . . . Daorii.
ΔΑΚ . . . . Dacicus.
ΔΑΜ . . . . Damascus.
ΔΑΡ . . . . Dardanum.
ΔΕ · . . . . Decelia.
ΔΕΚ . . . . Decius.
ΔΕΡ . . . . Derbe, in Lycaonia.
ΔΗ. (Δημος). . . The People.
ΔΗ . . . . Delos.

ΔΗΜΑΡΧ·ΕΞΟΥΣ With   Tribunician
                    Power.
ΔΙ . . . . Diospolis.
ΔΙΟ . . . . Diotus.
ΔΙΟΚΑΙ . . . . . . Diocaesarea.
ΔΙΟΣ . . . . Diospolis.
ΔΡΕ . . . . Drepanum.
ΔΥΡ . . . . Dyrrachium.

Ε . . . . Eryce.
Ε, ΕΡΕΣ . . . . . Eresus.
ΕΙΡ . . . . Eresus, Erythræ, Er-
                    etna.
ΕΛ . . . . Elea, Elatea.
ΕΛΕΥ . . . . Eleusis.
ΕΛΕΥΘ. (Ελευθε-
  ροι.) . . . . Free.
ΕΝ . . . . Enna, Entherna, En-
                    tella, Encheli.
ΕΠ., ΕΠΙ . . . . . Epidaurus.
ΕΡΙ . . . . Eriza in Caria.
ΕΡΜΟ . . . . Hermopolis.
ΕΡΥ . . . . Erythia.
ΕΡΧ . . . . Erchia.
ΕΣ . . . . Eppindus.
ΕΤ . . . . Etenna in Pamphylia.
ΕΤ., ΕΤΟ. (Ετους) A year.
ΕΥ., ΕΥΒΟ   Euboea.
ΕΥΑ . . . . Eva.
ΕΥΣ. (Ευσεβης) Pious.
ΕΥΤ. (Ευτυχης). Happy.
ΕΦ., ΕΦΕ . . . Ephesus.
ΕΧ. (Εχουσια.) . Power.

ΖΑ . . . . Zacynthus (then Sala-
                    mis, now Zanthus).
ΖΑΝΚΑ   . Zancle (afterward Mes-
                    sana).

Η . . . . Elium.
ΗΑΔΡ . . . . . . Hadrumentum.
ΗΑΤ . . . . Atna.
ΗΓ. (Ηγεμονος). President.
ΗΛΙΟΠ . . . . . Heliopolis.
ΗΡ . . . . Heracleia.
ΗΡΑΚ . . . . . . Heracleiopolis.
ΗΦΑΙ . . . . . . Ephaestia.

ΘΑ . . . . Thasus.
ΘΕ . . . . Thespiae.
ΘΕ., ΘΗΒ . . . . Thebae.
ΘΕΣ . . . . Thessalonica.
ΘΡ . . . . Thera.
ΘΥ . . . . Thurium.

Ι . . . . Iasus.
Ι., ΙΕΡ. (Ιερας) . Sacred.
ΙΕΡΑΠΥ . . . . Hierapythia.

174

PLATE LXXXIII.

GREAT SEAL OF CHARLES II.
(A.D. 1660-1685.)

IΘA . . . . Ithaca.
IKAP . . . . Hiccara, Icarius.
IΛ . . . . Ilisium.
IΛI . . . . Illium.
IOϒ . . . . Julius (meaning a city), or Julius (a man's name).
IOϒΛ . . . . Julia.
IΠA . . . . Hippana.
IP . . . . Irene.
IPP . . . . Irrhesia.
IΣ . . . . Isus, Istiaea.
IΣIN . . . . Isindus.
IΨϒ . . . . Ipsus.

K . . . . Caristus, Cyrene, Cyzicus, Callatea, Corcyra, Caius (a man's name).
K. (Κοιντος) . . Quintus.
K. KAIΣ . . . . . Caesar.
K. K. (Κοινον Κιλικιας) . . . . Community of Cilicia.
KA . . . . Carystus, Catana, Chalcis.
KAIΛ . . . . Caelius.
KAΛ . . . . Chalcedon.
KAΛΔI . . . . . . Calliopolis.
KAMA . . . . . . Camara.
KAN . . . . Canata.
KAΠ . . . . Capua.
KAΠΠ . . . . . . Cappadocia.
KAP, KAPP . . . Carrhae.
KAPT . . . . Carthage.
KANω . . . . . . Canopus.
KAΣT . . . . . . Castulo.
KAϒ., KAϒΛ . . Caulonia.
KE . . . . Ceos.
KE . . . . Cenchrae, Cephalenia, Cephalonia.
KEΛ . . . . Celenderis.
KEP . . . . Chersonesus.
KEΦ, KEΦAΛ . . Cephalaedis.
KI . . . . Ciamus, Cibacum.
KIΘ . . . . Cithaeron.
KIΛ . . . . Cilbrani.
KIΣ . . . . Cistena.
KΛ . . . . Cleonae, Claudius.
KΛA . . . . Clazomene.
KΛAϒΔIO . . . . . Claudiopolis.
KNΩ . . . . Cnopus.
KNI . . . . Cnidus.
KO . . . . Colophon, Corcyra.
KO, KOP . . . . . Corinth.
KOIN. (Κοινον.) A community.
KOΛ. (Κολονιας) Colony, Colophon.
KOM . . . . Commodus.
KOP . . . . Corcyra.

KP . . . . Cragus in Lycia.
KPA . . . . Cranos.
KPH . . . . Crete.
KPO . . . . Crotona.
KTH . . . . Ctemenae.
Kϒ . . . . Cydna, Cuma, Cyme, Cyrene, Cyzicus, Cytholus, Cydonium, Cyon.
KϒΔΩ . . . . . . Cydon.
KϒΘ . . . . Cythnus.
KϒΠ . . . . Cyprus.
KϒP . . . . Cyrene.

Λ . . . . A year, Lucius, Locris, Leucas.
ΛΛ . . . . Lacedaemon, Lampsacus, Larymna, Larissa.
ΛΛΛΛ . . . . . . Lalassa.
ΛΛM . . . . Launea, Lampsacus.
ΛΛMΠ . . . . . . Lampsacus.
ΛΛP . . . . Larissa.
ΛΛPI . . . . Larinum.
ΛE., ΛEϒ . . . . Leucas.
ΛEB . . . . Lebinus.
ΛEON . . . . . . Leontium.
ΛHM . . . . Lemnos.
ΛIΠ . . . . Lipara.
ΛIϒI . . . . Liviopolis.
ΛO., ΛΩK . . . . Locri.
ΛOΓ . . . . Longone.
Λϒ . . . . Lystus.
ΛϒΓ., ΛϒK . . . Lyctus.
ΛϒΣI . . . . . . Lysmachia.

M . . . . Marcus (a man's name), Melos, Maronea, Malca, Megalopolis, Mazaka.
M., MHTPO. . . . Metropolis.
MA . . . . Magnesia, Massyritus, Maronea, Massilia, Macedonia.
MAΓ . . . . Magnesia.
MAΘϒ . . . . . . Mathyma.
MAKPO . . . . . . Macrocephali.
MAΛ . . . . Mallus.
MAM . . . . Mamertini.
MAN . . . . Mantinea.
MAΣ . . . . Mazara.
MAΣΣ . . . . . . Massilia.
ME . . . . Menelais, on Syrian regal coins.
ME . . . . Messina, Metapontum, Melite.
ME., MEΓ . . . . Megara, Megalopolis, Megarsus.

PLATE LXXXIV.

1

2

3   4   3

5   4   5

M   6

ABBREVIATIONS ON GREEK COINS.

ΜΕΓ. (Μεγαλος)	Great.	**Π., ΠΡΥ.** (Πρυτα-	
ΜΕΝΔ	Mendes.	νος)	Praefect.
ΜΕΝΕ	Menelaus.	**Π., ΠΡΩΤ.** (Προ-	
ΜΕΝΕΚ	Menecrates.	τος)	First.
ΜΕΣ.	Messana, Messenia.	ΠΑ	Pales, Patrae.
ΜΕΤΑ	Metapontum.	ΠΑΙΣ	Paestum.
ΜΙ	Miletus.	ΠΑΙΩ	Paeonia.
ΜΙΝ	Minde.	ΠΑΝ	Panormus.
ΜΚ., ΜΛΣΑΚ	Mazaka, of Cappado-	ΠΑΡ	Paropinum, Paros.
	cia, on coins of Mith-	ΠΑΡΘ	Parthicus.
	ridates VI.	ΠΑΡΙ	Paros.
ΜΟΡ	Morgantia.	ΠΕ	Pelinna.
ΜΥ	Mycenae.	ΠΕ	Perinthus.
ΜΥΚΟ	Mycone.	ΠΕΛ	Pella.
ΜΥΛ	Mylasa.	ΠΕΡ	Pergus.
ΜΥΝΥ	Minya.	ΠΕΡΓ	Pergamus.
ΜΥΡ.	Myrlea.	ΠΕΡΤ	Pertinax.
ΜΥΤΙ	Mytilene.	ΠΕΣΚ	Pescennius.
		ΠΙ	Piasdarus.
Ν., ΝΑΥ	Naupactos.	ΠΙΝ	Pinarnytae.
Ν. **ΝΕΩΚ**	Neocori.	ΠΙΝΑ	Pinamus.
ΝΑ	Naxos, **Nape.**	ΠΛΑ	Plateae.
ΝΑΓΙΔ	Nagidus.	ΠΟ	Pontus.
ΝΑΞ	Naxos.	ΠΟΑΥ	Polyrrhenum.
ΝΑΥΑΡΧ. (**Ναυ-**		ΠΟΣ. ΠΟΣΕΙ	Posidonia.
αρχιδοι)	Enjoying a sea-port.	ΠΡ., ΠΡΕΣ.(Πρισ-	
ΝΕ	Nemea.	βεος)	Legate.
ΝΕΑΝ	Neandria.	ΠΡ, ΠΡΟ	Pronos.
ΝΕΟΠ	Neopolis.	ΠΡΑΙ	Praesus.
ΝΕΡ	Nerva.	ΠΡΑΣ	Prassus.
ΝΙΚ	Nicaeum, **Nicomedia.**	ΠΡΟ	Proconnesus.
ΝΥ	Nisyrus.	ΠΡΟΣΩ	Prosopis.
ΝΥΣ	Nysaei, on coins of	ΠΡΟΔΙ.(Προδικος)	Curator.
	Scythopolis.	ΠΤ	Ptolemais.
		ΠΥ	Pylos.
Ξ	Xanthus, **Xatynthus.**	ΠΥ	Pythopolis.
		ΠΥΛ	Pylos.
Ο	Opuntium.	ΠΥΘΟ	Pithopolis.
ΟΙ	Oethaei.	ΠΥΡ	Pyrnus.
ΟΛΒΙΟ	Olbiopolis.		
ΟΛΥ	Olympus.	**Ρ**	Rythymna.
ΟΝ. (Οντος)	being.	ΡΑΥ	Raucus.
ΟΠΕΛ	Opelius.	ΡΗ	Rhegium.
ΟΠ	Opus.	ΡΟ	Rhodes.
ΟΡΥ	Orycus.	ΡΥ	Rypae.
ΟΡΧ	Orchomenus.		
ΟΥΠ or ΥΠ. (Ου-		**Σ. ΣΑ**	Salamis, Samos, Syria,
πατος or Υπα-			Sacile, Sala, Seges-
τος)	**Consul.**		ta, Syracuse, Sycion.
ΟΦΡΥ	**Ophrynium.**	ΣΑ	Salamis, Salgania, Sa-
			mosate, Sacili, Same.
Π	Pitane, Pantecapaeum,	ΣΑΓ	Saguntum.
	Panormus.	ΣΑΛΑΠ	Salapia.
Π. (Παρα, Προς).	upon.	ΣΑΡ	Sardis.
Π., ΠΑ	Paphos, **or** Paros.	ΣΕ	Seriphus, Segeste, Sel-
Π., ΠΑΝ	Pantecapaeum.		gi, Seleucia.
Π., ΠΗ	Pelusium.	ΣΕΒ. (Σιβαστος)	Augustus.
Π., ΠΟΠΛ	Publius.	ΣΕΛ	Selinus, Seleucia.

178

PLATE LXXXV.

GREAT SEAL OF JAMES II.
(A.D. 1685–1688.)

ABBREVIATIONS ON GREEK COINS.

ΣΕΠΤ	Septimus.	ΤΡΟ	Triozene.
ΣΕΡ, ΣΕΡΙ	Seriphus.	ΤΥ	Tyndaris.
ΣΕΦΙ	Sephyrium.	ΤΥΑΝ	Tyana.
ΣΙ	Siphnos.	ΤΥΡ	Tyre (monogram).
ΣΙΔ	Side.		
ΣΙΚΙ	Sicinus, Sycion.	Υ, ΥΕ., ΥΕΛ	**Velia.**
ΣΙΝ., ΣΙΝΩ	Sinope.	ΥΠ., ΥΠΑΤ (Υπα-	
ΣΚ	Scepsis.	τος)	**Consul.**
ΣΜΥ	Smyrna.	ΥΡ	**Uria.**
ΣΟ	Soli.		
ΣΤΡ., ΣΤΡΑ.		Φ	Philip, Phoestus, Phi-
(Στρατηγος).	Praetor.		luntium, Phocis,
ΣΤΥ	Styria.		Phocaea, Phocians.
ΣΥ	Sicily.	ΦΑ	Phaselis, Phaestus,
ΣΥ., ΣΥΡΑ	Syracuse.		Pharos, Phanagoria,
ΣΥΒ	Sybaris.		Pharae.
ΣΥΡ	Syria.	ΦΑΙ	Phaestus.
ΣΩ	Solae.	ΦΑΛ	Phalanna.
		ΦΑΡ	Pharsalus.
Τ	**Tarentun, Tarsus,**	ΦΑΡΒΑΙ	Pharbaeshites.
	Teos, Titus.	ΦΙ	Vibius, Philippopolis,
ΤΑ	Terantum, **Tabae.**		Philadelphia.
ΤΑ., ΤΑΝΑ	Tanagra.	ΦΙΝΕ	Phineium.
ΤΑΒΑΛ	Tabala.	ΦΛ	Flavius.
ΤΑΡ	Tarentum, Tarsus.	ΦΟ	Phocis.
ΤΑΥΡ	Tauromenum.	ΦΟΚ	Phocaeum.
ΤΕ	Tementis, Tegea, Te-	ΦΟΥΑ	Fulvia.
	nedos, Terina.	ΦΥ	Phycus in **Cyrene.**
ΤΕΡ	Terina.	ΦΩ	Phocis.
ΤΗ	Teos, **Terpillas,** Tenus.		
ΤΙ., ΤΙΒ	Tiberius.	Χ	Chios.
ΤΟ	Tolistobegi.	ΧΑΛ	Chalcis.
ΤΡΑ	Trallis.	ΧΕΡ	Chersonesus.
ΤΡΙ	Tripolis.	ΧΙ	Chytri in Crete.
ΤΡΙΑ	Triadissa.		

PLATE LXXXVI.

1

2

3

ABBREVIATIONS ON ROMAN COINS.

WITH THEIR EXPLANATION.

A.

A.   Aulus, or annus.
A.A.   Anni, or annos.
A.A. A.A.A.   Augusti.
AA.A.F.F.   Auro, argento, **aere flando feriundo.**
ABN.   Abnepos.
ACCI.   Accitana.
ACCI.L.III.   Accitana legio iii.
ACT.   Actiacus, actia, or actium.
A. ACT. A.   Actiacus apollo.
AAD. FRV. EMV.   Ad fruges emundus.
AADI.   **Adjutrix.**
ADLOCVT. AVG.   **Adlocutio** augusti.
ADLOCVT. COH. PRÆTOR.   Adlocutio cohortium prætorianorum.
ADVENT. AVG. IVD. or MAV. or ACHA. or AFRIC. or ASI. or SIC. or GAL. or HISP.   Adventus augusti judeae, **or** mauritaniæ, or achaiæ, **or africœ,** or asiæ, or siciiliæ, **or** galliæ, or hispaniæ.
AED. CVR.   Aedilis curulis.
AED. DIVI. AVG. REST.   Aedes **divi augusti restitutae.**
AED. P.   Aedilitia potestas.
AED. PL.   Aedilitia plebis.
AED. S.   Aedes sacrae, or **aedibus sacris.**
AEM.   Aemilius, or aemilia.
ÆQVIT. AVG.   Æquitas augusti.
AET.   Aeternitas.
A. F.   Auli filius.
A. N.   Auli nepos.
AGRIP. F.   Agrippae filius.
AGRIPPA M. F. MA. C. CÆSARIS. AVGVSTI.   Agrippa marci filia **mater** caii cæsaris augusti.
ALE.   **Alexandria.**
ALIM. ITAL.   **Alimenta italiae.**
ALVIT.   **Alvitius.**
ANIC.   Anicius.
A. M. B.   Antiochiae moneta officina secunda.   Money of **Antioch b.**
AN. B. or ANT. B.   Antiochiae officina secunda.
A. N. F. F.   Annum novum felicem faustum.
ANN. DCCC. LXXII. NAT. VRB. P. CIR. CON.   Anno dccclxxii. natali urbis populo circenses constituti.
ANNONA. AVG.   Annona **augusti.**
ANT. P.   Antiochiae percussa.
ANT. S.   Antiochiae signata.

182

PLATE LXXXVII.

GREAT SEAL OF WILLIAM AND MARY.

(A.D. 1689-1694.)

A. P. F.   Auro populo feriundo or argento populo feriundo.
A. P. LVG.   Pecunia lugduni a.
APOL. MON.   Apollo monetalis.
APOL. PAL.   Apollo Palatinus.
APOL. SALVT. CONSERVATORI.   Apolloni salutari conservatori.
AQ. O. B.   Aquiliæ officina b.
AQ. P. S.   Aquiliae pecunia signata.
AQ. P.   Aquiliae percussa.
AQ. S.   Aquiliae signata.
AQVA. M.   Aqua marcia.
AQVA. TRAJ.   Aqua trajana.
AR. or ARL.   Arelate or arlate.
ARA. PAC.   Ara pacis.
ARAB. ADQVI.   Arabia adquisita.
ARMEN. CAP.   Armenia capta.
ARMENIA ET MESOPOTAMIA POTESTATEM P. R. REDACT.   Armenia et mesopotamia
potestatem populi **romani** redactae.
ASI. ASIA.   Asia.
A. SISC.   A. sisciae.
AST.   Astigitana.
AVG.   Augur or augustus, or augusta, **or augustalis.**
AVG. D. F.   Augustus divi filius.
AVGG. or AVGGG.   Augusti.
AVR. PIA. SIDON. COLONIA.   Aurelia pia sidonis colonia.

B.

B.   Berythus or bono, or braceara or officina secunda.
B. A.   **Braccara augustalis.**
BON. EVENT.   Bonus eventus, or bono eventui.
BRIT.   Britannicus or britannia.
B. R. P. N.   Bono republico nato.
BRVN.   Brundusium.
B. SIRM.   B. sirmii.
B. S. LG. B.   (Officina secunda) signata lugdunum.
B. T.   Beata tranquillitas.
BVTHR.   Buthrotum.

C.

C.   Caius or caesar.
C.   Carthago, or censor, or centum, or cives, or clypeus, or cohors, **or colonia,** or
consultum, or cornelius.
C. A. A. P.   Colonia augusta aroe patrensis, or colonia a. **augusta patrensis,** or co-
lonia agrippina.
CABE.   Cabellio.
C. A. BVT.   Colonia augusta buthrotum.
C. A. C.   Colonia augusta caesarea.
C. A. E.   Colonia augusta emerita.
C. A. E. AVG. PATER.   Colonia augusta emerita augustus **pater.**
CAES.   **Caesarea or** caesar.
CAESS. or CAESSS.   Caesares.
CAESAR. AVG. F. DES. IMP. AVG. COS. ITE.   Caesar augusti filius designatus impera-
tor augustus consul iterum.
CAESAR. DIVI. F.   Caesar divi filius.   Caesar, son of the **God.**
CAESAR. PONT. MAX.   Caesar pontifex maximus.
C. A. I. or C. I. A.   Colonia augusta julia.
CAL.   Calaguris, or calidius, or calidia.

PLATE LXXXVIII.

1

2

3

4

5

6

7

8

9

C. A. O. A. F. Colonia augusta oca antoniniana felix.
C.A. PI. MET. SID. Colonia aurelia pia metropolis sidon.
C. A. R. Colonia augusta rauracorum or colonia augusta regia.
C. C. Hundreds.
C. C. A. Colonia caesarea augusta.
C. CAESAR. AVG. PRON. AVG. P. M. TR. P. IIII. P. P. Caius caesar augusti proncpos augustus pontifex maximus tribunitia potestate iiii. pater patriae.
C. C. COL. LVG. Claudia copia colonia lugdunum.
C. C. L B. Colonia campestris julia babba.
C. C. I. B. D. D. Colonia campestris julia babba decreto decurionum.
C. C. I. H. P. A. Colonia concordia julia hadrumetina pia augusta.
C. CIV. D. D. P. Corona civica data decreto publico.
C. C. N. A. Colonia carthago nova augusta.
C. C. N. C. D. D. Colonia concordia norba caesarea decreto decurionum.
C. R. Centissima remissa, or circenses restituti.
C. C. S. Colonia claudia salaria.
C. CVP. Caius cupiennius.
CEN. Censor.
CENS. PER. Censor perpetuus, or censoris permissu.
CER. SACR. PER. OECVME. ISELA. Certamina sacra periodica oecumenica isclastica.
CERT. QVIN. ROM. CON. Certamina quinquennalia romae constituta.
C. E. S. Cum exercitu suo.
CEST. Cestius, or cestia.
C. F. Caius fabius.
C. F. Caii filius.
C. N. Caii nepos.
C. F. P. D. Colonia flavia pacensis develtum.
C. G. I. H. P. A. Colonia gemella julia hadriana pariana augusta.
C. I. C. A. Colonia julia concordia apamaea, or colonia julia carthago antiqua.
C. I. C. A. GENIO. P. R. D. D. Colonia julia concordia augusta genio populi romani decreto decurionum.
C. I. A. D. Colonia julia augusta dertona.
C. I. AVG. F. SIN. Colonia julia augusta felix sinope.
C. I. B. Colonia julia balba.
C. I. C. A. P. A. Colonia julia carthago augusta pia antiqua or colonia julia corinthus augusta pia antoniniana.
C. I. CAES. Caius julius caesar.
C. I. CAL. Colonia julia calpe.
C. I. F. Colonia julia felix.
C. I. G. A. Colonia julia gemella augusta.
C. I. I. A. Colonia immunis illice augusta.
C. I. IL. A. Q. PAPIR. CAR. Q. TER. MONT. II. VIR. Colonia immunis illice augusta quinto papirio carbone quinto terentio montano ii. viris quinquennalibus.
C. I. N. C. Colonia julia norba caesariana.
C. I. N. C. Colonia julia nova carthago.
CIR. CON. Circenses constituti, or circenses consessit.
C. I. V. Colonia julia valentia.
CL. Claudius, or claudia, or clypeus.
CLASS. PR. Classis praefectus or classis praetoriana.
C. L. AVG. F. Caius lucius augusti filius.
C. L. CAESS. Caius et lucius caesares.
C. L. I. COR. Colonia laus julia corinthus.
CL. V. Clypeus votivus.
C. M. L. Colonia metropolis laodicea.
CN. ATEL. FLAC. CN. POMP. FLAC. II. VIRIS. Q. V. I. N. C. Cnaeo atellio flacco cnaeo pompeio flacco ii. viris quinquennalibus victricis juliae novae carthaginis.
CN. DOM. AMP. Cnaeius domitius amplus.
CN. DOM. PROCOS. Cnaeo domitio proconsule.

PLATE LXXXIX.

GREAT SEAL OF WILLIAM III.
(A.D. 1694–1702.)

CN. F. Cnaei filius.
CN. MAG. IMP. Cnaeus magnus imperator.
CO. DAM. METRO. Colonia damascus metropolis.
COHH. PRÆT. VII. P. VI. F. Cohortes prætorianae vii. piae vi. fideles.
COH. I. CR. Cohortis i. cretensis.
COH. PRÆ. PHIL. Cohors prætoriana philippensium.
CO. AE. CAP. Colonia aelia capitolina.
COL. AEL. A. H. MET. Colonia aelia augusta hadrumetina.
COL. AEL. CAP. COMM. P. F. Colonia aelia capitolina commodiana pia felix.
COL. ALEX. TROAS. Colonia alexandriana troas.
COL. AMAS. or AMS. Colonia amastrianorum or colonia amstrianorum.
COL. ANT. or ANTI. Colonia antiochia.
COL. ARELAT. SEXTAN. Colonia arelate sextanorum.
COL. AST. AVG. Colonia astigitana augusta.
COL. AVG. FEL. BER. Colonia augusta felix berithus.
COL. AVG. FIR. Colonia augusta firma.
COL. AVG. IVL. PHILIP. Colonia augusta julia philippensis.
COL. AVG. PAT. TREVIR. Colonia augusta paterna trevirorum.
COL. AVG. TROA. vel TROAD. Colonia augusta troadensis.
COL. AVGVSTA. EMERITA. Colonia augusta emerita.
COL. AVR. ANTONI. AVG. TROA. Colonia aurelia antoniniana augusta troadensis.
COL. AVR. KAR. COMM. P. F. Colonia aurelia karrhæ commodiana pia felix.
COL. AVR. PIA. SIDON. Colonia aurelia pia sidon.
COL. AVR. P. M. SIDON. Colonia aurelia pia metropolis sidon.
COL. B. A. Colonia braccara augusta.
COL. BERIT. L. V. vel VIII. Colonia berithus legio v. or viii.
COL. CABE. Colonia cabellio.
COL. CAES. ANTIOCH. Colonia caesarea antiochia.
COL. CES. AVG. Colonia caesarea augusta.
COL. CAMALODVNVM. Colonia camalodunum.
COL. CASILIN. Colonia casilinum.
COL. CL. PTOL. Colonia claudia ptolomais.
COL. DAMAS. METRO. Colonia damascus metropolis.
COL. F. J. A. P. BARCIN. Colonia flavia julia augusta pia barcino.
COL. FLAV. AVG. COR. Colonia flavia augusta corinthus.
COL. FL. PAC. DEVLT. Colonia flavia pacensis deultum.
COL. H. Colonia heliopolis.
COL. HA. MER. Colonia hadriana mercuri.
COL. HEL. I. O. M. H. Colonia heliopolis jovi optimo maximo heliopolitana.
COL. IVL. AVG. C. I. F. COMAN. Colonia julia augusta claudia invicta felix coma-
    norum.
COL. IVL. AVG. FEL. BER. Colonia julia augusta felix berythus.
COL. IVL. AVG. FEL. CREMNA. Colonia julia augusta felix cremna.
COL. IVL. CER. SAC. AVG. FEL. CAP. OECVM. ISE. HEL. Colonia julia certamen sa-
    crum augustum felix capitolinum oecumenicum iselasticum heliopolitanum.
COL. IVL. CONC. APAM. AVG. D. D. Coloni julia concordia apamea augusto decreto
    decurionum.
COL. IVL. LAV. COR. Colonia julia laus corinthus.
COL. IVL. PATER. NAR. Colonia julia paterna narbonensis.
COL. ANT. COM. Coloniae antoninianae commodianæ.
COL. NEM. Colonia nemansus, or nemausensium.
COL. NICEPH. COND. Colonia nicephorium condita.
COL. PATR. Colonia patrensis, or patricia.
COL. P. F. AVG. F. CAES. MET. Colonia prima flavia augusta felix caesarea metro-
    polis.
COL. P. FL. AVG. CAES. METROP. P. S. P. Colonia prima flavia augusta caesarea me-
    tropolis provinciae syriae palestina.
COL. PR. F. A. CAESAR. Colonia prima flavia augusta caesarea.

PLATE XC.

Col. R. F. AVG. FL. **C. METROP.** **Colonia romana felix augusta flavia caesarea me**tropolis.

Col. ROM. **Colonia romulensis.**

Col. ROM. **LVGD.** **Colonia** romanorum lugdunum.

Col. **RVS. LEG. VI.** **Colonia** ruscino legio vi.

Col. SABAR. **Colonia** sabariae.

Col. SEBAS. Colonia sebastiae.

Col. SER. G. NEAPOL. Colonia servia galba neapolis.

Col. **TYR.** METR. Colonia tyras metropolis.

Col. **V. I.** CELSA. Colonia victrix julia celsa.

Col. **VIC.** IVL. LEP. Colonia victrix julia leptis.

Col. **VIM.** AN. I. Colonia viminacium anno i.

Col. **VLP.** TRA. Colonia ulpia trajana.

Com. ASI. ROM. ET. AVG. Commune asiae romae et augusto.

Com. IMP. AVG. Comes imperatoris augusti.

Comm. Commodus, or commodiana.

Co. M. O. B. vel. **Co. M. OB.** Constantinopoli **moneta** officina b. or **constantinopoli** moneta obsignata.

Con. vel CONS. vel **CONST.** Constantinople.

Con. AVG. VIII. Congiarium augusti viii.

Conc. Concordia.

Conc. APAM. Concordia apameae.

Cong. DAT. POP. Congiarium datum populo.

Congiar. PRIMUM. P. R. D. Congiarium primum populo romano datum.

Cong. P. R. vel Cong. PR. Congiarium populo romano, or congiarium **primum.**

Cong. **TER. P. R.** IMP. MAX. DAT. Congiarium tertium populo **romano** impensis **maximis datum.**

Con. M. Constantinopolis moneta.

Con. O. B. Constantinopoli officina **b.**

Con. OB. Constantinopoli obsignata.

Consensu. SENAT. ET. EQ. ORDINIS. P. Q. R. **Consensu senatus et** equestris ordinis populi que romani.

Cons. O. A. Constantinopoli officina a.

Cons. P. A. Constantinopoli percussa a.

Cons. SUO. Conservatori **suo.**

Coopt. **Cooptatus.**

Coopt. IN. OMN. CONL. SVPRA. NVM. EX. S. C. Cooptatus in omne conl egium supra numerum ex senatus consulto.

Co. P. F. CAE. METRO. Colonia prima flavia caesarea metropolis.

C. O. P. I. A. Colonia octavianorum pacensis julia augusta.

Co. R. N. B. Constantinopoli romae novae b.

Cos. ITER. ET. TER. DESIGN. Consul iter um et tertium designatus.

Coss. Consules.

Cos. VI. Consul vi.

C. P. FL. AVG. F. G. CAES. METRO. P. S. P. Colonia prima flavia augusta felix germanica caesarea, metropolis provincia syriae, palestina.

C. R. Claritas reipublicae.

Cras. Crassus.

C. R. I. F. S. Colonia romana julia felix sinope.

Crispina. **AVG.** COMMODI. Crispina augusta commodi augusti.

C. SACR. FAC. Censor sacris facundis.

C. T. T. Colonia togata taraco.

C. V. Clypeus votivus.

C. VAL. HOST. M. QVINTVS. Caius hostilianus messius **quintus.**

C. VET. LANG. **Caius** vettio languido.

C. VI. IL. Colonia victrix illice.

C. Q. P. P. Consul quintum pater **patriae.**

CVR. X. F. Curator x. flandorum.

PLATE XCI.

GREAT SEAL OF ANNE BEFORE THE ACT OF UNION.

(A.D. 1694-1707.)

C. v. t.   Colonia **victrix** taraco.
C. v. t. t. ÆTERNIT. AVG.   Colonia **victrix togata taraco** æternitati augustac.

D.

D. a.   Divus augustus.
Dac.   Dacia, dacicus.
Dac. cap.   Dacia capta.
Dacia avg. provincia.   Dacia augusti provincia.
Dama.   Damascus.
D. c. a.   Divus cæsar augustus.
D. c. c. n. c.   Decuriones coloniae concordiae norbae caesarianae.
D. cl. sept. albin. caes.   Decimus clodius septimus albinus caesar.
D. c. s.   De consulum sententia.
D. d. n. n.   **Domini** nostri or dominorum nostrorum.
Debellator. gent. barbar.   Debellatori gentium barbarorum.
Deci.   **Decius** or **decennalia.**
De. germ.   De germanis.
Deo. nem.   Deo nemausus.
Dert.   Dertosa.
D. f.   Decimi filius.
D. n.   Decimi nepos.
Diana. perg.   Diana pergensis.
Dict. per.   Dictator perpetuus.
Dii. pat.   **Dii** patrii.
Diis. cvst.   Diis custodibus.
Diis. genit.   **Diis** genitalibus.
D. i. m. s.   **Deo invicto** mithras sacrum.
Disciplina, or **discipvlina avg.**   Disciplina, **or discipulina** augusta, or augusti.
Divi. f.   Divi **filius.**
Divo. avg. vesp.   Divi augustus vespasiano.
Divo. avg.   Divo augusto.
T. divi. vesp. f. vespasiano.   Tito divi vespasiani filio vespasiano.
Div. pio.   Divo pio.
Divvs. traian. avg. parth. pater.   Divus traianus augustus parthicus pater.
Dom, or **Domit.**   Domitius, or domitianus.
Domitia avg. imp. caes. divi. f. domitiani avg.   Domitia augusta imperatrix caesaris divi, filii domitiani augusti.
D. p.   Divus pius.
D. p p.   Dii penates.
Dr. cæs. q. pr.   Drusus cæsar quinquennalis praefectus.
Drvsvs. cæsar. ti. avg. divi. avg. n.   Drusus cæsar tiberii **augusti filius, divi** augusti nepos.
D. s. i. m.   Deo soli invicto mithrae.

E.

Egn. gal. avg.   Egnatius gallienus augustus.
Eid. mart.   Eidibus martii.
Eq. coh.   Equestris cohors.
Eq. m.   Equitum magistri.
Eq. ordin.   Equitum ordinis.
Etr.   Etruscus.
Evr.   Europa.
Ex. ar. p.   Ex argento puro, or probato, **or publico.**
Ex. cons.   Ex consensu.
Ex. d. d.   Ex decreto decurionum.

PLATE XCII.

1

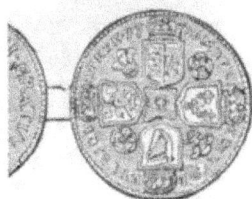

2

3

4

4

4

5

ABBREVIATIONS ON ROMAN COINS.

Ex. EA. P. Q. I. S. AD. AE. D. E.   **Ex ea** pecunia quae jussu senatus ad **aerarium** delata est.

EXERCITVS. VAC.   Exercitus vacccus.

EXERCITVS. YSC.   Exercitus yscanus.

EXERC. PERS.   Exercitus persicus.

Ex. S. C.   Ex senatus consulto.

Ex. S. D.   Ex senatus decreto.

F.

F.   Fabius, or faciundum, or fecit, or felix, or filius, or flamen, or fortunas.

FAB.   Fabius.

FABRI.   Fabricius.

FAD.   Fadius.

FÆCVND.   Fæcunditas.

FAN.   Fannia.

FATIS VICTRI.   **Fatis victricibus.**

FAVSTINA. AVG. ANTONINI AVG. PII. P. P.   **Faustina** augusta antonini augusti pii patris patriae.

F. B.   Felicitas beata.

F. C.   Faciundum curavit, or frumento convehendus.

FELICITATI AVG.   Felicitati augustæ, or augusti.

FEL PRO.   Felicitas provinciarum.

FEL. TEMP. REP.   Felix temporum reparatio.

FER. D.   Feronia dea.

FIDEI LEG.   Fidei legionum.

FIDES MILIT.   Fides militum.

FID. EXERC.   Fides exercitus.

FL.   **Flamen, or flavius.**

FLAM. D.   **Flamen divi.**

FLAM. DIAL.   **Flamen dialis.**

FLAM. MART.   **Flamen** martialis.

FL. FEL.   **Flaviae felicis.**

FOR.   Fortuna.

FORT. P. R.   Fortuna or fortitudo populi romani.

FORT. PRIM.   Fortuna primigenia.

FORT. RED.   Fortunae redux, or fortunae reduci.

FOVR.   Fourius.

FRVG. AC.   Fruges acceptae.

F. T. R.   Felix temporum **reparatio.**

FVL.   Fulvius.

FVLG.   Fulgurator.

FVLM.   Fulminator.

G.

G.   Galinicus, or gaudium, or genius, or germanus, or gnaea.

GADIT.   Gaditana.

GAL.   Galindicus, or galerius.

G. or GEN. AVG.   Genio augusti.

G. COR. SVPER.   Gnea cornelia **supera.**

G. D.   Germanicus dacicus.

GEM. L.   Gemina legio.

GEN. COL. COR.   Genio coloniae corinthiae.

GEN. ILLY.   Genius illyrici.

GENIO. COL. NER. PATR.   Genio coloniae neronianae patrensis.

GENIT. ORB.   Genitrix orbis.

GEN. LVG.   Genio lugdunensi.

Plate XCIII.

GREAT SEAL OF ANNE AFTER THE UNION WITH SCOTLAND.
(A.D. 1707–1714.)

ABBREVIATIONS ON ROMAN COINS.

GERM. CAPTA. Germania capta.
GER. P. Germanica provincia, or germaniae populus.
GL. E. R. Gloria exercitus romani.
GL. P. R. Gloria populi romani.
GL. R. Gloria romanorum.
G. L. S. Genio loci sacrum.
G. M. V. Gemina minerva victrix.
GOTH. Gothicus.
G. P. Græcia peragrata, or græciæ populus.
G. P. R. Genio populi romani.
GRAC. Gracchus.
G. T. A. Genius tutelaris aegypti, or geminae tutator africae.

H.

H. Hastati.
HADRIANVS AVG. COS. III. P. P. Hadrianus augustus consul iii. pater patriae.
HA. P. or H. P. Hastatorum principum.
HEL. Heliopolis.
HELV. PERT. Helvius pertinax.
Her. Hercules, or Herennius.
HERAC. Heraclitus.
HERC. COMMOD. Herculi commodiano.
HERC. GADIT. Herculi gaditano.
HERC. ROM. CONDIT. Herculi romano conditori.
HILARIT. TEMP. Hilaritas temporum.
Hip. Hippius.
HISP. Hispalis, or hispana, or hispalus.
Ho. Honor.
Hs. A sign for sestertium, the Sesterce, a piece of Roman money.

I.

I. Imperator, or jovis, or juno, or jussu, or I, or 1.
I. A. Imperator augustus, or indulgentiâ augusti.
I. C. Imperator caesar, or julius caesar.
II. IMP. CC. PHILIPPIS. AVGG. Ii. imperatoribus caesaribus philippis augustis.
III. VIR. A. A. A. AF. F. Trium viri auro argento aere flando feriundo.
I. IT. Imperator iterum.
II. VIR. QVINQ. Duum-vir quinquennalis.
IMP. CAES. ANTONINVS AVG. P.P.P. Imperator caesar antoninus augustus pius pater patriae.
IMP. CAES. AVG. COMM. CONS. Imperator caesar augustus communi consensu.
IMP. CAES. C. VIB. VOLVSIANO. Imperator caesari caio vibio volusiano.
IMP. CAES. DIVI. TRAIANI. AVG. F. TRAIANI. HADRIANO. OPT. AVG. DAC. PARTHICO. P. M. TR. P. COS. P. P. Imperatori caesari divi trajani augusti filio trajani hadriano optimo augusto dacico parthico pontifici maximo tribunitiae potestate consuli patri patriae.
IMP. CAES. DIVI. VESP. F. DOMIT. AVG. P. M. TR. P. P. P. Imperator caesar divi vespasiani filius domitianus augustus pontifex maximus tribunitia potestate pater patriae.
IMP. CÆS. G. M. Q. Imperator caesar gneus messius quintus.
IMP. CÆS. L. AVREL. VERVS. AVG. ARM. PART. Imperator caesar lucius aurelius verus augustus armeniacus parthicus.
IMP. CÆS. L. SEPT. SEV. PERT. AVG. TR. P. COS. Imperator caesar lucius septimus severus pertinax augustus tribunitia potestate consul.
IMP. CÆS. M. ANT. GORDIANVS. AFR. AVG. Imperator caesar marcus antoninus gordianus africanus augustus.

196

PLATE XCIV.

1

2

3

IMP. CÆS. M. OPEL. SEV. MACRINVS. AVG. Imperator cæsar marcus opelius **severus** macrinus augustus.

IMP. CÆS. NERVÆ. TRAIANO. AVG. GER. DAC. P. M. TR. P. COS. V. P. P. Imperatori cæsari nervæ trajano augusto germanico dacico pontifici maximo tribunitia potestate consul v. pater patriae.

IMP. CÆS. P. HELV. PERTIN. AVG. Imperator cæsar publius helvius pertinax augustus.

IMP. C. C. VA. F. GAL. VEND. VOLVSIANO. AVG. Imperator caesari caio valindico finnico galindico vendendico volusiano augusto.

IMP. C. M. CASS. LAT. POSTVMVS. P. F. AVG. Imperator caesar marcus cassius latienus postumus pius felix augustus.

IMP. C. M. TRAIANVS. DECIVS. AVG. Imperator caesar marcus trajanus decius **augustus.**

IMP. C. P. LIC. VALERIANVS. P. F. AVG. Imperator caius publius licinius valerianus pius felix augustus.

IMP. ITER. Imperator **iterum.**

IMP. M. IVL. PHILIPPVS AVG. Imperator marcus julius philippus augustus.

IMP. T. AEL. ANTONINO. Imperatori **tito** aelio antonino.

IMP. T. CÆS. DIVI. VESP. F. AVG. P. M. TR. POT. COS. REST. Imperator titus cæsar divi vespasiani filius augustus pontifex maximus tribunitia potestate consul restituit.

IMP. VI. Imperator vi.

INDVLGENT. AVGG. IN. CARTH. Indulgentia augustorum in carthaginenses.

INDVLG. PIA. POSTVMI. AVG. Indulgentia pia postumi augusti.

IO. CANTAB. Jovi cantabrico.

I. O. M. D. Jovi optimo maximo dicatum.

I. O. M. H. Jovi optimo maximo heliopolis.

I. O. M. S. Jovi optimo maximo sacrum.

I. O. M. SPONS. SECVRIT. AVG. Jovi optimo maximo sponsori securitatis augusti.

I. O. M. S. P. Q. R. V. S. PR. S. IMP. CAES. QVOD. PER. EV. RP. IN. AMP. ATQ. TRAN. S. E. Jovi optimo maximo senatus populus que romanus vota suscepta pro salute imperatoris caesaris quod per eum respublica in ampliori atque tranquilliori statu est.

I. O. M. V. C. Jovi optimo maximo victori conservatori.

IOV. OLYM. Jovi olympio.

IOV. STAT. Jovi statori.

IOV. TON. Jovi tonanti.

ISEL. OECVM. Iselastica **oecumenica.**

I. S. M. R. Juno sospita **magna regina, or** juno sospita mater romanorum.

ITAL. Italia.

ITAL. MVN. Italicum municipium.

IVD. CAP. Judæa capta.

IVL. Julius, or julia, or julianus.

IVL. AVG. CASSANDREN. Julia augusta cassandrensis.

IVL. AVG. GENIT. ORB. Julia augusta genitrix orbis.

IVLIA. AVGVSTA. C. C. A. Julia augusta colonia caesarea augusta.

IVLIA. IMP. T. AVG. F. AVGVSTA. Julia imperatoris titi augusti filia augusta.

IVL. V. MAXIMVS. C. Julius verus maximus caesar.

IVN. Junior, or junius, or Juno.

IVN. MART. Junoni martiali.

IVN. REG. Juno regina.

K.

K. Carthago **or kaeso.**

KAP. Capitolina.

KAR. Carthago.

KAR. O. Carthaginensis officina.

PLATE XCV.

GREAT SEAL OF GEORGE I.
(A.D. 1714-1727.)

KART. or KRT. E.   Carthago officina quinta.
KON. or KONS.   Constantinopolis.

L.

L.   Laus, or legatus, or **legio, or lucius, or ludi.**
L. C.   Lugdunum colonia.
LAPHR.   Laphria.
L. AUREL. COMMO. GERM. SARM.   Lucius aurelius commodus germanicus sarmaticus.
L. CAN.   Lucius caninius.
LEG.   Legio.
LEG. AUG. PR. PR.   **Legatus** augusti pro praetore.
LEG. GEM. PAC. or PARTH. or NEP. or VLP.   Legio gemina pacifica, or parthica, or neptunia, or ulpia.
LEG. I. ADI. P. F.   Legio i. **adjutrix pia fidelis.**
LEG. II. PART. V. P. V.F.   Legio ii. parthica v. pia fidelis.
LEG. III. PART.   Legio iii. parthica.
LEG. II. TRO. or TR. FOR.   **Legio ii.** trojanus or trajanus fortis.
LEG. IIII. VI. P. VI. F.   Legio iiii. vi. pia vi. fidelis.
LEG. M. XX.   Legio macedonica xx.
LEG. PRO. COS. or LEG. PRO. PR. or LEG. AVG. or LEG. A. P.   Legatus pro consul·, or legatus pro praetore, or legatus augusti, or legio armeniae provinciae.
LEG. VII. CL. GEM. FIDEL.   Legio vii. claudia gemina fidelis.
LEG. V. M. P. C.   Legio v. macedonica pia constans.
LEG. XI. CLAVDIA.   Legio xi. claudia.
LEG. XVI. FRE.   Legio xvi. fregellae or fregenae.
LEG. XXX. NEP. VI. F.   Legio xxx. neptuniana vi. fidelis.
LEN. CVR. X. F.   Lentulus curator x. flandorum.
LEP.   **Lepidus** or leptis.
LIB. AVG. IIII. COS. IIII.   Liberalitas augusti iiii. consul iiii.
LIBERALIT. AVG.   Liberalitas augusta or augusti.
LIBERIS. AVG. COL. A. A. P.   Liberis augusti colonia augusta aroe patrensis.
LIBERT. REST.   Libertas restituta.
LIB. II. or III.   Liberalitas ii. or iii.
LIB. P.   Libero patri.
LIB. PVB.   Liberalitas publica, **or libertas** publica.
LIC. COR. SAL. VALER. N. CÆS.   **Licinius** cornelius saloninus valerianus **nobilis** cæsar.
LIC. or licin.   Licinius licinianus.
L. I. MIN.   Legio i. minervium.
LOCVPLET. ORB. TERRAR.   Locupletatori orbis terrarum.
LON.   Longus.
L. P. D. AE. P.   Lucius papirius designatus aedilis plebis.
L. SEPTIM. SEVERVS. PIVS. AVG. P. M. TR. P. XV. COS. III. P. P.   **Lucius** septimus severus pius augustus pontifex maximus tribunitia potestate xv. consul iii. pater **patriae.**
L. SEPTIM. SEV. PERT. AVG. IMP. PARTH. ARAB. PARTH. ADIAB. COS. II. P. D.   Lucius **septimus** severus pertinax augustus imperator parthicus arabicus parthicus adia- **bicus** consul ii. pater patriae.
L. VAL.   **Lucius** valerius.
LVC.   **Lucanus,** or lucrio, or lucdunum.
LVC. P. S.   **Lucduni** pecunia signata.
LVC. AEL.   Lucius aelius.
LVCILLÆ. AVG. ANTONINI. AVG. F.   **Lucillæ** augustae antonini augusti filiae.
LVD. SÆC. FEC. COS. XIIII.   **Ludos** sæculares fecit consul xiiii.
LVP.   Lupercus.
LV. PC. S.   Lugduni pecunia signata.

PLATE XCVI.

1

2

3

M.

M. Maesia, or marcus, or memmius, or mensis, or minerva, or moneta, or municeps, or munitae.

M. A. Marcus aurelius.

MA. CANI. Manius caninius.

MA. C. AVG. Magna (aedes) caesaris augusti or macellum augusti.

M. ÆM. Marcus aemilius.

MAG. DECENT. Magnentius decentius.

MAG. PIVS. Magnus pius.

M. ANN. Marcus annius.

M. ANT. IMP. AVG. COS. DES. ITER. ET TERT. Marcus antonius imperator augur consul designatus iterum et tertium.

M. ANTON. AVG. GERM. Marcus antoninus augustus germanicus.

M. ANTONINVS. IMP. COS. DESIG. ITER. ET. TERT. III. VIR. REIP. C. Marcus antoninus imperator consul designatus iterum et tertium triumvir reipublicae constituendae.

MARC. Marcia, or marcus, or martius.

MARCIA OTACIL. SEV. AVG. Marcia otacilia severa augusta.

MAR. PROP. Mars propugnator.

MAR. VLT. Marti ultori.

M. CASS. LAT. POSTVMVS. Marcus cassius latienus postumus.

MAT. AVGG. Mater augustorum.

MAT. SEN. Mater senatus.

MAT. PAT. Mater patriae.

MAT. DEVM. CONSERVAT. Matri deum conservatrici.

MAT. DEVM. SALVT. Mater deum salutari.

MATER. AVGG. Mater augustorum.

MATR. CASTROR. Matri castrorum.

M. AVF. Marcus aufidius.

M. AVR. or MAR. AVR. Marcus aurelius.

M. AVR. ANTON. Marcus aurelius antoninus.

M. AVREL. ANTONINVS. AVG. ARMEN. P. M. Marcus aurelius antoninus augustus armeniacus pontifex maximus.

MAX. Maximus.

M. C. I. Municipium calaguris julia.

M. COMMODVS ANTONINVS AVG. BRIT. Marcus commodus antoninus augustus Britannicus.

MES. Messius.

MET. Metropolis.

MET. Metaccus.

MET. VLPIAN. PAN. Metallum ulpianum pannonicum.

MET. DEL. Metallum del. for dalmatianum.

MET. NOR. Metallum noricum.

M. F. Marci filius.

M. N. Marci nepos.

M. Π. ILLERGAVONIA. DERT. Municipium hibera illergavonia dertoza.

MINAT. Minatius.

MINER. VICT. Minervae victrici.

M. K. V. Moneta carthaginensis urbem.

M. L. Moneta lugdunensis.

M. LEP. C. REG. INST. Marcus lepidus civitatum reginensium instauravit.

M. LL. Moneta lugdunensium.

M. MARC. Marcus marcellus.

M. M. I. V. Municipes municipii julii uticensis.

M. N. Moneta narbonensis.

MON. Moneta.

MON. AVG. Moneta augusti.

MO. S. T. Moneta signata treveris.

PLATE XCVII.

GREAT SEAL OF GEORGE II.

(A.D. 1727-1760.)

M. s. AVGG. ET CAESS. NOSTR. Moneta sacra augustorum et caesarum nostrorum.
M. s. TR. Moneta signata treveris.
MVL. FEL. Multa felicia.
MVN. AVG. BILBILIS. C. CORN. REFEC. M. HELV. FRONT. II. VIR. Municipium augusta
bilbilis caio cornelio, refecto marco helvio frontone duumviri.
MVN. CLVN. Municipium clunia.
MVN. FANE. ÆL. Municipium fanestre ælium.
MVNICIP. STOB. Municipium stobensium.
MVNIC. ITALIC. PER. AVG. Municipium italicense permissu augusti.
MVN. STOB., or STOBENS. or STOBENSIVM. Municipium stobenso or stobensium.
MVN. TVR. or MV. TV. Municipium turcussae.

N.

N. Natalis, or nepos, or nobilis, or noster, or numen, or nummus.
NAT. Natalis or natus.
NAT. VRB. CIRC. CON. Natali urbis circenses constituti.
N. C. Nero caesar, or nobilis caesar.
N. C. A. P. R. Nummus cusus a populo romano.
NEP. RED. Neptuno reduci.
NEP. S. Neptuno sacrum.
NEPT. or NEPTVN. Neptunalia.
NER. Nero or nerva.
NER. I. Q. VRB. Nero i. quaestor urbis.
NERO. CLAVD. DRVSVS. GERMAN. IMP. Nero claudius drusus germanicus imperator.
NERO. ET. DRVSVS. CAESARES. QVINQ. C. V. I. N. C. Nero et drusus caesares quin-
quennales coloniae victricis juliae novae carthaginis.
N. F. Numerii filius.
N. N. Numerii nepos.
NICEPH. Nicephorium.
NIG. Niger.
NOB. C. Nobilis or nobilissimus caesar.
N. T. Numini tutelari.
N. TR. ALEXANDRIANÆ. COL. BOSTR. Nervae trajanae alexandrianæ coloniae bostrae,
or bostrensis.
NV. Numa.

O.

O. Ob, or officina, or ogulnius, or optimo.
OB. C. S. or OB. CIV. SER. or O. C. S. Ob. cives servatos.
OEc. OEcumenia.
OFF. III. CONST. Officinae tertiae constantinopoli.
OLY. Olympius.
O. M. T. Optimo maximo tonanti.
OP. or OPT. PRIN. or PR. Optimo principi.
OP. DIV. Opi divinae.
OPI. DIVIN. TR. P. COS. II. Opi. divinae tribunitia potestate consul ii. (ii. stands for
secundum).
OPPIVS. CAPIT. PROPR. PRÆF. CLA. Oppius capito propraetor praefectus classis.
ORB. TER. Orbis terrarum.

P.

P. Pater, or patriae, or per, or percussa, or perpetuus, or pius, or pontifex, or
populus, or posuit, or praefectus, or primus, or princeps, or provinciae, or publius, or publico.
P. A. Pietas augusti or augusta.

PLATE XCVIII.

PAC. or **PACI.** Pacifico.
PACE. P. R. TERRA. MARIQ. PARTA. IANVM. CLVSIT. Pace populi romani terra marique parta janum clusit.
P. ALITIO. L. MENIO. II. VIR. Publio alitio lucio menio duum-viri.
PANNON. Pannoniae.
P. AQ. Percussa aquileiae.
P. AR. Percussa arelate.
P. AR. AD. Parthicus arabicus adiabenicus.
PAR. Parthicus.
P. ARL. Pecunia arelatensis or percussa arelate.
PAT. Pater patriae.
PAX. AVG. Pax augusta.
PAX. P. ROM. Pax populi romani.
P. C. CÆS. Pater caii caesaris.
P. C. L. VALERIANVS. Publius cornelius licinius valerianus.
P. D. Populo datum.
PELAG. Pelagia.
PENATES. P. R. Penates populi romani.
PER. Permissu.
PER.,A. or **PERPET. AVG.** Perpetuus augustus.
PERM. DIVI. AVG. COL. ROM. Permissu divi augusti colonia romulea.
PERM. IMP. COR. Permissu imperatoris corinthi.
PERM. IMP. GERM. Permissu imperatoris germanici.
PERMISSV L. APRONI. PROCOS. III. Permissu lucii apronii proconsul iii.
P. R. P. Pecunia romae percussa.
PERT. Pertinax.
PESCEN. Pescennius.
P. F. Pius felix, or pia fidelis, or primus fecit.
P. F. Publii filius, or pii filia.
P. H. C. Provinciae hispaniae citerioris.
PH. COND. Philippus conditor.
P. I. or **PRIN. IVVEN.** Princeps juventutis.
PIET. AVG. Pietas augusta.
P. K. Percussa karthagine.
PLAE. TRAN. Plactorius tranquillus.
P. L. COR. SAL. Publius licinius cornelius saloninus.
P. L. O. N. Percussa lugduni officinâ novâ or nonâ.
P. M. Pontifex maximus.
P. M. S. COL. VIM. Provincae moesiae superioris colonia viminiacum or viminacium.
POL. Pollio.
POM. Pompeius.
PORT. OST. Portus ostiensis.
P. P. Pater patriae.
P. P. AVG. Perpetuus augustus.
P. POMPON. CR. II. VIR. Puplio pomponio crispo, or crispino duumviro.
P. R. Percussa romae.
PRÆ. CLAS. ET ORAE. MARIT. Præfectus classis et orae maritimae.
PRÆF. GERM. Præfectus germanorum.
PR. COS. Proconsul.
PRIMI. DECEN. Primi decennales.
PRINCIP. IVVENT. Principi Juventutis.
PROB. Probus.
PROC. Proconsul.
PROC. SIC. Proconsul siciliae.
P. ROM. Percussa romae.
PRON. Pronepos.
PROP. or **PRO. P.** Propraetor or propraetore.
PROQ. or **PRO. Q.** Proquaestor or proquaestore.

PLATE XCIX.

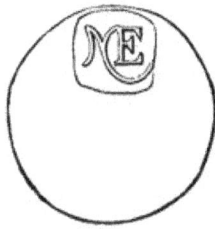
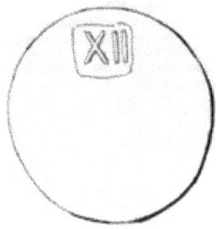

1

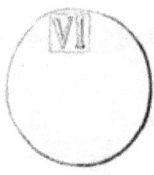

2

3

4

6

5

7

Prov. deor. Providentiae or providentiâ deorum.
Provident. senat. Providentia senatus.
Pr. s. p. Provinciae syriae palestinâ.
Pr. vrb. Praefectus urbis or praetor urbis.
P. s. Percussa sisciae.
P. t. Percussa treveris.
Pvdic. Pudicitia.
Pvpie. Pupienus.

Q.

Q. Quaestor, or quinarius, or quintus, or quinquennalis, or **quod**.
Q. cas. Quintus cassius.
Q. c. m. p. i. Quintus cecilius metellus pius imperator.
Q. des. Quaestor designatus.
Q. her. etr. mes. dec. nob. c. Quintus herennius etruscus messius decius nobilis caesar.
Q. hisp. Quaestor hispaniae.
Q. m. Quintus marcius.
Q. o. c. fab. Quinto ogulnio **(et)** caio fabio.
Q. p. Quaestor praetoris.
Q. papir. car. q. ter. mon. Quinto papirio carboni (et) quinto terentio montano.
Q. pr. q. pro. c. or **cos.** Quaestor provinciae, or quaestor pro consule or proconsulis.
Q. terent. cvlleon. pro. cos. iii. Quinto terentio culleoni proconsuli tertium.
Qvad. Quadratus.
Qvadrag. rem. Quadragesima remissa.
Qvin. iter. Quinquennalis iterum.
Q. v. or **qvod. v. m. s.** Quod viae munitae sint, or sunt.
Q. vrb. Quaestor urbis.

R.

R. Remissa, or roma, or restituit, **or romanus**.
Ra. Ravenna.
R. c. Romani cives.
R. cc. Remissa c c.
Rec. orb. Rector orbis.
Ref. Refecta.
Res. Restitutus or restituit.
Rest. ital. Restitutor italiae.
Rest. nvm. Restituta numidia or nummum restitutum.
Rex. arm. dat. Rex armeniae datus.
Rex. part. dat. Rex parthis datus.
Rex. Ptol. Rex ptolemaeus.
R. m. or **rei. mil.** Rei militaris.
Ro. Romae.
Rom. æter. Romae aeternae.
Rom. col. Romulea colonia.
Romvl. avg. Romulo augusto.
Romvl. condit. Romulo conditori.
Ro. p. s. Romae pecunia signata.
R. p. Romae percussa.
R. p. c. Rei publicae constituendae.
R. s. Romae signata.
R. v. Roma victrix.
R. p. s. Ravennae pecunia signata.
R. xl. Remissa xl.

PLATE C.

1

2

3

O   3

S.

S. Sacerdos, or sacra, or semissus, or senatus, or senator, or senior, or sextus, or soli, or spes, or suscepto, or sisciae.

S. A. Salus, or salus augusti, or securitas augusti, or signata antiochiae.

Sac. f. Sacris faciundum or sacra faciens.

Sacr. per. Sacra periodica.

Sæcvlar. avgg. Sæculares augustorum.

Sæcvlar. sac. Sæcularia sacra.

Sæcvl. frvgif. Sæculo frugifero.

Sag. Saguntum.

Sal. Salus, **or** salduba, or saloninus, or salonina.

Sal. gen. hvm. Salus generis humani.

Sall. barb. Sallustia barbia (Orbiana).

Salm. Salmantica.

S. arl. Signata arelate.

Sarm. Sarmaticus.

Savf. Sauffeia or sauffeius.

S. c. Senatus consulto.

Sci. af. Scipio africanus.

Scip. asia. Scipio asiaticus.

S. const. Signata constantinopoli.

Scr. Scribonia or scribonius.

Sec. or **sæc.** Securitas or sæculum.

Sec. orb. Securitas orbis.

Semp. Sempronius or sempronia.

Sen. Senior.

Senti. Sentia.

Sep. col. lavd. Septimia colonia laudicea.

Sept. sev. Septimius severus.

Sept. tyr. met. Septima tyrus metropolis.

Ser. Servius.

Seren. Serenus.

Sex. f. Sexti filius.

S. f. Saeculi felicitas.

Sicil. Sicilia.

Sider. recept. Sideribus receptis.

Sig. recept. Signis receptis.

S. i. m. Soli invicto mithrae.

Sir. or **sirm. Sirmium.**

Sisc. p. Sisciae percussa (moneta).

S. m. a. Signata, or sacra moneta antiochiae.

S. m. a. q. p. Sacra moneta aquileiæ percussa.

S. m. her. Signata moneta heracleae.

S. m. o. b. Signata moneta officina secunda.

S. m. n. Sacra **or** signata moneta narbonae or nicomediae.

S. m. r. Signata moneta romae.

S. m. r. q. Signata moneta romae officina quarta.

S. m. sisc. Signata moneta sisciae.

S. m. tr. Signata moneta treveris.

S. m. t. s. b. Sacra moneta treveris signata, officina secunda.

Sp. Spurius.

Sp. avgvsta. Spes augusta.

Spes. p. r. Spes populi romani.

S. p. q. r. adsert. libert. Senatus populus que romanus assertori libertatis.

S. p. q. r. a. n. f. f. Senatus populus-que romanus anno natali fieri fecit.

S. p. q. r. imp. cæ. qvod. v. m. s. ex. ea. p. q. is. ad. a. d. Senatus populus **que**

PLATE CI.

1

2   3

4   5   6

romanus imperator cæsari quod viae munitae sunt ex ea pecuniâ **quam is ad** aerarium detulit.

S. P. Q. R. IVLLÆ. AVGVST.   Senatus populus que romanus juliæ augustae.

S. P. Q. R. OPTIMO. PRINCIPI.   Senatus populus que romanus optimo principi.

S. P. Q. R. SVF. P. D.   Senatus populus que romanus suffamenta populo data.

S. P. Q. R. V. S. PRO. R. CÆS.   Senatus populus que romanus vota solvunt pro reditu cæsare.

S. R.   Senatus romanus, or salus romanorum, or spes reipublicae, or sacris receptis, or restitutis.

S. T.   Signata treveris or securitas temporum.

STABIL.   Stabilitas.

SVLL.   Sulla or sylla.

Ss.   Sestertium.

T.

T.   Titus, or treveris, or tribunus, or tutelaris.

T. AR.   Tertia arelate.

T. CAES. **DIVI. VESP.** F. AVG. **P. M. TR.** P. P. COS. VIII.   Titus caesar divi vespasiani filius augustus pontifex maximus tribunitiâ potestate pater patriae consul viii.

TEMPL. DIV. AVG. REST. COS. IIII.   Templum divi augusti restitutum consul quartum.

TER.   Terentius.

TES.   Tessalonicae.

T. F.   Titi filia or temporum felicitas.

T. FL.   Titus flavius.

T. G. A.   Tutelaris genius aegypti.

TI.   Tiberius.

TI. N.   Tiberii nepos.

TI. F.   Tiberii filius.

T. M. AP. CL.   Titus manlius (et) appius claudius.

T. P., **or** TR. POT., or TRIB. POT.   Tribunitia potestas.

T. P., **or** TR. POT., or TRIB. POT. V. etc.   Tribunitia potestas, or tribunitia potestas v.

TR.   Treveris.

TRAI.   Trajanus.

TRAN.   Tranquillus.

TRANQ.   Tranquillitas.

TREBAN.   Trebanius.

TREBON or TREB.   Trebonianus.

TR. F.   Trajana fortis.

TRIVMPH.   Triumphator.

TR. OBS. or O. B. S.   Treveris obsignata or officina **b. signata.**

TR. LEG. II.   Tribunus legionis ii.

TR. P.   Treveris percussa or pecunia.

TR. PL. D.   Tribunus plebis designatus.

TR. V. M.   Triumviri monetales.

T. T.   Trevirorum.

TVL. H. or HOST.   Tullus hostilius.

V.

V.   Quinque, or verus, or victrix, or vir, or virtus, or voto, or votivus, or urbs.

V. AET.   Virtus aeterna.

VAL. or VALER.   Valerius or valerianus.

VAR. RVF.   Varius rufus.

VEN. FEL.   Veneri felici.

VENER. VICTR.   Veneri victrici.

VENT.   Ventidius.

VESP.   Vespasianus.

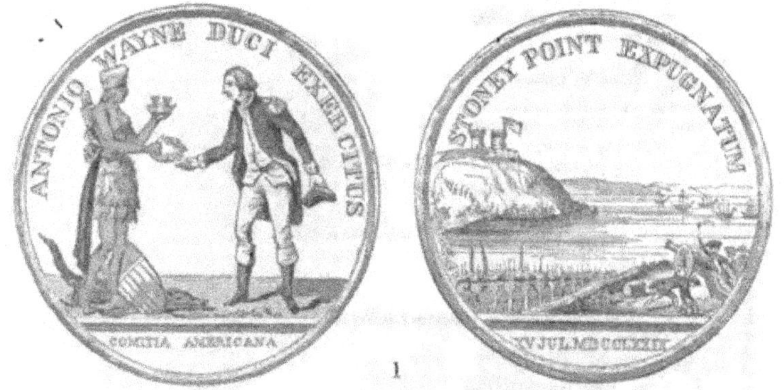
ANTONIO WAYNE DUCI EXERCITUS
COMITIA AMERICANA
STONEY POINT EXPUGNATUM
XV JUL. MDCCLXXIX

1

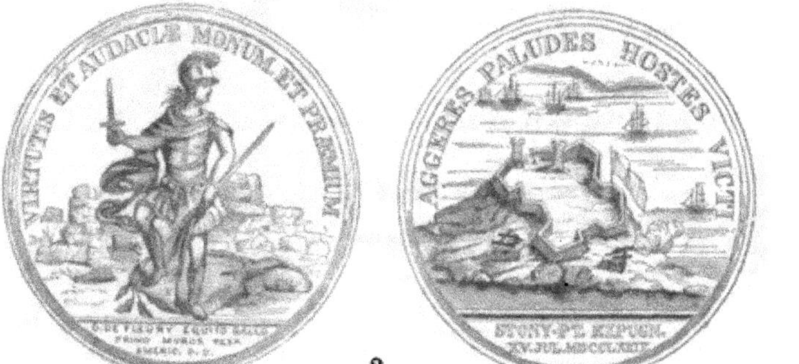
VIRTUTIS ET AUDACIÆ MONUM ET PRÆMIUM
AGGERES PALUDES HOSTES VICTI
STONY-PT. EXPUGN.
XV. JUL. MDCCLXXIX.

2

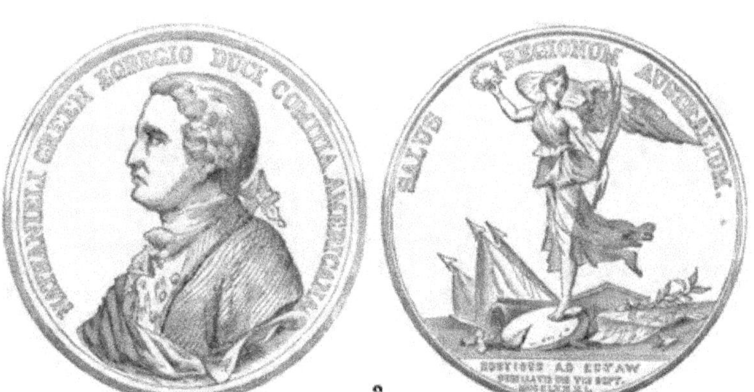
NATHANAELI GREEN EGREGIO DUCI COMITIA AMERICANA
SALUS REGIONUM AUSTRALIUM

3

VETER. Veteranorum.
VET. LANG. Vettius languidus.
V. I. Vota imperii.
VIB. Vibius.
VIC. AVG. Victoria augusti.
VIC. GERM. Victoria germanica.
VIC. PAR. M. Victoria parthica maxima.
VIC. S. Victoria sicilia.
VIC. BEATISSIM. CAESS. Victoria beatissimorum caesarum.
VIC. BRIT. P. M. Victoria britannica pontifex maximus.
VICTOR. ROM. Victoria romanorum.
VICT. P. GAL. AVG. Victoria parthica gallieni augusti.
VII. VIR. EPV. Vii viri epulonum.
VIR. Virtus.
VI. VIR. A. Vi. vir. augustus.
V. N. M. R. Urbis nicomediae moneta restituta.
VOL. Volusius.
VOTA. PVB. Vota publica.
VOT. DECEN. Vota decennalia.
VOT. XX. MVL. XXX. Vota xx. multiplica xxx.
V. P. Vota publica or vota populi.
V. V. Vota v.

X.

X. Decem. Ten, or Decennalia.
X. F. X. faciendum.
XL. R. Xl. remissa.
Xv. Xv. Money worth fifteen denarii.
XVI. Sixteen (denarii).
Xv. VIR. SAC. FAC. Xv. viri sacris faciundis.
Xx. V. Xx. vota.

214

PLATE CIII.

1

2

3

4

5

6

PRICES OF ENGLISH COINS.

(FROM HUMPHREYS.)

ALL are silver pennies till Edward III.

WILLIAM I., from 2s. to £1.

WILLIAM II., from 15s. to £2 10s.

HENRY I., from £1 to £4.

STEPHEN, from 15s. to £3.

HENRY II., from 3s. to 10s.

RICHARD I., from 2s. to 6s.

HENRY III., from 2s. to 5s.

EDWARD I. and II., from 2s. to 5s.

EDWARD III. pennies, half groats, and groats, about 4s. each.

    GOLD. Noble, about £2; half do., about 21s.; quarter do., about 12s.

EDWARD BLACK PRINCE pennies, about 7s.

RICHARD II. pennies, about 6s.; half groats, about 15s.; groats, about 20s.

    GOLD. Noble and half do., about £3; quarter do., about £1.

HENRY IV., V., VI. pennies, from 4s. to 20s.; half groats, from 4s. to 20s.; groats, from 4s. to £1.

    GOLD. Nobles, about £2; half do., about 25s.; quarter do., about 12s.

EDWARD IV. pennies, about 5s.; half groats, about 4s. and 5s.; groats, 3s. to 10s.

    GOLD. Noble, about £2; half do, 25s.; quarter do., about 21s.; angel and half do., about 30s.

RICHARD III. pennies, about £1; half groats, very rare; groats, about 25s.

    GOLD. Angel, about £5.

HENRY VII. pennies, about 4s.; half do., about 4s.; groats, about 5s.; shillings, from £10.

    GOLD. Sovereign, about £10; angel, about 25s.; half do., about £2.

HENRY VIII. pennies, 2s. 6d.; half groats and groats, 4s. and 5s.; shilling, about £2.

    GOLD. Sovereign, about £8; half sovereign, about 25s.; angel, about £1; half do., about 25s.; crown, about £1.

EDWARD VI. pennies, from 10s.; half groat, base, about £4; groat, base, very rare, in Durrant's sale, sold for £10 10s.; quarter shilling, about 20s.; sixpence, about 10s.; shilling, from 4s.; half crowns, £2; crowns, about £2.

    GOLD. Double sovereign, Colonel Durrant's, sold for £38 10s.; sovereign, about £4; half do., about £2; quarter do., about £4; half crown, about £3.

MARY I. pennies, about 10s.; half groats, about £3; groats, about 12s.; half shillings, about £2; shillings, about £2.

    GOLD. Sovereign, about £6; rial, one of the rarest coins in the series, Colonel Durrant's, sold for £66; angel, about £4.

ELIZABETH, three-farthing pieces, about 10s.; pennies, about 2s.; three-halfpenny pieces, about 10s.; half groats, about 4s.; threepenny pieces, about 4s.; groats, about 10s.; half shillings, about 3s.; shillings, about 10s.; half crowns, about £2; crowns, about £2.

PLATE CIV.

1

2

3

PRICES OF ENGLISH COINS.

GOLD. Sovereigns, about £4; rial, the average of Colonel Durrant's was £7 15s.; angel, about £2; half do., about 20s.

JAMES I. pennies, about 4s.; half groats, about 3s.; sixpences, about 10s.; shillings, from about 7s. 6d.; half crowns, about £2; crowns, about £2.

GOLD. Sovereigns, or rose rials, about £4; unites, or twenty-shilling pieces, about £2; half sovereign, about £1; crowns, about 12s.; half crowns, about 10s.; angel, about £2; half do., about £3.

CHARLES I. COPPER. Farthings, about 6d.

SILVER. Pennies, 2s. to £1; half groats, about 4s.; threepenny pieces, about 4s.; groats, about 5s.; sixpences, about 5s.; shillings, about 10s.; half crowns, about £2; crowns, about £2; ten-shilling pieces, about £2 10s.; pound-pieces, about £10.

GOLD. Angels, about £4; unit, or broad, about £2; half do., about £2; crowns, about £1; treble unit, or three-pound piece, Oxford Mint, about £8.

COMMONWEALTH. SILVER. Half pennies, about 4s.; pennies, about 4s.; half groats, about 3s.; sixpences, about 12s.; shillings, about 7s.; half crowns, about £3; crowns, about £2 10s.

GOLD. Twenty-shilling piece, about £3; half do., about £2 10s.; crowns, about £2 10s.

OLIVER CROMWELL. The set of his silver coins, crown, half do., and shilling, is worth from £7 to £12.

GOLD. Broad, about £7.

CHARLES II. COPPER. Half pennies, about 5s.; farthings, about 1s.

SILVER. The set of Maunday money, 1d., 2d., 3d., and 4d., given by the monarch on Maunday Thursday to certain poor persons, about 3s. 6d.; sixpences, about 3s.; shillings, about 5s.; half crowns, about 10s.; crowns, from 15s. upward, according to preservation.

GOLD. Half guineas, about £2; guineas, about £3; two-guinea pieces, about £3; five-guinea pieces, about £7.

From this time till the present, the COPPER COINS can be purchased for from 1s. to 2s. and 3s. per specimen, with the exception of ANNE'S FARTHING, a fine specimen of which, of the common type, can be procured for about 14s. to £1. The SILVER COINS can be purchased for about double currency, and upward, according to preservation; and the GOLD COINS can be obtained for about 50 per cent. advance on the current value.

PRICES OF MODERN COINS OF FOREIGN NATIONS.

THE ordinary coins of nearly every modern nation on the face of the earth may be found in New York city. The great immigration, and the wide-spread commerce which brings seamen here from every port, necessarily produces a constant supply. Hence, as a general rule, none of them are worth more than their intrinsic value in copper and silver, or, at the most, three or six cents each for fine specimens of copper coins, while silver coins are never worth more than their weight. Foreign tradesmen's cards are of no more value than coins. Very fine sets of the English can be imported at about five cents each, in uncirculated condition.

PLATE CV.

1

2

3

4

5

6

7

REMARKS ON SOME RARE COINS OF THE UNITED STATES SERIES.

THE tables will serve to show the collector what coins of the regular series he may expect to find readily and without trouble, as well as what coins it will be difficult to procure except at high prices. But it is of course impossible to give, in the form of a table, the relative rarity of those coins which belong to the general class denominated very rare. We therefore make some notes on these coins for the special benefit of young and inexperienced collectors.

DOLLARS.

The dollar of 1794—the first silver dollar of the series—is now very rare, and commands a large premium. It is worth, in ordinary condition, from $4 to $5, and in fine condition much more. The dollars from 1794 to 1804 are not worth any premium above the weight of the silver, unless in extra fine condition. One variety of 1798—that with the eagle on the reverse like the eagle of 1797—is rare, and worth about $2.

The dollar of 1804 is very rare—so rare that not more than two or three specimens are known. It has even been doubted whether these are not manufactured coins; but this suspicion is groundless. The dies are in existence at the Mint, and it is stated that these two specimens were struck from them about 1827.

The dollars of 1836, 1838, and 1839 are but pattern pieces, with a flying eagle on the reverse, never issued in circulation. They are rare in the order of their dates, the last being most rare. They command prices varying from $6 to $18, according to date and condition.

The dollar of 1848 is becoming scarce. In 1851 and 1852 no dollars were issued for circulation, and the specimens struck at the Mint are of the highest degree of rarity. They command $15 to $18 each at auction sales.

The dollar of 1854 is becoming very rare. That of 1858 was never issued for circulation, and the Mint proofs command a price from $6 to $8.

With the foregoing exceptions, the dollars may be easily procured. It should be borne in mind, however, that they are worth a premium of 6 to 7 per cent. over the coins of smaller denomination since 1853, and they are therefore seldom found in circulation, and usually go to the silversmiths. Hence they are fast disappearing, and in a few years all the dates will be very rare. The same is true of all the silver coinage prior to July, 1853.

PLATE CVI.

1

2

3

HALF DOLLARS.

The half dollar of 1794 is seldom found in good condition, and when so found is worth $1 to $2. That of 1795 is more common; but 1796 and 1797 are exceedingly rare, bringing readily, if in fine order, $10 to $15 each at auction and private sale. 1801 and 1802 are rarely found in even fair keeping, and it is very difficult to supply them in collections. They are worth $1 to $2 each, in good order. The remarks made on the dollar of 1804 apply also to the half dollar of the same year. We have never seen a specimen, and might doubt that it ever existed but for the fact that a variety of 1805 is known of which the die was altered from the die of 1804, and the alteration is so poorly executed that the 4 is more distinct than the 5. It is impossible to name any price for the dollar or the half dollar of 1804, for they have never been sold.

The die of 1807, with the head like that of 1808, is scarce in good condition, though very common in poor condition.

1813 is difficult to find in good keeping. 1815 is rare in good condition, and worth $1.50 to $2.50.

The milled-edge variety of 1836 is scarce, and worth $1 to $1.50. 1840 is scarce in good condition, but rubbed specimens are common. 1851 is quite scarce—worth $1 to $2; and 1852 is almost equally rare.

With these exceptions, all the half dollars are to be had with little trouble from any silver dealer of your acquaintance.

QUARTER DOLLARS.

This coin, being one in most common use, is seldom found in first-rate condition in any of the early years. The quarter dollar of 1796 is sufficiently rare to be worth about $2.50 in good condition. 1804 is worth 50 cents to $1. 1823 is a very rare coin—in fact one of the rarest of the series. The price marked for it is not higher than it will command in first-rate order. 1827 is very rare. The other dates are comparatively common, though nearly all before 1837 are difficult to find, except more or less rubbed.

DIMES.

The dime of 1796 is rare—worth $1.50 to $2.50. The dime of 1797 is of the highest rarity, and commands $7.50 to $8.50. 1798, 1801, and 1803 are worth $1 each. 1804 is very rare, and worth $5. 1809 and 1811 are very rare in good condition, and worth $2 to $3. 1822 is rare also, and worth $1.50 to $2. 1844 is becoming very scarce. 1846 is rare, and worth $1.50 to $2.50 in first-rate order. 1853, without arrow-heads at the sides of the date, is rare, and brings $1.

HALF DIMES.

1794 is seldom found. It is worth $3 if in first-rate order, or $2 in ordinary condition. 1796 and 1797 are worth about $1 each. 1801 and 1803 are worth $2 each. 1846 is scarce, and brings $1 to $1.50. 1853, without the arrow-heads on each side

PLATE CVII.

1

2

3

5

4

6

8

7

9

of the date (which arrow-heads were placed on the coinage in July, 1853, to mark the new and reduced weight), is now rare, and brings 75 cents to $1.

CENTS.

The desire to make collections of cents has made so much variation in the prices that it is impossible to say that any date has a fixed and definite value.

In general, all the cents can be procured in ordinary circulation, with very little trouble, by a diligent searcher, excepting only 1793, 1799, and 1804. It is, in fact, unnecessary for any collector to pay a premium for any cent except these years, unless he desires to enrich his collection with proof or uncirculated coins. We have already explained the difference between a proof and an uncirculated coin. But it may be repeated here with benefit. The proof coins are those struck in the Mint from the master-die, the original die cut by the engraver. The custom of the Mint has been to strike about a hundred sets, more or less, of the entire coinage of the year from the master-die. These are very beautiful and perfect specimens, and are known as proofs. They always command a premium, which increases as years advance. The master-die is afterward used to impress in soft steel and make other dies, from which the great bulk of the coinage is struck.

In the cents the difference between the proofs and other issues is very great, and the former command extravagant prices, as the annexed table shows. The collector, however, must not be misled by this table into supposing that he will have to pay these prices for fine or uncirculated specimens. Patience in collecting will enable him in time to make his set of cents fine enough at little cost except for the rare years, 1793, 1799, and 1804.

The numerous varieties of 1793 command various prices. The rarest is the Liberty-cap cent, like that of 1794. In fine condition it brings from $4 to $6. The Link cent, having the chain around the words ONE CENT, is worth $3 to $5 in first-rate condition. The Wreath cent, in various varieties, brings about the same price; but this cent of 1793 has so varied in price of late years that it is impossible to name a fixed value to any variety. The mania for coins has largely increased the supply, while it has also increased the number of collectors and the demand.

The cent of 1799 is the rarest of the copper coins. The collector must beware of counterfeits, which abound in the cities, well executed by altering cents of 1797 and 1798. A first-rate 1799, of undoubted genuineness, is worth about $10—but the price falls rapidly as the condition of the piece deteriorates. Close examination with the aid of a magnifying-glass will not in all cases detect these counterfeits. The collector should at least adopt this rule, not to purchase a 1799 which has the slightest scratch or flaw on the surface any where near the last 9 in the date.

1804 is not so rare a cent as it is commonly reputed, and yet it commands from $3 to $7.50, according to condition. We recommend the collector not to purchase this date, but search diligently among old coppers until he finds it. We have had no difficulty in finding some fair specimens among copper cents in bulk. It is, however, very rare in first-rate condition, and the same is true of all the dates from 1800 to 1811, except perhaps 1802 and 1803. The cent of 1808, with filleted head resembling 1807, is rarely found except in very poor condition. Its existence even has been disputed, so rarely is the date legible.

224

PLATE CVIII.

1

2

3

4

P

5

RARE AMERICAN COPPER.

In 1815 no cent was coined; any specimens that are exhibited must be alterations from other years. It is by some disputed that this cent is unknown. We can affirm, however, that we never saw a cent of 1815, never saw a person who had seen one, and never heard of a collector who either possessed one or had heard of one in any other person's possession. If the coin ever existed, it has absolutely disappeared. Counterfeits are easily made from 1813; but no one need be imposed on by such coppers after this information.

The cents from 1830 to 1849 are rarely found in uncirculated condition, and this will explain the high prices paid for proof specimens, as shown by the table.

HALF CENTS.

These little coins are fast disappearing. 1793 has become very rare. 1796 is much rarer; and, with few exceptions, all the early years are becoming scarce. These exceptions are 1803, 1804, 1806, and 1807, which are perhaps more common than others. 1831 and 1836 are of the highest rarity, commanding, for the former, $5 to $7.50, and the latter, $3 to $5.

In 1841, 1842, 1843, 1844, 1845, 1846, 1847, and 1848 none were issued for circulation, and the specimens coined at the Mint are of the highest rarity, as also is true of 1852. The table gives the prices recently paid for these.

226

PLATE CIX.

1   2

3

4

5   7   6

TABLE

[N.C., none coined.   Greatest rarity, 6.]

Years.	Dollars.	Half Dollars.	Quarter Dollars.	Dimes.	Half Dimes.	Three Cents.	Cents.	Half Cents.
1793............	N.C.	N.C.	N.C.	N.C.	N.C.	N.C.	5	6
1794............	6	4	N.C.	N.C.	5	N.C.	2	3
1795............	2	2	N.C.	N.C.	4	N.C.	2	4
1796............	2	6	5	4	4	N.C.	2	6
1797............	2	6	N.C.	5	4	N.C.	3	5
1798............	1	N.C.	N.C.	4	N.C.	N.C.	2	N.C.
1799............	1	N.C.	N.C.	N.C.	N.C.	N.C.	6	N.C.
1800............	2	N.C.	N.C.	3	4	N.C.	3	3
1801............	2	4	N.C.	3	4	N.C.	3	N.C.
1802............	2	4	N.C.	4	5	N.C.	2	5
1803............	1	1	N.C.	3	5	N.C.	1	4
1804............	6	6	3	3	N.C.	N.C.	5	1
1805............	N.C.	2	2	2	4	N.C.	3	3
1806............	N.C.	2	2	N.C.	4	N.C.	3	2
1807............	N.C.	1	2	2	N.C.	N.C.	2	2
1808............	N.C.	3	N.C.	N.C.	N.C.	N.C.	4	1
1809............	N.C.	3	N.C.	5	N.C.	N.C.	4	1
1810............	N.C.	2	N.C.	N.C.	N.C.	N.C.	3	3
1811............	N.C.	2	N.C.	5	N.C.	N.C.	3	5
1812............	N.C.	2	N.C.	N.C.	N.C.	N.C.	3	N.C.
1813............	N.C.	3	N.C.	N.C.	N.C.	N.C.	3	N.C.
1814............	N.C.	2	N.C.	2	N.C.	N.C.	2	N.C.
1815............	N.C.	4	3	N.C.	N.C.	N.C.	N.C.	N.C.
1816............	N.C.	N.C.	N.C.	N.C.	N.C.	N.C.	2	N.C.
1817............	N.C.	3	N.C.	N.C.	N.C.	N.C.	1	N.C.
1818............	N.C.	2	3	N.C.	N.C.	N.C.	1	N.C.
1819............	N.C.	2	2	N.C.	N.C.	N.C.	1	N.C.
1820............	N.C.	2	2	2	N.C.	N.C.	2	N.C.
1821............	N.C.	2	2	2	N.C.	N.C.	2	N.C.
1822............	N.C.	2	2	5	N.C.	N.C.	1	N.C.
1823............	N.C.	2	6	2	N.C.	N.C.	3	N.C.
1824............	N.C.	2	2	2	N.C.	N.C.	2	N.C.
1825............	N.C.	2	2	2	N.C.	N.C.	2	2
1826............	N.C.	2	N.C.	N.C.	N.C.	N.C.	2	2
1827............	N.C.	2	6	2	N.C.	N.C.	1	N.C.
1828............	N.C.	1	3	2	N.C.	N.C.	1	1
1829............	N.C.	1	N.C.	2	3	N.C.	1	2
1830............	N.C.	1	N.C.	2	2	N.C.	2	N.C.
1831............	N.C.	1	2	2	1	N.C.	1	6

PLATE CX.

1

2

3

4

Years.	Dollars.	Half Dollars.	Quarter Dollars.	Dimes.	Half Dimes.	Three Cents.	Cents.	Half Cents.
1832	N.C.	1	2	2	1	N.C.	1	1
1833	N.C.	1	2	2	1	N.C.	1	1
1834	N.C.	1	2	2	1	N.C.	1	1
1835	N.C.	1	2	2	1	N.C.	1	1
1836	6	2	2	2	1	N.C.	1	6
1837	N.C.	2	2	2	1	N.C.	1	N.C.
1838	6	2	2	2	1	N.C.	1	N.C.
1839	6	2	2	2	1	N.C.	1	N.C.
1840	3	3	2	2	1	N.C.	2	6
1841	2	1	2	2	1	N.C.	2	6
1842	2	1	2	2	1	N.C.	2	6
1843	2	1	2	2	1	N.C.	2	6
1844	2	2	1	4	3	N.C.	1	6
1845	2	1	1	1	2	N.C.	1	6
1846	2	1	1	5	5	N.C.	1	6
1847	2	1	1	1	2	N.C.	1	6
1848	2	1	1	1	1	N.C.	1	6
1849	2	1	1	1	1	N.C.	1	2
1850	2	1	1	1	1	N.C.	1	2
1851	6	3	1	1	1	1	1	2
1852	6	2	1	1	1	1	1	6
1853	2	1	1	1	1	1	1	1
1854	4	1	1	1	1	1	1	2
1855	2	1	1	1	1	4	1	2
1856	2	1	1	1	1	1	5	1
1857	1	1	1	1	1	1	3	1
1858	5	1	1	1	1	1	1	N.C.
1859	1	1	1	1	1	1	1	N.C.

The Table of Comparative Rarity is based on only six orders. It is of course impossible to distinguish all coins exactly by these six numbers. Thus the dollar of 1804 might well be ranked as more rare than almost any other of the coins. But the table will serve the purposes of the collector without more minute distinctions. We have classed the dollars of 1836, 1838, and 1839 as very rare. They are, in fact, pattern pieces (especially the dollar of 1839, of which very few were struck), and should perhaps be omitted from the table. The cent of 1856 referred to in the table is the nickel cent, and that of 1857 the copper.

PLATE CXI.

1   2   3

4   5

6   7   8

9   10

WEIGHT AND FINENESS OF GOLD AND SILVER.

GOLD is never found in a pure state when taken from the earth. It is always alloyed more or less with silver. The process of parting the gold from the silver is very simple. Being melted and poured into cold water, it is granulated; then boiled, each 3½ ounces of alloyed metal with 4 ounces of nitric acid, which dissolves the silver and copper, leaving the gold in a brown powder. This is washed with hot water to remove the nitrate of silver, and is then as pure as it is practicable to obtain it. It still contains from three to ten thousandths of silver.

All coin is alloyed. The difference in the color of gold coins is caused by the difference in the comparative quantity of silver and copper used for the alloy. Thus the present standard of coin is 900 parts of fine gold to 100 parts of alloy. The 100 parts of alloy may be entirely copper, but never are so in fact. The law requires that of this 100 parts alloy not more than 50 parts shall be silver. The quantity of the silver will determine the comparative paleness or ruddiness of the coin. The Mint practice is to add 100 parts of copper to 900 parts of fine gold, it being supposed that enough copper will oxidize in the melting to reduce the entire alloy, both copper and silver, to 100.

The same standard of fineness (900 to the 1000 parts) is preserved in the silver coins of the present day. There have been several changes in this respect in both gold and silver coinage, which the following will illustrate:

WEIGHT AND FINENESS OF GOLD COINS.

Before July 1, 1834, gold coin was 916⅔ thousandths fine, the eagle weighing 270 grains.

From July 1, 1834, to January 1, 1837, gold coin was 899¼ thousandths fine, the eagle weighing 258 grains.

Since January 1, 1837, gold coin was 900 thousandths fine, the eagle weighing 258 grains.

WEIGHT AND FINENESS OF SILVER COINS.

Before January 1, 1837, silver coin was 892$\frac{4}{10}$ thousandths fine. One ounce coined into $1.15.2$\frac{4}{10}$.

From January 1, 1837, to July, 1853, silver coin was 900 thousandths fine. One ounce coined into $1.16.3$\frac{6}{10}$.

Since July 1, 1853, silver coin was 900 thousandths fine. One ounce coined into $1.25.

PLATE CXII.

1   2   3   4

5   6   7   8

9   10   11

12   13   14

FINENESS OF GOLD AND SILVER.

The preceding statement of silver coins excepts dollars since 1853. They remain of the former weight—412½ grains—and are, therefore, never used for circulation. Three-cent pieces, since July, 1853, are of the same fineness of silver with the other coins. Before July, 1853, they were 750 thousandths fine. It will be observed that a very simple weight may be used by persons not having Troy weights at hand. Five new, uncirculated, and clean quarter dollars, since July, 1853, weigh one ounce Troy, and of course each weighs one-fifth of an ounce.

The term carat, as applied to gold and silver, may be interpreted in this way: Gold or silver which is chemically pure, that is absolutely without alloy, is 24 carats fine, and gold or silver 12 carats fine is one half pure metal and one half some other metal or metals. The other degrees of fineness in carats are determined on the same proportions.

A new, more convenient, and intelligible nomenclature has been recently adopted. It is this: Gold or silver chemically pure, that is 24 carats fine, is now called 1000 fine. It is understood as consisting of 1000 parts, all of which are pure metal. If 500 parts be gold and 500 parts some other metal, then the gold is said to be 500 fine, or $\frac{500}{1000}$ fine, and of course such gold is equivalent to 12 carats fine.

The following table will be convenient for reducing carats to thousandths:

TABLE OF CARATS AND THOUSANDTHS.

GOLD OR SILVER CALLED

1 carat should contain of pure gold or silver	41⅔ thousandths.
2 carats should contain of pure gold or silver	83⅓ thousandths.
3 carats should contain of pure gold or silver	125 thousandths.
4 carats should contain of pure gold or silver	166⅔ thousandths.
5 carats should contain of pure gold or silver	208⅓ thousandths.
6 carats should contain of pure gold or silver	250 thousandths.
7 carats should contain of pure gold or silver	291⅔ thousandths.
8 carats should contain of pure gold or silver	333⅓ thousandths.
9 carats should contain of pure gold or silver	375 thousandths.
10 carats should contain of pure gold or silver	416⅔ thousandths.
11 carats should contain of pure gold or silver	458⅓ thousandths.
12 carats should contain of pure gold or silver	500 thousandths.
13 carats should contain of pure gold or silver	541⅔ thousandths.
14 carats should contain of pure gold or silver	583⅓ thousandths.
15 carats should contain of pure gold or silver	625 thousandths.
16 carats should contain of pure gold or silver	666⅔ thousandths.
17 carats should contain of pure gold or silver	708⅓ thousandths.
18 carats should contain of pure gold or silver	750 thousandths.
19 carats should contain of pure gold or silver	791⅔ thousandths.
20 carats should contain of pure gold or silver	833⅓ thousandths.
21 carats should contain of pure gold or silver	875 thousandths.
22 carats should contain of pure gold or silver	916⅔ thousandths.
23 carats should contain of pure gold or silver	958⅓ thousandths.
24 carats should contain of pure gold or silver	1000 thousandths.

A necessary result of this table is the rule to convert thousandths into carats, viz.: Divide the number of thousandths by 41⅔; and to convert carats into thousandths, multiply the number of carats by 41⅔.

Pure gold, 1000 fine, is valued at the United States Mint, per ounce Troy, at $20.67.183468.

1

2

3

4

5

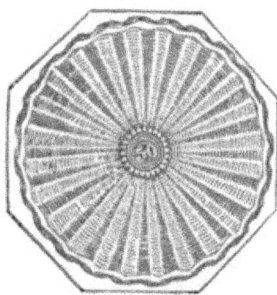

4

6

7

8

To find the value per ounce of gold of any degree of fineness, specified in thousandths, multiply the above value by the number of thousandths. Thus, one ounce of gold of 900 thousandths is worth $20.67.183468 × .900 = $18.60.4651212.

Pure silver, 1000 fine, is valued, in purchasing at the Mint, per ounce Troy, at $1.34.444 +, or $1.34⅖ exactly.

The same rule applies as given above for gold.

UNITED STATES GOLD COINAGE.

TABLE SHOWING THE YEARS WHEN GOLD WAS COINED.

[O indicates a coinage; N.C., none coined.]

Years.	Double Eagles.	Eagles.	Half Eagles.	Quarter Eagles.	Three Dollars.	Dollars.
1793	N.C.	N.C.	N.C.	N.C.	N.C.	N.C.
1794	N.C.	N.C.	N.C.	N.C.	N.C.	N.C.
1795	N.C.	O	O	N.C.	N.C.	N.C.
1796	N.C.	O	O	O	N.C.	N.C.
1797	N.C.	O	O	O	N.C.	N.C.
1798	N.C.	O	O	O	N.C.	N.C.
1799	N.C.	O	O	N.C.	N.C.	N.C.
1800	N.C.	O	O	N.C.	N.C.	N.C.
1801	N.C.	O	N.C.	N.C.	N.C.	N.C.
1802	N.C.	N.C.	O	O	N.C.	N.C.
1803	N.C.	O	O	N.C.	N.C.	N.C.
1804	N.C.	O	O	O	N.C.	N.C.
1805	N.C.	N.C.	O	O	N.C.	N.C.
1806	N.C.	N.C.	O	O	N.C.	N.C.
1807	N.C.	N.C.	O	O	N.C.	N.C.
1808	N.C.	N.C.	O	O	N.C.	N.C.
1809	N.C.	N.C.	O	N.C.	N.C.	N.C.
1810	N.C.	N.C.	O	N.C.	N.C.	N.C.
1811	N.C.	N.C.	O	N.C.	N.C.	N.C.
1812	N.C.	N.C.	O	N.C.	N.C.	N.C.
1813	N.C.	N.C.	O	N.C.	N.C.	N.C.
1814	N.C.	N.C.	O	N.C.	N.C.	N.C.
1815	N.C.	N.C.	N.C.	N.C.	N.C.	N.C.
1816	N.C.	N.C.	N.C.	N.C.	N.C.	N.C.
1817	N.C.	N.C.	N.C.	N.C.	N.C.	N.C.
1818	N.C.	N.C.	O	N.C.	N.C.	N.C.
1819	N.C.	N.C.	O	N.C.	N.C.	N.C.
1820	N.C.	N.C.	O	N.C.	N.C.	N.C.
1821	N.C.	N.C.	O	O	N.C.	N.C.
1822	N.C.	N.C.	O	N.C.	N.C.	N.C.
1823	N.C.	N.C.	O	N.C.	N.C.	N.C.
1824	N.C.	N.C.	O	O	N.C.	N.C.
1825	N.C.	N.C.	O	O	N.C.	N.C.

PLATE CXIV.

1

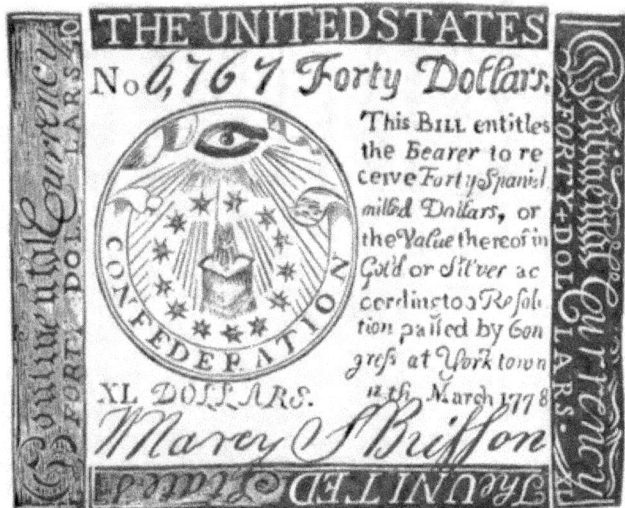

2

UNITED STATES GOLD COINAGE.

Years.	Double Eagles.	Eagles.	Half Eagles.	Quarter Eagles.	Three Dollars.	Dollars.
1826	N.C.	N.C.	O	O	N.C.	N.C.
1827	N.C.	N.C.	O	O	N.C.	N.C.
1828	N.C.	N.C.	O	N.C.	N.C.	N.C.
1829	N.C.	N.C.	O	O	N.C.	N.C.
1830	N.C.	N.C.	O	O	N.C.	N.C.
1831	N.C.	N.C.	O	O	N.C.	N.C.
1832	N.C.	N.C.	O	O	N.C.	N.C.
1833	N.C.	N.C.	O	O	N.C.	N.C.
1834	N.C.	N.C.	O	O	N.C.	N.C.
1835	N.C.	N.C.	O	O	N.C.	N.C.
1836	N.C.	N.C.	O	O	N.C.	N.C.
1837	N.C.	N.C.	O	O	N.C.	N.C.
1838	N.C.	O	O	O	N.C.	N.C.
1839	N.C.	O	O	O	N.C.	N.C.
1840	N.C.	O	O	O	N.C.	N.C.
1841	N.C.	O	O	N.C.	N.C.	N.C.
1842	N.C.	O	O	O	N.C.	N.C.
1843	N.C.	O	O	O	N.C.	N.C.
1844	N.C.	O	O	O	N.C.	N.C.
1845	N.C.	O	O	O	N.C.	N.C.
1846	N.C.	O	O	O	N.C.	N.C.
1847	N.C.	O	O	O	N.C.	N.C.
1848	N.C.	O	O	O	N.C.	N.C.
1849	N.C.	O	O	O	N.C.	O
1850	O	O	O	O	N.C.	O
1851	O	O	O	O	N.C.	O
1852	O	O	O	O	N.C.	O
1853	O	O	O	O	N.C.	O
1854	O	O	O	O	O	O
1855	O	O	O	O	O	O
1856	O	O	O	O	O	O
1857	O	O	O	O	O	O
1858	O	O	O	O	O	O
1859	O	O	O	O	O	O

SCALES FOR MEASURING COINS.

THE size of a coin or medal is determined among collectors by its diameter. The ordinary scale in use in Europe is that known as the Scale of Mionnet. This is arbitrary in construction, and the collector can only make use of it by having it always with him. One much more convenient, which we have adopted in this volume, is that of sixteenths of an inch. With this the collector can determine the size of a coin wherever he can find an ordinary measuring rule. It is to be hoped that this scale may be universally adopted and used in America, where it originated with the Philadelphia collectors.

There are many coins and medals closely resembling each other in their designs and inscriptions, but differing in size. This is true of a large number of American political or Presidential medalets and tokens.

In some old works on coins we find scales for measuring the thickness of the planchet. This is, however, of little use, because the thickness of ancient coins varies according to the amount of corrosion they have undergone, and a difference in this respect, in either an ancient or a modern coin, can hardly be said to make a variety in the specimens.

SCALE OF MIONNET.

[In general use in Europe.]

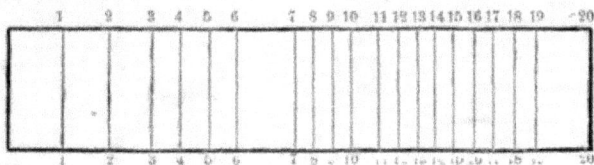

SCALE OF SIXTEENTHS OF AN INCH.

[Adopted in this Volume, and now much used in America.]

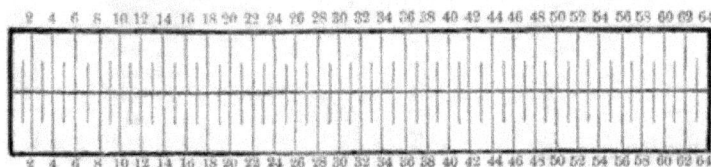

PRICES

OF UNITED STATES SILVER AND COPPER COINS AT RECENT SALES
BY AUCTION.

[p. indicates proof coins; u. uncirculated coins. Blanks indicate either no coinage, or no sales by which to establish prices.]

Years.	Dollars.	Half Dollars.	Quarter Dollars.	Dimes.	Half Dimes.	Cents.	Half Cents.
1793						$10.00	$4.13
1794	$7.50	$1.25			$2.13	1.00	1.00
1795	1.25	1.25			.55	u. 11.00	.75
1796	1.25	17.00	$2.50	$2.25	2.00	u. 4.50	12.00
1797	1.25	23.00			1.00	u. 4.00	1.00
1798	1.25			2.38		u. 2.50	
1799	1.25					11.00	
1800	1.25			.50	.55	u. 2.00	.70
1801	1.25	1.00		2.00	2.10	u. 2.00	
1802	1.25	1.00		.50		u. 2.63	2.13
1803	1.25	1.00		1.00	2.50	.75	.30
1804			.95	7.50		8.00	1.38
1805		1.00	.35	.50		.80	.45
1806		.75	.35			u. 3.75	.30
1807		.75	.35	.55		u. 2.13	.25
1808		.65				1.00	.40
1809		1.20		.45		p. 4.50	.30
1810		.60				.70	.70
1811		.60				u. 2.00	1.88
1812		.60				1.00	
1813		.60				u..2.00	
1814		.75		.20		.80	
1815		3.00	.50				
1816						.80	
1817		.75				.80	
1818		.75	.50			.30	
1819		.75	.30			1.60	
1820		1.10	.35	1.25		u. 2.55	
1821		.75	.35	.70		p. 8.00	
1822		.70	.60	1.75		1.00	
1823		.75	25.00	.15		.80	
1824		.55	.75	.15		u. 2.13	
1825		.60	.35	1.50		u. 3.25	.22
1826		.60				u. 3.00	.22
1827		.85		.15		u. 4.00	
1828		.60	.35	.15		1.13	.22
1829		.55		.15	.55	p. 5.13	.22
1830		.65		.15	.25	u. 2.00	
1831		.60	.35	.25	.12	p. 3.25	p. 10.50

Years.	Dollars.	Half Dollars.	Quarter Dollars.	Dimes.	Half Dimes.	Cents.	Half Cents.
1832		$ .60	$ .35	$ .12	$ .12	u. $4.00	$ .25
1833		.55	.75	.25	.50	u. 1.75	p. .25
1834		.55	.25	.25	.30	u. 1.25	.25
1835		.80	.50	.45	.12	u. 1.85	.25
1836		.70	.35	.50	.13	.65	p. 5.25
1837		.70	.45	p. .75	.25	p. 3.00	
1838		.55	.45	.25	.15	.55	
1839		.60	.60	.45	.15	u. 1.62	
1840	$1.25	.65	.35	.60	.30	p. 3.00	
1841	1.25	.75	.35	.65	.10	p. 3.38	p. 4.50
1842	1.25	.70	.30	.20	.10	u. 2.50	p. 9.50
1843	1.25	.65	.35	.45	.30	p. 4.00	p. 4.00
1844	1.25	.60	.40	.20	.15	u. 2.13	p. 5.00
1845	1.25	.80	.30	.15	.25	u. 1.25	p. 4.75
1846	1.25	.60	.50	.80	1.20	u. 1.88	p. 8.75
1847	1.50	.60	.40	.12	.40	p. 4.88	p. 8.25
1848	1.75	.60	.70	.12	.30	p. 4.50	p. 5.75
1849	1.25	.60	.40	.12	.25	u. 1.13	.25
1850	1.25	.80	.35	.12	.30	u. .40	p. 1.10
1851	15.00	1.20	.50	.12	.30	.35	.05
1852	15.00	1.35	.55	.45	.30	u. .35	p. 5.50
1853	1.25	.50	.25	1.10	.95	u. .15	.45
1854	3.00	.50	.25	.10	.05	p. 4.00	.05
1855	1.25	.50	.25	.10	.05	p. 3.50	.05
1856	1.25	.50	.25	.10	.05	p. 2.37	p. 1.10
1857	1.25	.50	.25	.10	.05	p. 2.25	p. .65
1858	5.00	.50	.25	.10	.05	p. .15	
1859	1.25	.50	.25	.10	.05	p. .10	

Q

REMARKS ON PRICES OF COINS, MEDALS, MEDAL-ETS, ETC.

The tables which follow can not, for various reasons, be perfect. They are made up from recent sales at auction and in private, and the prices stated have in most instances been paid for the coins. But few coins, medals, or tokens have as yet a fixed market value in this country. The first table which we present, of the comparative prices at different sales, will illustrate this; and on many of these coins the prices have more than doubled since the last-mentioned sale, as indicated by our estimated prices in the other tables. Much of the difference in prices may be owing to the condition of the pieces; but many pieces have doubled or trebled in value within a few months from the sudden demands of inexperienced collectors, while others have as greatly depreciated. And the prices vary in different cities. There are an immense number of medals, medalets, tokens, etc., to which we have made no allusion in the tables. They are omitted, because any attempt to assign to them a value, in a book which is designed to be of permanent use, would be more likely to mislead than to aid a collector. Many of those which we have mentioned have been or will be restruck, and will thus become common. It is by no means to be regretted that they are so made plenty. No collector has a right to complain. If he has foolishly paid an extravagant price for a medal or token struck within a few years, relying on the dies having disappeared, he has taken the risk, and must be content to let others supply themselves from the dies if found. The absurdities into which American collectors have been led, by the mere desire to possess rare pieces of stamped metal, have been well checked by the reproduction from original dies of these highly-prized trifles. It should rather be a subject of congratulation that coins or medals of comparative rarity are multiplied and placed in the hands of all collectors. But these reasons explain the imperfections of the price tables. It will be many years before such tables can be more than a temporary assistance.

We have given the prices of very few medals. Few have been sold at public or private sales, and we have preferred to reserve a full table of prices of American medals for a future edition of the present work.

EXPLANATION OF THE TABLES.

In the tables the scale used to measure sizes is the scale of sixteenths of an inch. A medalet of size 16 is one inch in diameter. The metals are indicated thus: c., copper; b., brass; w. m., white metal; G. s., German silver.

TABLE

	February 28, 1859.	May 4, 1859.	June 7, 1859.	June 21, 1859.	Novem'r 2, 1859.
1. Erie Canal medal, by Wright	$2.				
2. Masonic medal of Franklin	3.50				
3. Henry Clay (small medal)	3.				$4.
4. Webster, by Wright	3.75				4.
5. Clay, by Wright (the large medal)	15.				21.
6. Washington, by Wright; reverse, the Declaration of Independence	8.				10.
7. Washington, Manley medal	2.50				
8. Washington, Sansom medal	1.75				
9. Washington before Boston	3.25		$4.	$4.75	2.75
10. Washington, by Wyon	2.				
11. New Haven medal	3.				
12. Herndon medal	5.50				4.25
13. De Fleury medal	1.75				
14. Paul Jones	3.25			4.	2.
15. Gates	2.25				
16. Morgan	1.75				
17. William Washington	1.		2.	3.50	1.
18. Washington Alston (bronze)			1.50	1.75	1.75
19. Washington Alston (silver)					6.
20. Cyrus W. Field (silver)	3.				4.
21. Cyrus W. Field (bronze)					1.75
22. Mexican volunteer			4.50	3.50	2.50
23. Howard Association					3.25
24. Ludovicus Warrington					5.
25. Washington cent, 1791, large eagle	10.50	$7.		6.	
26. Washington cent, 1791, small eagle	17.				
27. Washington half penny, 1793; reverse, a ship	2.75	3.50		4.12	
28. Washington half dollar, 1792	57.				
29. Washington token, 1783, Unity States	1.	.75	.65	.50	
30. Washington token, 1783, United States	2.37	1.87	.50	1.25	.56
31. Washington token, 1783, small head	1.50		1.12		.55
32. Washington token, 1783, double head	1.75	1.	.75	.62	.50
33. Washington; Liberty and Security, large	3.50	3.	2.50		2.50
34. Washington; Liberty and Security, small					
35. Washington token; Success to the United States	3.	2.50			
36. Washington grate	1.75			2.87	
37. Washington North Wales	3.75		2.50	3.50	
38. New Jersey	.37	.55	.10	.25	.25
39. Virginia	2.	3.12	1.75	2.50	1.25
40. U. S. A. bar cent		5.25		7.05	
41. Pine-tree shilling	4.		5.	3.75	
42. Pine-tree sixpence					
43. Pine-tree threepence	4.50		4.75		
44. Pine-tree twopence	3.75				
45. Chalmers shilling	13.				

	February 28, 1859.	May 4, 1859.	June 7, 1859.	June 21, 1859.	Novem'r 2, 1859.
46. Kentucky or triangle copper..................	$3.25	$4.12	$2.13	$3.25	$3.25
47. Georgius Triumpho.............................		2.25	1.75		
48. Franco-Americana Castor-land, silver.....	8.				
49. Franco-Americana Castor-land, copper ...			5.50	5.50	3.75
50. Granby copper.................................	14.50			13.	
51. Louisiana piece, 1721..........................	2.75				
52. Louisiana piece, 1722..........................	2.75				
53. Louisiana piece, 1767..........................	2.75		1.50		2.
54. Rosa Americana penny, without date......	6.				
55. Rosa Americana penny, 1723................	2.75			1.75	
56. Rosa Americana half penny, 1722..........	1.50		1.75	2.12	
57. Rosa Americana half penny, 1723.........				4.25	
58. Rosa Americana farthing, 1722.............	1.37				
59. Rosa Americana farthing, 1723	5.25				
60. Massachusetts cent, 1787	.75	.30	.75	.37	.30
61. Massachusetts cent, 1788		.50	.75	1.	.62
62. Massachusetts half cent, 1787...............	3.		3.00	4.	2.25
63. Massachusetts half cent, 1788...............				2.75	
64. Vermon Auctori..............................		.50	.10	.62	.31
65. Vermonts Respublica		2.12		2.	
66. Vermontensium Respublica...................				1.12	1.75
67. Nova Constellatio		.65	.62	.50	.62
68. Pitt token; no stamps, 1766.................			3.25		
69. New England elephant piece.................					
70. Auctori. Connec.	.62	.60	.60	.10	.07
71. Nova Eborac.................................	2.75	2.50	1.50	2.75	2.25
72. Immunis Columbia............................	5.25		5.25	5.50	
73. Fugio coppers................................	.50	.35	.20	.50	.15
74. Continental pewter money....................	4.50				
75. New York Excelsior copper; rev., an eagle					17.

UNITED STATES MINT PATTERN, TRIAL, OR EX-PERIMENTAL PIECES,

WITH PRICES LATELY REALIZED.

1792. Disme .... $15.
1792. Half disme .... 15.
1792. Large copper; Liberty, Parent of Science and Industry.................. 66.50
1792. Small copper, like the last.. 50.
1792. Like the last, with silver centre-piece................................ 50.
1792. Copper, eagle piece. No sales.
1836. Silver dollar, flying eagle .... 9.
1836. Silver dollar, flying eagle, with engraver's name in the field (*Gobrecht*) 25.
1836. Gold dollar, Liberty-cap, etc. .... —
1836. Gold dollar, alloyed with silver...................................... 12.
1836. Two-cent piece; nickel, edge plain.................................... 5.
1836. The same, with milled edge.. 2.50
1836. The same, in copper... 3.75
1836. Medalets—first steam coinage; three varieties...................... 3.

PATTERN AND TRIAL PIECES.—(*Continued.*)

1838. Flying-eagle silver dollar	$16.
1838. Half dollar, flying eagle	7.50
1838. Half dollar, spread eagle	7.
1839. Silver dollar	20.
1839. Half dollar	31.50
1849. Three-cent pieces: **(1)** Liberty seated; (2) Liberty seated, III.; (3) Liberty-cap and rays; each	3.
1850. Three-cent pieces; Liberty-cap, etc.	3.
1850. Ring cent: (1) with date; (2) without **date; struck in nickel and also in** copper; each	2.50
1851. Cent, Liberty seated	4.25
1852. Gold ring dollar	16.
1852. Gold ring half dollar	14.
1852. Gold ring dollar, struck in silver	8.
1853. Cent; Liberty-head, nickel	3.50
1854. Cent; Liberty-head, nickel	1.50
1854. Flying-eagle cent (varieties)	3.
1855. Flying-eagle cents; two sizes, and various proportions of nickel and copper, making eight or ten varieties; each	$1 to 2.50
1856. Cents, nickel size, two varieties	2.
1856. Half cent, struck in nickel	3.50
1857. Quarter-eagle, in copper	3.25
1858. Quarter dollar	23.
1858. Nickel cents, twelve varieties; each	1.50
1859. Nickel cent, with reverse of 1860	1.50
1859. Mule half dollar; head of Liberty; **reverse, spread eagle; silver and** copper; each	6.00
1859. Half dollars, four varieties, in silver and copper; **each**	2.50

COLONIAL AND RARE AMERICAN COINS,

WITH PRICES ESTIMATED FROM LATE SALES.

(**Prices** vary according to condition of the pieces; but pieces must be in fair condition to bring the lowest price named.)

1. Somer Islands or Bermuda coin, no sale.
2. New England shilling and sixpence, $20 to $25 each.
3. Massachusetts Pine-tree, Oak-tree, and other varieties; shilling, sixpence, threepence, and twopence, $4 and $5 each.
4. Good Samaritan shilling (doubtful), no sale.
5. Lord Baltimore shilling, sixpence, and groat, $75 the set.
6. Lord Baltimore penny, no sale.
7. James II. tin piece, $2 to $3.
8. Carolina elephant piece, no sales, probably worth $30 or $40.
9. New England elephant piece, no sales, worth $30 to $50.
10. Louisiana copper piece of 1721, 1722, and brass piece of 1767, $2.50 to $7.50 **each.**
11. Rosa Americana pieces—

1722. Penny without crown	$4.	1723. Penny, crowned	**$7.25**
1722. Half penny without crown.	4.	1723. Half penny, crowned	4.75
1722. Half penny, *utile dulci*	4.75	1723. Farthing Americana,	
1722. Farthing Americana, without crown	5.	crowned	6.
		1733. Penny	5.
1722. Farthing Ameri	5.25	Penny without date	7.50

12. Granby or Higley copper, **five** varieties, 1737, $13 to $25.
13. Pitt or No Stamps token, 1766, $3 to $7.
14. Virginia half penny, 1773, two sizes, $2 to $4.
15. Continental pewter piece, two varieties, $3 to **$6.**
16. Janus-head copper of 1776 (doubtful), no sale.
17. Massachusetts copper piece of 1776, LIBERTY AND VIRTUE, no sale.
18. Massachusetts copper of 1776, AMERICAN LIBERTY, no sale.
19. Massachusetts copper of 1776; obverse, an eagle; reverse, a shield and arms; no sale.
20. U. S. A. copper, with thirteen bars, $5 to **$9.**
21. NON DEPENDENS STATUS copper, no sale.
22. Nova Constellatio coppers, many varieties, $0.50 to $1.
23. Immune Columbia pieces, silver and gold, no sale.
24. Immune Columbia copper; **reverse,** Nova Constellatio, $35.
25. Georgius Triumpho, $3.
26. Chalmers Annapolis shilling, **$8.**
27. Chalmers sixpence and threepence, **$15 each.**
28. Confederatio copper (two varieties known), **no sale.**
29. Vermonts Respublica copper, **$1.75.**
30. Vermontis Respublica copper, **$2.50.**
31. Vermontensium Respublica copper, **$1 to $3.**
32. Vermon Auctori coppers (many **varieties in 1787 and 1788), $0.50 to $1.**
33. Vermon Auctori baby-head (so called), $2.
34. Georgius III. Rex, with reverse Inde. et Lib., $0.50 to $1.
35. Vermon Auctori; reverse, Brittania, 50 cents.
36. Connecticut coppers, an immense variety in 1785, 1786, 1787, 1788, $0.10 to $2. (The Auctori Connect., the Et Lib. Inde., and other rare and odd varieties, bring prices varying from $1 to $2. The Et Lib. Inde. of 1786 is more rare than of 1787.)
37. AUCTORI PLEBIS copper, $5.
38. New Jersey coppers, a large variety in 1786, 1787, 1788, $0.25 to $1. The one with horse's head **to** the left brings $2.50; the E PLURIBS, $2 to $3.
39. New York gold **coin,** NOVA EBORACA COLUMBIA EXCELSIOR, no sale.
40. New York eagle piece; reverse, arms of the State, $25.
41. New York copper coins; obverse, Nova Eborac; reverse, Virt. et Lib.; **two va-** rieties, $2 to $4. .
42. NEO EBORACENSIS, or New York Washington piece, $25.
43. Immunis Columbia copper, $10.
44. LIBER NATUS LIBERTATEM DEFENDO, New York copper, two varieties, no sale.
45. George Clinton copper, no sale.
46. Fugio, or Mind your Business copper, several varieties, 10 to 50 cents.
47 Kentucky copper (so called), two varieties, lettered edge and plain edge, $3.25.
48. Massachusetts cent, 1787 and 1788, $0.25 to $1.
49. Massachusetts half cents of 1787 and 1788, $3.
50. Myddleton token, copper, of Kentucky, no sale.
51. Myddleton token in silver, $35.
52. Danske Americansk, copper and silver, several sizes and varieties, 25 to 50 cents.
53. Franco Americana Colonia, copper, $3; silver, $5. This piece is struck to order in France, and a new supply is constantly sent to America.
54. North American token, 25 cents.

WASHINGTON COINS, MEDALS, AND TOKENS,

WITH PRICES.

(Many varieties are omitted because no sales have been made.)

	Size.	Price.
1. Washington and Ind. token, 1783; Unity States, etc.	18	$1.25
2. Similar token; United States	18	1.25
3. Washington double-head token	18	1.25
4. Washington and Ind. ; small military bust	18	1.25
5. Washington cent of 1791, large eagle, in ordinary condition, $5, fine proof	19	9.
6. Washington cent, 1791, small eagle	19	26.
7. Washington cent, 1791, small eagle, different variety	19	no sale.
8. Washington half dollar, 1792	21	`57.
9. Washington half dollar struck in copper (commonly called the large eagle cent of 1792), is worth from $40 upward; a splendid proof brought	21	64.
10. Washington cent, 1792, small eagle	19	no sale.
11. Liberty and Security medal, large size, **head to left**	22	4.
12. Liberty and Security, small, head **to** right	18	5.50
13. Washington token, North Wales	18	6.
14. Liverpool half pennies, several **varieties of ships**	19	4.35
15. He is in Glory, the **World in Tears** copper	19	6.50
16. The same in white **metal**		3.
17. Washington token; reverse, **a grate**	18	2.50
18. Medalet, with Courage and **Fidelity**, etc.		7.
19. Washington medal; Reunit par un rare, etc.	24	7.50
20. Washington before Boston **medal**		5.
21. Washington President; reverse, **Genl. of the Am.** Armies, 1775, resigned, etc. c.		12.
22. Geo. Washington, born Virginia, Feb. 11, 1732; reverse like the last c.		7.
23. George Washington; obverse, 14 Dec., 1799, head with curious wig; reverse, Late President, etc. c.		8.50
24. George Washington, by Davis; **reverse, arms of New York** **w. m.**	16	2.
25. George Washington; Success to the United States **b.**	16	5.
26. The same token in several sizes and varieties, each **b.**		5.
27. Washington medal (Eccleston)		9.
28. Washington medal (Sansom) bronze	26	5.50
29. Washington medal (Sansom) w. m.		2.
30. Centennial medal, struck and distributed **in civic** procession, February 22, 1832 c.	20	2.
31. The same w. m.		1.
32. Washington **Benevolent** Society; bust of Washington on a pedestal, **1808** silver	27½	4.
33. George Washington; **head to left, w. ft. WRIGHT & BALE**; reverse, **Born** Feb. 22d, 1732, etc. bronze	29	5.
34. The **same in** silver		10.
35. The **same** in white metal		3.
36. The same, plain reverse, also wreath reverse silver & w. m.		no sales.
37. Washington Temperance Society; reverse, the pledge b. & c.	27	1.50

	Size.	Price.
38. Washington Temperance Society; reverse, the pledge w. m.		$ .75
39. The same; reverse, House of Temperance; same metals and same prices.		
40. Washington Temperance Society; reverse, head of Franklin, etc. w. m.		1.
41. Washington Temperance Benevolent Society; reverse, a fountain w. m.	14	.40
42. Washington surrounded by seven other Presidents; reverse, names of Presidents to Van Buren, inclusive bronze	21	2.
43. The same w. m.		1.50
44. Washington's head; The Union must, etc.; reverse, back, cannon, etc. bronze	30	2.
45. The same w. m.		1.25
46. G. Washington; bust surrounded by names of Presidents and Lafayette; reverse, an eagle covering the field, Independence, all men are free, etc., 1834 (very rare) lead	32	no sales.
47. The Father of his Country; reverse, national monument w. m.	25	.75
48. George Washington; reverse, Washington on horseback silver	20	14.50
49. The same c.		2.88
50. George Washington; born, etc., died, etc. (Lovett's dies) silver	20	1.25
51. The same c.		.30
52. The same w. m.		.30
53. Geo. Washington; North Point and Fort M'Henry silver	20	1.50
54. The same c.		.40
55. Genl. Washington; reverse, an eagle b.	17	.18
56. Genl. Washington; reverse, head of Liberty b.	17	.18
57. Other varieties and sizes of these tokens, with the Capitol, the New York City Hall, etc., etc., ten varieties in all b.		.18
58. George Washington on horseback; carry me to Atwood's, etc.; three varieties, now highly prized, each c.	15	5.
59. Washington Temperance Benevolent Society; We serve the Tyrant Alcohol no longer silver	13½	3.50
60. Head of Washington; reverse, Wright & Bale, Die-cutters, etc. c.	12	5.
61. Washington and Lafayette; reverse, Par nobile fratrum silver	18	2.75
62. The same copper		1.50
63. The same w. m.		1.
64. Washington and Franklin; same reverse, same metals, sizes, and prices.		
65. Washington; reverse, Franklin silver	13½	1.50
66. The same in copper and white metal, each		1.
67. Head of Washington; store-card of Abrahams, Weston, Missouri b.	18	1.50
68. The same; Independence, Missouri b.	18	1.50
69. Washington on horseback before Boston; reverse, R. Lovett, Jr., Die-sinker, etc. G. s.	20	.25
70. The same w. m.		.25
71. Washington; head in an oval; reverse, head of Jackson in an oval; Wolf, Clark, & Spies' card b.	16½	4.
72. The same; Jackson's bust in an octagon, and the word over it *President* b.	16½	4.
73. The same; head of George IV. b.	16½	4.
74. Washington on horseback; reverse, a movable calendar b.		.50

	Size.	Price.
75. Copies of the half dollar of 1792, from die cut in Philadelphia silver		$3.25
76. The same in copper and brass		.50
77. Washington medalet issued at United States Mint in connection with the Washington Cabinet; George Washington; reverse, Time increases his Fame silver	18	4.
78. The same c.		3.
79. Another; Pater Patriae; reverse, a Memorial of the Washington Cabinet, etc. silver	14	4.
80. The same c.		3.
81. Another; obverse, head of Washington; reverse, born 1732, died 1799 silver	12	4.
82. The same c.		3.
83. Washington token; Baker, music, etc. b.	12	no sale.
84. Several varieties of Washington tokens, cut by Bale & Smith, all rare and highly prized.		
85. Patriae Pater, 1732; Providence left him Childless, etc. c.	18½	.90
86. Pater Patriae; Good for a Chance in Raffle, etc. c.	13	.80

PRESIDENTIAL AND ELECTION MEDALS AND MEDALETS.

	Size.	Price.
JACKSON.		
1. Andrew Jackson; reverse, an urn, willow-tree, etc., born, etc., died, etc. w.m.	18	$1.
2. Andrew Jackson; an eagle; reverse, The gallant and successful Defender, etc. w.m.	28	1.
3. Andrew Jackson; reverse, The Union must and shall be Preserved—the Bank must Perish c.	17	2.
4. Andrew Jackson, President; reverse, Elected A.D. 1828, etc.—We Commemorat the glorious Victories, etc. b. and c.	17	.25
5. Andrew Jackson, Prest. of the U.S.; otherwise like the last b.	17	.55
6. Andrew Jackson, President of the U.S.; reverse, Elected A.D. 1829, etc. b.	17	.30
7. Genl. Andrew Jackson, Hero of New Orleans b.	16	.40

		Size.	Price.
8. And. Jackson, President of the, etc.; reverse, The gallant and successful Defender of New Orleans b.		16½	$ .75
9. Genl. Andrew Jackson, The Nation's Pride b.		15½	.55
10. Genl. Andrew Jackson, The Nation's Good b.		15½	.50
11. Obverse, a head of Jackson; reverse, And. Jackson inaugurated Presidt. U. S., etc. silver		11	3.
12. Andrew Jackson, Pres. of the U. S.; reverse, eagle, 8 Jan., 1815 b.		16½	.20
13. A head of Jackson in an oval, *Jackson* over the head; reverse, Washington in an oval; card of Wolfe, Clarke, & Spies b.		16	4.
14. Similar to last, but head of Jackson in an octagon, and *President* over the head b.		16	4.
15. Andrew Jackson on horseback; reverse, The Advocate of the American System w. m.		24	.65

HARRISON.

1. Maj. Gen. W. H. Harrison; reverse, a log cabin and flag on it, eagle lighting, four soldiers standing in a row, The People's Choice, etc. w. m.		22	1.25
2. William H. Harrison, the Hero and Statesman; reverse, Candidate of the People b.		16	.45
3. William Henry Harrison; reverse, Bunker Hill Monument, Harrison Jubilee, Bunker Hill, Sept. 10, 1840 w. m.		26½	1.50
4. Maj. Gen. W. H. Harrison (Turpin engraver); reverse, scales, Locos, Wigs, Weighed in the Balance, etc. b.		16	.20
5. Major Gen. Wm. H. Harrison; reverse, Resolution of Congress, etc. c.		19½	1.20
6. Maj. Gen. W. H. Harrison; reverse, an eagle with a ribbon inscribed Tippecanoe b.		16	.25
7. Maj. Gen. W. H. Harrison; reverse, a log cabin, etc., The People's Choice, etc., six soldiers in a row w. m.		24	1.70
8. Maj. Genl. W. H. Harrison; reverse, scales, Democrats, Whigs, Weighed in the Balance and found wanting b.		15	.50
9. Maj. Gen. W. H. Harrison; reverse, a battle, Harrison on horseback, Tippecanoe b.		15	.50
10. Maj. Gen. W. H. Harrison; reverse, Go it Tip, come it Tyler c.		16½	.25
11. The same in brass		16½	.50
12. Maj. Gen. W. H. Harrison; reverse, a steamboat, Steamboat Van Buren, Locofoco Line, for Salt River direct b.		15	.30
13. Maj. Gen. W. H. Harrison; reverse, a log cabin, The People's Choice, the Hero of Tippecanoe b. and c.		18	.25
14. Similar to the last, but under the head *March* 4, 1841, *He redeems his Country* b.		18	.35
15. Same as No. 13, except in size and metal w. m.		24	1.50
16. Maj. Gen. W. H. Harrison; reverse, He leaves the Plough to save his Country b.		18	.37

	Size.	Price.
17. Maj. Genl. W. H. Harrison; reverse, a log cabin, etc., The Choice of the People, etc. b.	15	$ .12
18. Like No. 17; but reverse, The People's Choice in the Year 1840 b.	15	.15
19. Like No. 18, but the bust has a full face b.	15	.22
20. Like No. 18; reverse, date reads 1841 b.	15	.25
21. Genl. W. H. Harrison, Honor where Honor is due; reverse, Bunker Hill Monument	24	2.
22. William H. Harrison, Head facing the right; reverse, Born, etc. w. m.	24	

VAN BUREN.

	Size.	Price.
1. The Sober Second Thoughts, etc.; reverse, eagle and safe, The Independent Sub Treasury, etc. c.	18	.17
2. The same in brass	18	.17
3. Martin Van Buren, born Dec. 5, 1782; reverse, a pair of scales, Weighed in the Balance, etc. b.	15	.50
4. M. Van Buren, 26 stars; reverse, a temple, etc., Democracy and our Country w. m.	16½	1.75
5. The same in brass		.55
6. Martin Van Buren; reverse, a flag, Democrats to the Polls, and the Victory is ours b.	15	.50
7. M. Van Buren, two sprigs under the bust; reverse, a temple, etc. w. m.	23	1.50
8. M. Van Buren; reverse, an eagle on a safe, Van Buren, The Country demands his re-election w. m.	22½	1.75
9. Martin Van Buren and Democracy; reverse, a temple, A uniform and sound Currency, The Sub Treasury w. m.	23½	1.30
10. Obverse like the last; reverse, an eagle holding scales, Federal. Democ., March 4, 1841, Our Principles are Justice and Equity	23½	1.60
11. Martin Van Buren; reverse, Free Soil, Free Labor, Free Speech, hollow shell b. and silvered	16½	.50
12. Martin Van Buren and Democracy; reverse, Our next President	21	1.
13. A head of Van Buren; The Principles and Prudence of our Forefathers; reverse, a man plowing, the Democracy who can justly appreciate, etc. w. m.	22	2.
14. Martin Van Buren; reverse, a safe and dog b.	15	1.
15. Martin Van Buren; reverse, Temple of Liberty, Democracy and our Country w. m.	23	1.25

	Size.	Price.
CLAY.		
1. Henry Clay; reverse, Young Men's Convention, Baltimore, May, 1844, The Flag we wear at our Mast should be, etc. w. m.	26½	$1.75
2. Henry Clay; reverse, the Baltimore Monument, In Commemoration of the great Convention held at Baltimore, May, 1844 w. m.	24	1.50
3. The same in bronze	24	2.
4. Henry Clay; reverse, Time writing on a monument, Every end he aimed at was his Country's w. m.	26½	.75
5. Henry Clay; reverse, a ship, factories, etc., The Wealth of a Nation is indicated by its Industry w. m.	26	1.05
6. Henry Clay; reverse, Henry Clay, the Champion of a Protective Tariff, a ship, etc. w. m.	32	1.70
7. Henry Clay; reverse, Born in Virginia, Ap. 12, 1777, 1799 opposes the Alien and Sedition Law, 1806 elected, etc. w. m.	22	1.
8. Henry Clay of Kentucky; reverse, a wreath of flags, anchor, shield, etc., Equal and full Protection, etc. w. m.	24	1.50
9. Henry Clay, the Ashland Farmer; reverse, a plow, O. K., The same old Coon w. m.	20½	1.
10. Henry Clay; reverse, A Tariff for Protection w. m.	17	1.
11. Harry of the West, 1845; reverse, The Protector of Home Industry	16½	.55
12. Henry Clay and the American System; reverse, United we Stand b.	17	.30
13. The same in copper	17	.30
14. Henry Clay, 26 stars; reverse, an eagle, Protection to American Industry c.	16½	1.
15. The same in brass	16½	.80
16. H. Clay, I would rather be Right than be President; reverse, an eagle, United States of America, 1848 c.	15	.37
17. President Henry Clay, 1845; reverse, an eagle, etc. w. m.	13½	.85
18. Similar to the last, slightly varying w. m.	13½	.75
19. Obverse like the last; reverse, two hands grasping, United we Stand, Divided we Fall w. m.	13½	.75
20. Henry Clay, the Farmer, etc.; reverse, The Noble and Patriotic Supporter of the People's Rights b.	15	.45
21. Henry Clay elected President A.D. 1844; reverse, The Mill-Boy of the Slashes inaugurated March 4th, 1845. (This medalet serves to show that numismatology may deceive in history.) b.	16	.50
22. H. Clay, the **Man** of the People, the Star of the West, 1844 w. m.	20	.35
23. Henry Clay, the Ashland Farmer, 1844, born, etc.; reverse, The Noble and Patriotic Supporter of Protection b.	15	.45
24. Henry Clay; reverse, Clay and Frelinghuysen, etc. b.	16	.81
25. Henry Clay, the Ashland Farmer; reverse, Weighed in the Balance, etc. b.		.30
26. Henry Clay, "A Halo shines as bright as Day," etc. w. m.	21½	1.13
27. Obverse like No. 6; reverse, factories, **etc.,** in bas-relief	32	1.50

	Size.	Price.
CASS.		
1. **Gen.** Lewis Cass; reverse, The Constitution and the Freedom of the Seas w. m.	20	$ .87
2. General Lewis Cass, 1848; reverse, a female figure, a boy with a torch, etc. b.	18	.40
3. General L. Cass (by Leonard); **reverse,** The Sub Treasury and the Tariff of '46 w. m.	26	1.
4. Gen. Lewis Cass (by **Bird**), **Principles, not Men;** reverse, Liberty, Equality, etc. w. m.	22	1.75
POLK.		
1. **James K.** Polk, Friend of Equal Rights; reverse, a head of **Dallas**, Young Hickory, Dallas and Victory b.	16½	1.25
2. James **K.** Polk, head cut by Leonard; reverse, a bust of Dallas, George M. Dallas w. m.	26	1.50
3. Jas. **K.** Polk, G. M. Dallas, busts of Polk and Dallas; reverse, The Firm and Fearless Advocates of Democratic Principles, etc. w. m.	19½	1.70
4. Obverse, a head of Polk, Young Hickory, Press Onward, Enlarge the Boundaries of Freedom; reverse, a head of Dallas, Dallas and Victory, Equal Protection to all Classes	24	1.55
TAYLOR.		
1. Maj. **Gen.** Zach. Taylor; reverse, Fort Harrison, Okeechobee, etc. w. m.	19	.50
2. The same in brass	19	.50
3. The same in copper	19	.50
4. Maj. Gen. Zach. Taylor; reverse, "A little more Grape, Capt. Bragg," and names of battles w. m.	20	1.81
5. Zachary Taylor, Whig Candidate, etc., 1848; reverse, Born, etc., and names of battles w. m.	23	1.75
6. Major Genl. Z. Taylor never surrenders; **reverse,** A little more Grape, etc., **I ask no favor, etc.** w. m.	26	1.25
7. Major General Zachary **Taylor**; reverse, **Entered** according to Act, etc. w. m.	25	1.80
8. Major Gen. Taylor, born 1790; reverse, General Taylor never Surrenders, etc. b.	17	.95

	Size.	Price.
9. Major General Zachary Taylor, Hero of Palo Alto, etc., 1847; reverse, an eagle, etc. c. and b.	15	$ .40
10. Zachary Taylor; reverse, Taylor and Filmore, shell b. and silvered	16	.50
11. Gen. Z. Taylor, Hero of Palo Alto, etc.; reverse, an eagle, etc., Rio Grande, Texas, May 9 and 10, 1846 b.	17	1.
12. Major General Zachary Taylor, born 1790; reverse, In Honor of the Hero of Palo Alto, etc. w. m.	21½	.80

FILLMORE.

1. Millard Fillmore, engraver's name, Odling; reverse, The Union w. m.	24	1.
2. Obverse like the last; reverse, Born in N. Y., Jan. 7, 1800, etc. w. m.	24	1.30
3. Like the last, in copper	24	2.50
4. Millard Fillmore; reverse, Be Vigilant and Watchful, etc. w. m.	21½	.25
5. The same in copper	21½	.50
6. Millard Fillmore, For the whole Country; reverse, an eagle, United States, etc. b.	18	.12
7. Like the last, with the addition of 31 S. under the eagle b.	18	.10

SCOTT.

1. Maj. General Winfield Scott; reverse, Chippewa, Lundy's Lane, etc. b.	16	.25
2. Maj. Gen. Winfield Scott, U.S.A.; reverse, Scott wounded Lundy's Lane b. and c.	17½	.35
3. Maj. Gen. Win. Scott; reverse, Lundy's Lane, Vera Cruz, Cerro Gordo, etc. w. m.	20	.55
4. Obverse like the last; reverse, United we Stand, Divided we Fall b., c., and w. m.	20	1.
5. Obverse like the last; reverse, our next President w. m.	20	1.
6. Gen. Winfield Scott, First in War, etc.; reverse, Scott and Graham, etc. b.	18	.25
7. Major Genl. Winfd. Scott (Leonard, ft.); reverse, A Gallant and Skillful Hero, etc.	26	1.50

	Size.	Price.
PIERCE.		
1. Gen. Franklin Pierce, the Statesman and Soldier; reverse, Pierce and King, the People's Choice b.	17½	$1.
2. Gen. Frank. Pierce, the Statesman and Soldier; reverse, For President, etc., for Vice President, etc. b.	16	.55
3. General F. Pierce; reverse, United we Stand, etc. w. m.	26	1.50
BUCHANAN.		
1. James Buchanan, XVth President, etc., engraver, Paquet; reverse, The Union must, etc. w. m.	38½	1.10
2. James Buchanan; reverse, Buchanan, The Crisis demands, etc. w. m.	21½	.30
3. The same in copper	21½	.50
4. A Buck at full run, a cannon, and Breckenridge; reverse, Washington w. m.	30	1.
5. The same in bronze	30	2.
6. James Buchanan, No Sectionalism; reverse, an eagle, United States, etc.	18	.20
7. Similar to last, with three stars under the eagle b.	18	.50
8. Similar to last, 31. S. under the eagle b.	18	.20
9. James Buchanan; reverse, The Union one, etc. w. m.	21½	.25
FREMONT.		
1. John C. Fremont; reverse, mountains, the White House, surveyors, etc., Honor to whom, etc. c.	27	2.
2. The same in white metal	27	1.
3. John C. Fremont; reverse, Free Soil, Free Speech, Free Labor, etc. c.	22	.50
4. The same in white metal	22	.25
5. Col. John C. Fremont, engraver's name, Paquet; reverse, The People's Choice for 1856, etc. w. m.	38½	.75
6. John C. Fremont, Free Soil and Free Speech; reverse, an eagle, Wm. L. Dayton, Free Speech, etc. b.	18	.40
7. Col. John C. Fremont, Jessie's Choice; reverse, Fremont and Dayton, etc. b.	18	.90
8. John C. Fremont, Free Soil, etc.; reverse, an eagle, United States of America b.	18	.55

	Size.	Price.
9. John C. Fremont, Free Soil, etc. ; reverse, an eagle, United States of America, with 31. S. under the eagle b.	18	$ .50
10. J. C. Fremont, born, etc. ; reverse, an eagle on a globe	14½	.25

MEDALETS OF VARIOUS INDIVIDUALS.

		Size.	Price.
1. William H. Seward, our next Governor; reverse, The Glory and Pride, etc. b.		17	$ .80
2. Obverse like the last; reverse, A faithful Friend to our Country b.		17	.55
3. Gulian C. Verplanck, our next Govnr. ; reverse, A faithful Friend, etc. b.		17	.50
4. Thomas Swann, Mayor of Baltimore w. m.			.25
5. Kossuth, three varieties, head to right b.		18	.15
6. Kossuth, head to the left b.		18	.55
7. Herr Alexander, 1847 c.		18	1.

POLITICAL TOKENS, ETC.

		Size.	Price.
1. A cow, a friend, etc. ; reverse, a ship, Agriculture and Commerce		18	$1.10
2. The Glorious Whig Victory of 1835; Fellow-citizens, save your Constitution		17	2.50
3. For the Constitution Hurra ; Whigs of New York Victorious, etc.		16½	2.
4. American Republicans beware, etc. ; reverse, Bunker Hill w. m.		23	1.50
5. The same in copper		23	.75
6. Natives beware, etc., 1844; reverse, Our Flag trampled upon w. m.		26½	.75
7. Millions for Defence, not One Cent for Tribute ; all the ordinary varieties, in uncirculated order ; each c.		18½	.05
8. The same, fillet head, inscribed United c.		17½	.50
9. The same, head surrounded by stars, two varieties c.		17½	.50
10. Loco Foco Mint Drop c.		19	.10
11. Mint Drops, two other varieties c.		18	.05
12. Turtle and Safe, Executive Experiment, two varieties c.		18½	.05
13. Turtle and Safe, Executive Financiering		18½	.25
14. Webster Credit Current and Currency, five varieties c.		18½	.05
15. General and Safe, two ordinary varieties c.		18½	.05
16. General and Safe, large head and fat donkey c.		18½	.15
17. General and Safe, reverse, a ship b.		18½	.40

			Size.	Price.
18.	A plain System, void of Pomp	c.	18½	$ .20
19.	Substitute for Shinplasters, two varieties	c.	18½	.03
20.	Specie Payments suspended, several varieties	c.	18½	.03
21.	Perish Credit, etc. ; a hog running	c.	18½	.10
22.	The same	b.	18½	.50
23.	Not One Cent, but Just as Good	b.	18	.65
24.	The same, with various reverses of tradesmen's cards and other devices, have brought from $1.25 to $1.75.			
25.	Success to Republican Principles	b.	15	.20
26.	The same	c.	15	1.

TEMPERANCE MEDALETS, ETC.

			Size.	Price.
1.	American Juvenile Temperance Society; reverse, Temperance pledge	c.	22½	$1.
2.	The same	w. m.	22½	.50
3.	Obverse the same; reverse, a man at a well	c.	22½	1.
4.	The same	w. m.	22½	.50
5.	Man at a well; reverse, Temperance leads, etc.	b.	16	.15
6.	The same	oreide	16	.30
7.	Man at well (well without pole); reverse, Declaration of the Cold Water Army	b.	15½	.30
8.	Temperance pledge; reverse, Our Country's Freedom, etc.	b.	16½	.50
9.	Man at a well with windlass, B. & S. N. Y.; reverse, Pledge	w. m.	21½	.55
10.	In Commemoration of the National Celebration of the Sons of Temperance; reverse, Sons of Temperance insignia	c.	24	1.
11.	The same	w. m.	24	.30
12.	House of Temperance; reverse, Pledge	w. m.	27	.70
13.	The same in copper, and also in brass		27	1.
14.	American Total Abstinence Society, the pledge; reverse, I.H.S. on a shield, man and woman, two children		28	.50
15.	American Temperance Mission	w. m.	26½	.50
16.	American Temperance Mission, another variety	w. m.	26½	.50
17.	Father Matthew giving the pledge	w. m.	26½	.65
18.	Father Matthew; reverse, St. James Temperance Society	w. m.	21	.65
19.	Man at well; reverse, The Bearer of this, etc.	w. m.	23	.25
20.	Man at well (by Thomas); reverse, Pledge	w. m.	22½	.50
21.	Man at well; reverse, St. James Temp. Soc.	b.	15	.30
22.	Tobacco medalet, boy trampling on leaves	b.	16½	.80

TEMPERANCE MEDALETS.

	Size.	Price.
23. No Repeal, State of New York c. gilt and silvered Other temperance medalets will be found among Washington coins, etc.	18	$ .25

MISCELLANEOUS MEDALETS AND TOKENS.

		Size.	Price.
1. Am I not a Man and a Brother? (not American) two sizes			$1.50
2. Am I not a Woman and a Sister? (proofs)	c.	18	.50
3. California Counter, 1852; obverse, head of Liberty; reverse, a flag	b.	23	.25
4. California Counter; obverse, an eagle; reverse, a flag	b.	17½	.20
5. California Counter; obverse, head of Liberty; reverse, a flag	b.	17½	.20
6. California Counter; obverse like reverse of $20 gold piece; reverse, a flag	b.	23	.35
7. Little Samuel; reverse, the Lord's Prayer, cut by Lovett	w. m.	22½	.50
8. Boy and dog, cut by Bridgens; reverse, John Bull and Jonathan	c.	20	1.
9. The same	w. m.	20	.50
10. Boy and dog, with other reverses; same metals and prices.			
11. Gen. Tom Thumb; reverse, head of Liberty	b.	14	.05
12. Gen. Tom Thumb; reverse, head of Victoria	b.	14	.05
13. Mobile Jockey Club, members' medal	silver	18	
14. The same	b.	18	.20
15. The same	c.	18	.25
16. The same	w. m.	18	.10
17. We all have our hobbies, witch medalet	G. s.	18	
18. The same	silver	18	
19. The same	w. m.	18	.10
20. The same	c.	18	.30
21. The same	b.	18	.20
22. Odd Fellows' Hall; reverse, Odd Fellows' insignia	w. m.	24	1.25
23. St. Matthen's Kirche, Walker St., N. Y.	w. m.	24½	1.
24. N Y. Crystal Palace; reverse, flags of all nations	w. m.	25	1.
25. N Y. Crystal Palace; reverse, The first Pillar, etc.	w. m.	33	.25
26. N. Y. Crystal Palace; reverse, the globe, etc.	w. m.	46	.50
27. N. Y. Crystal Palace; reverse, Liberty seated, Inimitate, etc.	w. m.	29	1.12
28. New Merchants' Exchange, New York	c.	18½	.05
29. St. Thomas's Church, N. Y., Robert Raikes	w. m.	22	.70

		Size.	Price.
30. German Musical Festival medal; reverse, trumpets, etc.			
	w. m.	37	$ .63
31. Balloon medalets; great air ship	c.	22	.50
32. The same	w. m.		.25
33. Nassau Water Works, 1859	c.	22	.50
34. The same	w. m.		.20
35. The same, differently executed	w. m.	22	.50
36. Eleanor Rugg Byrne medalet	b., w. m., and c.	19½	.30
37. The same, with milled edge	c.	19½	1.38
38. Honesty is the best Policy; Dedicated, etc.	b.	14	.25
39. Bunker Hill Monument; reverse, All Hail, etc.	w. m.		1.25
40. Lovett's series of Presidents of the U. S., each	c.	22	.50
41. The same	w. m.		.25
42. Sage's historical tokens, each	c.	22	.25
43. Sage's numismatic gallery, each	c.	22	.25
44. Ohio, 1855, sun rising, a grain-field, etc. ; reverse, a mova-ble calendar	b.	23½	.70
45. Other States of the Union, with same reverse, each	b.	23½	.70
46. Ships, Colonies, and Commerce; ship with American flag	c.		.45
47. The same; W. & B., N. Y., under the ship	c.		.50
48. Half cent's worth of pure copper	c.	15	.75
49. Massachusetts and California Co., 1849	c.	15	3.
50. The same	silver	15	3.50
51. National Jockey Club, New York	b.	16½	.65
52. Communicant's token, oval	w. m.		1.50
53. The Champagne Fountain; In Vino Veritas	silver	10	1.50

AMERICAN MEDALS

AWARDED BY CONGRESS TO MILITARY AND NAVAL OFFICERS.

1. GEORGE WASHINGTON. On the taking of Boston, 17th March, 1776.
2. JOHN PAUL JONES. On the capture of the *Serapis*, 23d September, 1778.
3. JOHN STEWART. On the taking of Stony Point, 15th July, 1799.
4. ANTHONY WAYNE. On the taking of Stony Point, 15th July, 1799.
5. D. DE FLEURY. On the taking of Stony Point, 15th July, 1799.
6. HORATIO GATES. On the surrender of Burgoyne, Saratoga, 17th October, 1777.
7. CAPTORS OF ANDRE.
8. NATHANIEL GREENE. For gallant conduct at Eutaw Springs, 8th September, 1781.
9. DANIEL MORGAN. For the victory at Cowpens, 17th January, 1781.
10. JOHN EAGER HOWARD. For the victory at Cowpens, 17th January, 1781.
11. WILLIAM A. WASHINGTON. For the victory at Cowpens, 17th January, 1781.
12. HENRY LEE. On the attack at Paulus Hook, 19th August, 1779.
13. THOMAS TRUXTON. On the capture of the French frigate *Vengeance* by the *Constellation*, 1st February, 1800.
14. EDWARD PREBLE. On the attack upon Tripoli in 1804.
15. WINFIELD SCOTT. On the battles of Chippewa and Niagara, July 5 and 25, 1814.
16. EDMUND P. GAINES. On the battle of Erie, 15th August, 1814.
17. JAMES MILLER. On the battles of Chippewa, Niagara, and Erie, July 5 and 25, and September 17, 1814.
18. JACOB BROWN. On the battles of Chippewa, Niagara, and Erie, July 5 and 25, and September 17, 1814.
19. ELEAZAR W. RIPLEY. On the battles of Chippewa, Niagara, and Erie, July 5 and 25, and September 17, 1814.
20. PETER B. PORTER. On the battles of Chippewa, Niagara, and Erie, July 5 and 25, and September 17, 1814.
21. ALEXANDER MACOMB. On the battle of Plattsburgh, September 11, 1814.
22. ANDREW JACKSON. On the battle of New Orleans, January 8, 1815.
23. ISAAC SHELBY. On the battle of the Thames, October 5, 1813.
24. WILLIAM HENRY HARRISON. On the battle of the Thames, October 5, 1813.
25. GEORGE CROGHAN. On the defense of Fort Sandusky, August 2, 1813.
26. ISAAC HULL. On the capture of the *Guerriere* by the *Constitution*, July, 1812.
27. JACOB JONES. On the capture of the *Frolic* by the *Wasp*, 18th October, 1812.
28. STEPHEN DECATUR. On the capture of the *Macedonian*, October 25, 1812.
29. WILLIAM BAINBRIDGE. On the capture of the *Java*, December 29, 1812.
30. W. BURROWS. On the capture of the *Boxer*, September 4, 1813.
31. EDWARD R. M'CALL. On the capture of the *Boxer*, 4th September, 1813.
32. JAMES LAWRENCE. On the capture of the *Peacock*, 24th February, 1813.
33. THOMAS M'DONOUGH. On the battle of Lake Champlain, 11th September, 1814.
34. ROBERT HENLEY. On the battle of Lake Champlain, 11th September, 1814.
35. STEPHEN CASSIN. On the battle of Lake Champlain, 11th September, 1814.
36. LEWIS WARRINGTON. On the capture of the brig *L'Epervier*, 29th March, 1814.

AMERICAN MEDALS.

37. **Johnson Blakeley.** On the capture of the *Reindeer*, 28th June, 1814.
38. **Charles Stewart.** On the capture of the *Cyane* and the *Levant*, 20th February, 1815.
39. **James Biddle.** On the capture of the *Penguin*, 23d March, 1815.
40. **Oliver Hazard Perry.** On the battle of Lake Erie, September 10, 1813.
41. **Jesse Duncan Elliott.** On the battle of Lake Erie, September 10, 1813.

Note.—The above catalogue comprises only medals relating to the Revolution and the war of 1812. Of the Revolutionary medals some may be obtained at moderate prices, as indicated in the price tables elsewhere. But very many of the series are unknown except in the original gold presentation medal. A fine series of electrotype copies of all the medals has been made, with great labor and diligence, by **Thomas Wyatt,** Esq., of New York, from whom they may be obtained.

Of many other American medals—Indian and others—the dies remain at the Philadelphia Mint, and it is hoped that Congress may authorize the supply of specimens to collectors at a moderate price.

262

EXPLANATION OF THE PLATES.

FRONTISPIECE.

1. Silver coin of Seleucus, B.C. 280.
2. Silver coin of Philip V. of Macedon, B.C. 220–178.
3. Silver coin of Macedonia, about B.C. 280.
4. Silver coin of Lysimachus, B.C. 286–280.
5. 6. Silver medal of Syracuse. This is one of the splendid remains of ancient art. It seems probable that it was struck as a prize in the races, or as a token. Several specimens are extant.
7. A copper coin of Chalcis, showing the seven-stringed lyre.
8. Silver coin of Demetrius Poliorcetes, B.C. 294–287.
9. Silver coin of Perseus, B.C. 178–167.
10. Silver coin of Ptolemy Soter, B.C. 285.

PLATE I.

1. Egyptian ring money. No specimens are known; but it is found painted, in countless instances, on tombs, and colored to indicate both gold and silver.
2. Ancient Egyptian method of weighing money, the weights being a lamb, a half lamb, etc. From the wall of a tomb.

PLATE II.

1. Gold stater of Miletus; the earliest known coin in any metal.
2. Gold stater of Lydia; by some supposed to be the earliest coin.
3. Persian silver daric; probably struck in Egypt during the Persian dynasty.
4. Persian gold daric, found in Western Asia; date uncertain, probably a very early coin.
5. Quarter stater of Phocea, gold.
6. Drachma of Ægina; the earliest silver coin. The tortoise was the emblem of Ægina.
7. Silver coin of Caulonia, showing the punch corresponding with the die.
8. Drachma of Archelaus I. of Macedonia, B.C. 413; the first coin with the portrait of a prince.
9. Drachma of Ægina, later than No. 6.
10. Silver coin of Alexander I. of Macedonia, B.C. 450; one of the first coins with a human figure.

PLATE III.

1. Large Ptolemaic copper coin; head of Jupiter on the obverse; an eagle on the reverse; with legend BASILEOS PTOLEMAIOU. These immense coppers are by some supposed to have been medals.
2. Ancient Greek coin, showing the theatre of Dionysius, on the slope of the Acropolis at Athens.

3. **Ancient Greek coin,** showing the Acropolis, the statue of Minerva, **the Parthe-**
   non, etc.
4. Silver **coin of** Ptolemy Philadelphus.
5. Silver **coin of a** Ptolemy, showing a man cutting millet with a sickle. This coin
   is interesting as showing the millet, a species of Indian corn or maize, in existence in Egypt at that early date.
6. Jewish shekel; obverse, the pot of manna; reverse, **the** rod of Aaron. The
   shekel was never coined till the time of the Maccabees. There are several
   varieties, some of them of the highest rarity.

PLATE IV.

1. **Silver** coin (tetradrachm) of Pyrrhus, **B.C.** 275 (King of Epirus, etc.); obverse,
   head of the Dodonean Jupiter.
2. Silver coin (tetradrachm) of Antiochus the Great, B.C. 192.
3. Gold stater of Alexander the Great (found at Sidon recently).
4. **Gold stater of** Philip II., father of Alexander (found at Sidon). These coins
   were **found in a** jar, with a large quantity like them, **where** they were probably left by **a** paymaster in Alexander's army.
5. Gold stater of Alexander, another variety.
6. Silver coin (tetradrachm) of Perseus, last King of Macedon, B.C. **178.**
7. Silver coin (tetradrachm) of Attalus I. of Pergamus, B.C. 170.

PLATE V.

1. Silver tetradrachm of Mithridates VI., King of Pontus, B.C. 89.
2. Silver coin of Philip **V.** of Macedon.
3. Silver coin of Corinth.
4. Silver drachma of Athens.
5. Silver tetradrachm **of** Athens.
6. A Greek coin, having on the reverse a palm-leaf and an arrow; date unknown.

PLATE VI.

1. Silver coin of Cyrene, showing the Silphium.
2. Silver coin of Acarnania.
3. Phoenician coin, probably **of** some place on the Syrian coast under Persian
   power.
4. Parthian gold coin; legend "Of the Great King Arsaces."
5. Coin of Amphipolis, showing a lamp on the reverse.
6. Parthian silver coin, probably of Arsaces Orodes, B.C. 55; perhaps minted in
   Syria.
7. Silver **coin of** Artaxerxes Ardshir, A.D. 226, founder of the dynasty of the Sas-
   sanidæ.
8. **Silver coin of Carthage;** obverse, **head of Dido;** reverse, horse, with Punic inscription.

PLATE VII.

1. Roman Quincussis, five ases.—See page 22.

EXPLANATION OF THE PLATES.

PLATE VIII.

1. Obverse of the as, head of Janus.
2. Reverse of the as, prow of a galley or ship.
3. Sextans, sixth part of the as. The two balls indicate the weight, two ounces.
4 and 5. Triens, third part of the as. The four balls indicate the weight, four ounces. Figures 3, 4, and 5 on this plate are each one half the diameter of the original coin.

PLATE IX.

1. A medalet in copper, possibly a sextans; obverse, an eagle; reverse, the wolf of the capitol.
2. Silver coin of the Samnites, showing on the reverse the Samnite bull goring the Roman wolf, about B.C. 340.
3. Roman denarius of Livineius, the head on which is supposed to be the head of Regulus, B.C. 256.
4. Early Roman coin, with Janus head; probably an as of the time of Pompey, and the heads portraits of Pompey and his son Sextus.
5. Coin of Epidaurus, or a coin of Rome, commemorating the sacred snake (emblem of Æsculapius) which the embassadors who were sent to Epidaurus about B.C. 290 brought back with them.—See page 12.
6. Reverse of a denarius of the Cassian gens, showing a person voting. The tablet or ballot is marked A. for "*Absolvo*."
7. Denarius of P. Porcius Lacca, who, B.C. 256, introduced the Porcian law, "*de capite et tergo civium*," which was the law of appeal under which Paul "appealed to Cæsar."
8. Denarius of Metellus Scipio, referring to the battle of Panormus, B.C. 250.
9. Silver coin of Marcellinus, B.C. 215.

PLATE X.

1. Silver coin with head of Jupiter Capitolinus on the obverse, and temple of Jupiter on the Capitoline Hill on the reverse.
2. Denarius of the Quinctian gens.
3. Denarius commemorating the triumph of the consul L. Emilius Paullus over Persens, B.C. 168.
4. Denarius of the Clodian gens; obverse, head of Flora; reverse, a vestal; probably struck in honor of the splendid Floralia during the ædileship of C. Clodius Pulcher, B.C. 99.
5. Denarius of the eight Italian nations, commemorating a confederacy about B.C. 90.
6. Denarius of the last two nations who held out; legend in Oscan characters.
7. Denarius with Castor and Pollux on the reverse, and head of Minerva on the obverse. A very common form of the denarius.
8. Denarius of Acilius, showing a triumphal car on the reverse.
9. Gold coin of Antony, minted at Antioch. This is a very rare coin.
10. Denarius of Cæsar in his fourth dictatorship, indicated by the words DICT. QUART.

PLATE XI.

1. Obverse of a very rare and splendid silver coin of Cleopatra. No. 10 shows the reverse, with head of Marc Antony.

EXPLANATION OF THE PLATES.

2. **Denarius** of Julius Cæsar; reverse, Marc Antony.
3. Denarius of Julius Cæsar, commemorating the conquest of Egypt.
4. Denarius of Julius Cæsar, commemorating the conquest of Gaul.
5 and 6. Denarii of the Triumvirs.
7. Denarius of Cæsar.
8 and 9. Denarii commemorating the death of Cæsar.
10. Head of Marc Antony. Reverse of No. 1 on this plate.

PLATE XII.

1. Denarius of Publius Licinius Crassus, censor with Julius Cæsar.
2. Aureus of Augustus Cæsar.
3. **Silver denarius**; the common form, known as a quadrigatus from the four horses on **the reverse**.
4. Gold coin, four scrupula, or sixty sestertii.
5, 6, and **7.** Silver denarii of different families, whose names they bear.
8. Silver denarius, on which is a biga, whence these coins were called bigati
9. Silver denarius, with a quadriga, hence called quadrigatus.
10. Gold coin of Agrippa, with the head of Augustus.
11. Copper coin of the colony of Nismes.

NOTE.—The denarius, of which so many illustrations are given on this **and the** preceding plates, is the most common form of Roman silver. The young collector will bear in mind that he must classify these coins according to their general character and date. There are great numbers of them which are "family coins"—that **is,** denarii bearing the names of distinguished Roman families. These were issued **before the empire** was established. Then follow denarii of the emperors, of which **the variety is** very great; some bearing **the heads of the** emperors, others of empresses; some with the names and banners of certain legions; some commemorating great events, **victories, etc.** The illustrations given will enable the collector to judge of the general character of many of his coins by comparison, even if they are not identical; **and it need not be** repeated here that our object is only to introduce **him** to his subject, that he may follow the study **in** other works.

PLATE XIII.

1, 2, 3, 4, 5, 6. Reverses of six consular denarii, showing the costumes, sella curulis, fasces, etc., of Roman lictors.
7. Silver denarius of the Cœlian gens, representing an Epulo preparing a conch for Jupiter, on which is inscribed L. CALDUS VII. VIR. EPUL..
8 and 9. Reverses of denarii, showing the rostra. No. 8, a denarius of the Lollian gens, shows probably the old rostra. No. 9, a denarius of the Sulpician gens, shows probably the new rostra.
10 and 11. Reverses of denarii, showing the puteal or well in the forum, called *Puteal Libonis* or *Scribonianum.*
12. Reverse of a **coin of** Claudius, showing the emperor sitting as censor, and a servant holding a horse.
13. Denarius of Flamen Martialis, high-priest of Mars, with head of Augustus.
14. Colonial silver coin of Cœla in the Thracian Chersonesus, with figure of Silenus standing, having his hand raised, emblematical of municipal freedom.
15. Copper coin of Antoninus, showing a triumphal car.

EXPLANATION OF THE PLATES.

PLATE XIV.

1. **Medal** of Marc Antony, showing the corona radiata.
2. **Medal** of Nero, showing an organ and a sprig of laurel; probably designed as a prize medal to a musician.
3. Medal of Augustus, showing the myrtle crown, or corona ovalis.
4. Medal of Ventidius, lieutenant of Marc Antony, showing the corona **triumphalis**; probably struck on occasion of his victory over the Parthians.
5. Medal of Lepidus, showing the corona oleagina, or olive-leaf crown.
6. Medal of Lepidus. The letters **H. O. C. S.** stand for **HOSTEM OCCIDIT, CIVEM SERVAVIT.**
7. Medal of Agrippina, showing **the carpentum, or wagon in which Roman ladies** were accustomed to ride.

PLATE XV.

1. Reverse of a brass coin of Antoninus Pius, which is also an example of a very common reverse of the large brass coins of Rome.
2, 3, and 4. Reverses of Roman brass coins, showing galleys.
5. Large brass coin of Nero, showing the temple of Janus closed.
6. Brass coin of Corcyra.
7. Brass coin of Commodus.
8. Medal of Albinus Brutus; probably commemorative **of the close of the civil war with** Antony. (Showing the sacerdotal crown.)

PLATE XVI.

1. Brass coin of Gordianus and Tranquillina, struck at Singara.
2. Brass coin of Trajan, struck at Nineveh.
3. Brass coin of Maximinus, struck at Nineveh.
4 and 5. Pigs of lead, with the stamp of Hadrian, found in England.
6. Brass coin of Faustina.
7 Brass coin of Septimus Severus.

PLATE XVII.

1. Colonial **coin** of **Corinth** in the time of Antoninus (silver).
2. Silver coin of Philip **V.**
3. Silver coin of Hadrian.
4. Silver coin of Theodosius **the Great.**
5. Silver coin of Arcadius.
6. Silver coin of Honorius.
7. Silver coin of Theodosius II.
8. Gold coin of Leo III., A.D. 719; obverse, D. LEON. P. AUG.; reverse, VICTORIA AUGU. CONOB.
9. **Silver** denier of Charlemagne, A.D. 770.
10. **Gold** coin of Irene, A.D. 800, struck during her **sole reign; obverse and reverse** alike.

PLATE XVIII.

1. Medal of the Emperor Justinian.
2. Medal of Martin V., A.D. 1417, who first of the Popes, after an interval of 300 years, resumed the royalty of coining, and whose medals are the first of the Papal series.
3. Medal of John Palæologus II., **by Pisani, A.D. 1438.**

EXPLANATION OF THE PLATES.

PLATE XIX.

1. Gold coin of Basil I. and his son Constantine; obverse, busts of the Emperors, BASILIOS ET CONSTANT. AUGG.; reverse, Christ seated, + IHS XPS REX REGNANTIUM + (A.D. 867).
2. Gold coin of John I. Zimisces; obverse, ΘΕΟΤΟΚ. ΒΟΗΘ. ΙΩ. ΔΕΣ., busts of the Emperor and Virgin Mary, over the Virgin M. Θ. (Μητηρ Θεου); reverse, + IHS. XPS. REX. REGNANTIUM., figure of Christ (A.D. 1000).
3. Gold coin of John II.; obverse, figures of the Emperor and the **Virgin Mary.** Legend, Ιω. Δεσποτ. Τω. Η. Φυρογενητ; reverse, Christ seated. **Legend, IC.** XC. (A.D. 1180).
4. Gold coin of Haroun Al Raschid; obverse, No Deity but God, He hath no partner. In the name of God, this Dirhem was made at El Basrah, Anno Hegirae 182; reverse, Mohammed is God's Apostle. By order of Emir El Amin Mohammed, Son of the Prince of the Faithful. Mohammed is God's Apostle, sent with the command and religion of truth to exalt it over all religions in spite of their upholders (A.D. 800).
5. Gold coin of the Calif El Mustansir Billah; obverse, Allah. No Deity but God. He has no partner. Mohammed is God's Apostle, God's friend. Mohammed, God's Apostle, sent with command and religion of truth to exalt it over all religions in spite of their upholders; reverse, Maad Abdallah, servant of God and his vicar Imaum Abou Temim El Mustansir Billah, Prince of the Faithful. In the name of God, the Compassionate, the Merciful, **this Denarius** was struck at Misr (El Fostat, Cairo in Egypt), A.H. 439.
6. Gold sequin of Roman Senate; obverse, S. PETRUS SENATOR URBIS, Peter delivering a banner to a Senator; reverse, ROMA CAPUT MUNDI S. P. Q. R. Christ holding a book (A.D. 1140).
7. Silver coin of Alexius II., Emperor of Trebizond; obverse, the Emperor on horseback. Αλε. ΗΕΝ. (Αλειος ὁ Κομνηνου); reverse, Ο. Α. Ε. Γ. Ν. (Ὁ Αγιος Ευγενιος), the saint on horseback (A.D. 1204).
8. **Silver** coin of Senator BRANCALEONE of Rome, A.D. 1252–1258.

PLATE XX.

1. **Medal** of Pope Eugenius **IV.**, A.D. 1438.
2. **Dutch** medal on the overthrow of the Armada, **A.D. 1588; reverse, the Church on a rock** in the midst of the sea.
3. **Medal of Cosmo** dei Medici.

PLATE XXI.

1. A coiner at work; **from the** capital of a column at St. George de Boucherville, in Normandy.
2. Coining in the Middle Ages; from a wood-cut made by order of the Emperor Maximilian, and published in his life (Der Weiss Kunig), by Keiser.

PLATE XXII.

1. Medal **of Lorenzo** de Medici.
2. Medal of Gregory XIII. commemorating the massacre of St. Bartholomew.
3. An ancient patera. This is an engraved plate or dish, and illustrates the use of the simple scales for weighing. The scene represented is the examination by Mercury and Apollo of the fates of Achilles and Memnon by weighing their respective genii against each other.

EXPLANATION OF THE PLATES.

PLATE XXIII.

1. **English torques,** or ring money. The larger ones were worn around the body, or even over the shoulder, as ornaments. Some were wristlets, and others **smaller** ornaments. They are all multiples of one unit, the unit being the weight of the smallest one yet found. This regularity of weight **leaves** no doubt of their uses.
2. **Earliest** English coins (gold), which, if struck as coins, were of a **period between** the invasion of Cæsar and the reign of Claudius. By some these are supposed to be tokens, or masonic pledges of a later period. The one having an ear of wheat is a reverse, which has been found with **other** obverses, as in Plate XXVII., and is probably of Cymbeline. That **marked Boduo is perhaps** of Boadicea or Bodnodicea.

PLATE XXIV.

Great Seal of Edward the Confessor.

PLATE XXV.

1. Copper coin of Hadrian, relating to Britain, A.D. **120.—See Humphreys, p. 32.**
2. Coin of Claudius, relating to Britain, **representing his triumph in Britain, A. D. 43.**
3. **Gold** coin of Claudius, **relating to Britain; struck in honor of the triumphal arch** which the Senate decreed **to him, about A.D. 46, after his conquest of Britain.** —See Humphreys, p. 31.
4. Copper coin of Antoninus Pius, about A.D. 138, showing figure of Britannia, which was adopted afterward in the reign of Charles II.
5. Copper coin of Antoninus Pius, commemorating his victory in Britain, about A.D. 138.
6. Gold coin of the Emperor Carausius, who reigned in Britain A.D. 290–297.
7. Silver coin of Edward the Confessor, A.D. 1042.
8. Another silver coin of Edward the Confessor.

PLATE XXVI.

Great Seal of William the Norman.

PLATE XXVII.

1. Gold coin (aureus) of Emperor Carausius; obverse, IMP. CARAUSIUS P. F. AUG. (Imperator Pius Felix Augustus); reverse, RENOVAT. ROMANO. (Renovatio Romanorum).
2. Silver coin of Offa, about **A.D. 780.**
3. Silver coin of Egbert, about A.D. **832.**
4. Silver coin of Ethelwulf, A.D. 837–857.
5. Silver coin of Canute, A.D. 1017–1035.
6 and 7. Silver coins of Alfred, A.D. 871–901.
8. Silver penny of Ethelbert II., King of Kent **and Bretwalda, about A.D.** 616. This coin is evidently an imitation of the Roman—see **coin of Carausius, No.** 1—but the genuineness of this coin is doubtful.
9. Gold coin of Cynobelin, **or** Cunobelinus, about A.D. 40; obverse, CAML reverse, CUXO. This monarch **is** supposed to be the Cymbeline of Shakspeare.

10. Silver penny of William I., A.D. 1066–1087.
11. Silver penny of William II., A.D. 1087–1100.
12. Silver penny of Henry I., A.D. 1100–1135.

PLATE XXVIII.

Great Seal of William Rufus.

PLATE XXIX.

1. Silver penny of Stephen.
2. Silver penny of Henry II.
3. **Irish** silver penny of John.
4. Silver penny of Henry III.
5. Silver penny **of** Edward I.
6. Silver **penny (probably)** of **Edward II.**
7. **Groat of Edward III.**
8. **Noble of Edward III.**

PLATE XXX.

Great Seal of Henry I.

PLATE XXXI.

1. Half groat of Edward III.
2. Penny of Edward III.
3. Groat of Richard II.
4. Penny of Richard II.
5. Half groat of Richard II.
6. Half noble of Henry V.
7. Quarter noble of Henry **V.**
8. Noble of Henry V.

PLATE XXXII.

Great Seal of Stephen.

PLATE XXXIII.

1. Penny of Henry V.
2. Half groat of Henry V.
3. Groat of Henry V.
4. Groat of Henry VI.
5. Half groat of Henry VI.
6. Penny of Henry VI.
7. Angel of Edward IV.

PLATE XXXIV.

Great Seal of Henry II.

EXPLANATION OF THE PLATES.

PLATE XXXV.

1. Half groat of Edward IV
2. Half angel of Edward IV.
3. Groat of Edward IV.
4. Penny of Edward IV.
5. Half groat of Richard III.
6. Groat of Richard III.
7. Perkin Warbeck's groat.
8. Penny of Richard III.

PLATE XXXVI.

Great Seal of Richard I. (Cœur de Lion).

PLATE XXXVII.

1. Sovereign of Henry VII.
2. Rose real of Henry VII.
3. Groat of Henry VII.
4. Half groat of Henry VII.
5. Penny of Henry VII.

PLATE XXXVIII.

Great Seal of King John.

PLATE XXXIX.

1. Gold noble of Henry VIII.
2. Gold crown of Henry VIII.
3. Gold half crown of Henry VIII.
4. Shilling of Henry VIII.
5. Cardinal Wolsey's groat.
6. Wolsey's half groat.
7. Wolsey's penny.

PLATE XL.

Great Seal of William of Scotland.

PLATE XLI.

1. Gold sovereign of Edward VI.
2. Gold crown of Edward VI.
3. Sixpence of Edward VI.
4. Groat of Edward VI.
5. Shilling of Edward VI.

PLATE XLII.

Great Seal of Henry III.

271

EXPLANATION OF THE PLATES.

PLATE XLIII.

1. Silver medal of Henry VIII.
2. Gold medal of Henry VIII. The legends, on the obverse in Latin, and on the reverse in Hebrew and in Greek, are of similar purport: "Henry the Eighth, King of England, France, and Ireland, Defender of the Faith, and in the Land of England and Ireland, under Christ, the Supreme Head of the Church."
3. Medal of Philip and Mary.

PLATE XLIV.

Great Seal of Edward I.

PLATE XLV.

1. Shilling of Edward **VI.**
2. Penny of Edward VI.
3. Gold sovereign of Mary.
4. Gold real of Mary.
5. Penny of Mary.
6. Groat of Mary.

PLATE XLVI.

Great Seal of Edward II.

PLATE XLVII.

1. Medal struck in honor of the Earl of Essex, about A.D. 1640; obverse, portrait of the Earl; reverse, the two Houses of Parliament, the King presiding in the Lords and the Speaker in the Commons. From the parliamentary series by Simon.
2. Medal of James **I.** Curious from **the** use of the title Imperator.
3. Medal of Sir Thomas Fairfax.
4. Medal given for service in the action with the Dutch, July 31, 1653. **Monk and** Penn commanding the English, and Van Tromp commanding the **Dutch.**

PLATE XLVIII.

Great Seal of Edward III.

PLATE XLIX.

1. Shilling of Philip and Mary.
2. Sixpence of Philip and Mary.
3. Penny of Elizabeth.
4. Groat of Elizabeth.
5. Sixpence of Elizabeth.
6. Gold real of Elizabeth.
7. Gold angel of Elizabeth.

EXPLANATION OF THE PLATES.

PLATE L.

Great Seal of Richard II.

PLATE LI.

Medal of James, Duke of York, afterward James II., commemorating the naval victory over the Dutch, June 3, 1665.

PLATE LII.

Great Seal of Henry IV

PLATE LIII.

1. Silver crown of Elizabeth.
2. Shilling of Elizabeth.
3. Penny of James I.
4. Twopence of James I.
5. Half penny of James I.
6. Silver crown of James I.

PLATE LIV.

Great Seal of Henry V.

PLATE LV.

1. Medal of Charles II. and Catharine ; probably relating to the Queen's dowry.
2. Medal struck to commemorate the appointment of James, Duke of York, Lord High Admiral.
3. Medal struck to commemorate the flight of James II. from Ireland, and the supremacy of the house of Orange; obverse, bust of King James; reverse, an orange-tree in full fruit, and an old oak broken down.

PLATE LVI.

Great Seal of Henry VI.

PLATE LVII.

1. Gold thirty-shilling piece of James I.
2. Half sovereign of James I.
3. Sixpence of James I.
4. Sovereign of James I.
5. Fifteen-shilling piece of James I.
6. Shilling of James I.

PLATE LVIII.

Great Seal of Edward IV.

S   273

EXPLANATION OF THE PLATES.

PLATE LIX.

1 and 2. Medals struck to commemorate the murder of **Sir** Edmondbury Godfrey.
A.D. 1677.
3. Titus Oates medal, in commemoration of the Popish plot.
4. Medal struck to commemorate the acquittal of Earl Shaftesbury.

PLATE LX.

Great Seal of Edward **V**.

PLATE LXI.

1. Oxford crown of Charles I., 1644.   Exurgat Deus, Dissipenter inimici.
2. Groat of Charles I.
3. Sixpence of Charles I.
4. Gold twenty-shilling piece of Charles I.
5. York half crown of Charles I.

PLATE LXII.

Great Seal of Richard III.

PLATE LXIII.

1. Medal relating to the Rye House Plot; obverse, the King as Hercules menaced
by a hydra-headed monster, the heads representing the supposed conspirators,
a hand in the clouds holding a thunder-bolt; reverse, a shepherd—the King
—with his flock, in the middle of which two wolves are hung, London in the
distance.
2. Medal of Archbishop Sancroft and the seven bishops arrested with him in 1688.
3. Medal of James II. and Mary of Modena.
4. Medal of William III.

PLATE LXIV.

Great Seal of Henry VII.

PLATE LXV.

1. Shilling of Charles I.
2. Pattern for a broad of Charles I.
3. Colchester shilling, siege-piece of Charles I.
4. Beeston Castle shilling, siege-piece of Charles I.
5. Half penny of Charles I.
6. Penny of Charles I.
7. Scarborough half crown, siege-piece of Charles I.
8. Newark shilling, siege-piece of Charles I.

PLATE LXVI.

Great Seal of Henry VIII.

EXPLANATION OF THE PLATES.

PLATE LXVII.

1. Medal commemorating the raising of the siege of Londonderry; obverse, the English fleet advancing to relieve Londonderry, in front a bust of King William crowned by Valor and Abundance; reverse, Poverty and Slavery take from the head of Louis XIV. a broken wreath of laurel.
2. Medal commemorating the battle of the Boyne, A.D. 1690. King William crossing the river at the head of his troops.
3. Medal in honor of the Queen, after the defeat of the English and Dutch fleets in the Channel in June, 1690.

PLATE LXVIII.

1. Angel of Charles I.
2. Ten-shilling piece of Charles I.
3. Twopence of the Commonwealth.
4. Penny of the Commonwealth.
5. Crown of the Commonwealth.
6. Copper farthing of the Commonwealth.

PLATE LXIX.

Great Seal of Edward VI.

PLATE LXX.

1. Medal of Queen Anne in honor of the Union; struck at Leipzig.
2. Medal struck to commemorate the battle of Blenheim; obverse, portraits of Prince Eugene and the Duke of Marlborough; reverse, the battle.
3. Medals commemorating the trial of Dr. Sacheverell, February 27, 1710. The Doctor's portrait was accompanied by different reverses, to suit the taste of the purchasers, whether Romish or English Episcopal.

PLATE LXXI.

Great Seal of Mary.

PLATE LXXII.

1. Twenty-shilling piece of the Commonwealth.
2. Pewter farthing of the Commonwealth.
3. Ten-shilling piece of the Commonwealth.
4. Shilling of the Commonwealth.
5. Sixpence of the Commonwealth.
6. Half penny of the Commonwealth.
7. Shilling of Oliver Cromwell.

PLATE LXXIII.

Great Seal of Elizabeth.

EXPLANATION OF THE PLATES.

PLATE LXXIV.

1. Medal commemorating the battle of Ramilies; obverse, Union of England and Holland between busts of Marlborough and D'Ouwerkerke; reverse, the battle.

PLATE LXXV.

Great Seal of James I.

PLATE LXXVI.

1. Silver crown of Cromwell.
2. Copper farthing of Cromwell.
3. Sixpence of Cromwell.
4. Copper halfpenny of Charles II.
5. Silver crown of Charles II.

PLATE LXXVII.

Great Seal of Charles I.

.

PLATE LXXVIII.

1. Medal struck to commemorate the surrender of Lille, A.D. 1708; obverse, Victory taking the crown from prostrate Lille; reverse, Britannia with the ægis striking France with terror.
2. Medal commemorating the battle of Dumblane, A.D. 1773.
3. Medal commemorating the victory of Oudenarde, A.D. 1708; obverse, Marlborough and Eugene as Castor and Pollux; reverse, the battle of Oudenarde and the town.

PLATE LXXIX.

Great Seal of the Commonwealth.

PLATE LXXX.

1. Shilling of Charles II.
2. Silver crown of James II.
3. Guinea of Charles II.
4. Halfpenny of James II.
5. Silver crown of William and Mary.

PLATE LXXXI.

Great Seal of Scotland under the Protectorate.

EXPLANATION OF THE PLATES.

PLATE LXXXII.

1. Medal of George I.; reverse, the horse of Brunswick leaping across the map of the northwest part of Europe.
2. Medal of James III., the elder Pretender, and Clementina, his wife.
3. Medal of George II.

PLATE LXXXIII.

Great Seal of Charles II.

PLATE LXXXIV.

1. Shilling of William and Mary.
2. Shilling of William III.
3. Copper half penny of Queen Anne.
4. Crown of Queen Anne.
5. Shilling of Queen Anne.
6. Half penny of William III.

PLATE LXXXV.

Great Seal of James II.

PLATE LXXXVI.

1. Medal commemorating the capture of Porto Bello by Admiral Vernon, A.D. 1740.
2. Medal of the young Pretender, A.D. 1745.
3. Medal commemorating Sir Edward Hawkes's victory in Quiberon Bay, A.D. 1759.

PLATE LXXXVII.

Great Seal of William and Mary.

PLATE LXXXVIII.

1. Shilling of George I.
2. Farthing of Queen Anne.
3. Farthing of Queen Anne.
4. Farthing of Queen Anne.
5. Farthing of Queen Anne.
6. Farthing of Queen Anne.
7. Farthing of Queen Anne.
8. Farthing of Queen Anne.
9. Half penny of George I.

PLATE LXXXIX.

Great Seal of William III.

EXPLANATION OF THE PLATES.

PLATE XC.

Medal of George II., commemorating the Battle of Dettingen, A.D. 1743, in which he commanded in person.

PLATE XCI.

Great Seal of Anne before the Union.

PLATE XCII.

1. Crown of George I.
2. Shilling of George II.
3. Half penny of George II.
4. Half pennies known as Wood money, with three different reverses.
5. Crown of George II.

PLATE XCIII.

Great Seal of Anne after the Union.

PLATE XCIV.

1. Medal commemorating the battle of Minden, in which Frederic of Brunswick defeated the French, A.D. 1759.
2. Medal commemorating the battle of Plassy, A.D. 1758.
3. Medal commemorating the battle of Trafalgar, A.D. 1805.

PLATE XCV.

Great Seal of George I.

PLATE XCVI.

1. Medal in honor of Lord Howe's victory over the French fleet, A.D. 1794.
2. Medal in honor of Lord North; struck by the University of Oxford at the time of the American troubles, A.D. 1775.
3. Victoria medal of the battle of Aliwal.

PLATE XCVII.

Great Seal of George II.

PLATE XCVIII.

Medal of Washington before Boston; struck by order of Congress, March 25, 1776. The original medal was gold.

EXPLANATION OF THE PLATES.

PLATE XCIX.

1. New England shilling, silver; first issue of the Massachusetts Mint.
2. New England sixpence, silver.
3. Pine-tree shilling, silver.
4. Virginia half penny, copper.
5. Copper piece of Louis XIII., said to have been issued for Louisiana in 1721. It was probably issued for all the French colonies, and had no special reference to Louisiana.
6. Lord Baltimore shilling, issued for Maryland.
7. Granby or Higley copper of 1737, issued at Granby, in Connecticut.

PLATE C.

1 and 3. Medal presented to Paul Jones by resolution of Congress, October 16, 1787; struck in Paris under the direction of Mr. Jefferson.
2. Medal presented by Congress to General Morgan, in honor of his conduct at Cowpens.

PLATE CI.

1. Rosa Americana penny.
2. Vermont copper, usually known as the Vermontensium Res Publica.
3. Vermont copper; known as the Vermon Auctori. The reverse of this coin is usually the same as the reverse of the Connecticut copper, Plate CIII., No. 3.
4. Pitt or No Stamps token of 1766; struck in England for American circulation.
5. Nova Constellatio copper.
6. Nova Constelatio copper, another variety.

PLATE CII.

1. Medal awarded by Congress to General Anthony Wayne, after the storming of Stony Point, A.D. 1779.
2. Medal awarded by Congress to Lieutenant-Colonel De Fleury, "first over the walls" at the storming of Stony Point, A.D. 1779.
3. Medal awarded to General Greene by Congress, after the battle at Eutaw, A.D. 1781.

PLATE CIII.

1. Georgius Triumpho copper. There should be thirteen bars in the barrier behind which Liberty is standing.
2. Massachusetts copper cent of 1786.
3. Connecticut copper of 1787, commonly called Auctori. Connec.
4. New Jersey copper of 1786.
5. Kentucky token, copper; so called because Ky. appears uppermost among States on the stars, also called the Triangle cent.
6. Immunis Columbia copper of 1787.

EXPLANATION OF THE PLATES.

PLATE CIV.

1. Medal awarded by Congress to Major Stewart, after the battle of Stony Point, A.D. 1779.
2. Medal awarded by Congress to Lieutenant-Colonel Howard, "because, rushing suddenly on the line of the wavering enemy, he gave a brilliant specimen of martial bravery at the battle of Cowpens," A.D. 1781.
3. Medal awarded by Congress to Major Henry Lee, for brilliant conduct at Paulus's Hook, 19th August, 1779.

PLATE CV.

1. George Clinton copper of New York, A.D. 1787.
2. Confederatio copper. (Unique piece in the collection of Benjamin Haines, Esq., of Elizabeth, New Jersey.)
3. A Spanish (Mexican) pistareen, of the kind called Cob money, in circulation in the northern part of America during the latter part of the 18th century (silver). Similar coins were struck in gold.
4. Chalmers shilling of Annapolis, A.D. 1788.
5. New York copper, commonly called Nova Eborac.
6. New York copper, commonly called the New York Washington piece.
7. Talbot Allum & Lee token or card of 1794.

PLATE CVI.

1. The captors' medal, awarded by Congress to the captors of Major André—Paulding, Williams, and Van Wart—A.D. 1780. The originals were in silver.
2. Medal presented by Congress to General Gates in honor of the surrender of Burgoyne at Saratoga, 1777.
3. Medal presented to Colonel William Washington, for valor at Cowpens, 1781.

PLATE CVII.

1 and 2. The Washington half dollar of 1792 (silver), and also known, in copper, as the Washington cent of 1792.
3. Washington token, brass, SUCCESS TO THE UNITED STATES.
4. Obverse of the large eagle Washington cent of 1791.
5. Reverse of the small eagle Washington cent of 1791.
6. Reverse of the large eagle Washington cent of 1791.
7. Obverse of a Washington cent of 1792. This is a very rare coin, and is, in fact, the only Washington cent of 1792.
8. Washington and Independence token of 1783, laureated head.
9. Washington and Independence token of 1783, military bust.

PLATE CVIII.

1. Seal of the Old Colony, Plymouth, Massachusetts.
2. Seal of Tryon, Governor of North Carolina, 1765-1771, and of New York from 1771 till nominally superseded in 1780.
3. Seal of William Penn.
4. Seal of Virginia.
5. Seal of Thomas Jefferson.

EXPLANATION OF THE PLATES.

PLATE CIX.

1. U. S. A. or thirteen bar copper.
2. Fugio or Franklin cent of 1787.   First national copper coinage.
3. Continental pewter piece, 1776.
4. First United States dollar, 1794.
5. U. S. cent of 1793, obverse.
6. Another variety of U. S. cent of 1793.
7. Reverse of the U. S. Link cent of 1793.

PLATE CX.

1. Dollar of 1795, as it **appeared** in the latter part of the year, and continued till 1804.
2. Reverse of the dollar as adopted 1798, latter part of the year.
3. Flying eagle (pattern) dollar of 1836 and 1838.
4. Dollar of 1841, being the pattern still in use.

PLATE CXI.

1. Reverse of the half dollar of 1794.
2. Obverse of half dollar **as** adopted in 1795, **and continued till 1807.**
3. Reverse of half dollar as adopted in 1801.
4. Half dollar of 1846.   The reverse was adopted in 1836, **and** the obverse in the latter part of 1839.
5. Half dollar of 1853, after July 1, when **the** change occurred in the weight of the coin.
6. Quarter dollar, reverse, of 1796.
7. Quarter dollar, obverse, adopted **in 1804.**
8. Quarter dollar, reverse, adopted in **1804.**
9. Quarter dollar as adopted in 1839.
10. Quarter dollar of 1853, after July, **when the change occurred in the weight of** the coin.

PLATE CXII.

1. Reverse of dime of 1796.
2. Dime as adopted in 1797, and continued until **1807.**
3 and 4. Dime as adopted in 1838.
5. Half dime of 1794.
6. Reverse of half dime as adopted in 1800.
7. Reverse of half dime adopted in 1837.
8. Three-cent piece of 1841.
9. Reverse of gold eagle of 1795.
10. Reverse of gold eagle adopted in 1838.
11. Reverse of gold double eagle, 1849.
12. Half eagle of 1795.
13. Reverse of half eagle of 1798.
14. Reverse of half eagle of 1808.

EXPLANATION OF THE PLATES.

PLATE CXIII.

1. Half eagle of 1846 (adopted in 1838).
2. Quarter eagle of 1796.
3. Three-dollar piece.
4. Fifty-dollar piece.
5. Gold dollar.
6. Five-dollar piece of Bechtler (private coinage in North Carolina).
7. One dollar of Bechtler.
8. Private coinage of San Francisco, half eagle.

PLATE CXIV.

1. Specimens of continental money.
2. A counterfeit continental bill.

INDEX OF SUBJECTS.

283

INDEX OF SUBJECTS.

INDEX OF SUBJECTS.

INDEX OF SUBJECTS.

283

INDEX TO THE PLATES.

T
289

INDEX TO THE PLATES.

INDEX TO THE PLATES.

292

THE END.

www.ingramcontent.com/pod-product-compliance
Lightning Source LLC
Chambersburg PA
CBHW020508270326
41926CB00008B/786